LOCOMOTION PAPERS LP245

THE
YORKSHIRE LINES
OF THE
LNWR

by
Neil Fraser

A railway dray in King Street, Huddersfield about 1949. The carter is Mr Frank Spence.
W.B. Stocks

THE OAKWOOD PRESS

© Neil Fraser, 2019.

ISBN 978-0-85361-561-3

Printed by
Claro Print Ltd, Office 26/27, 1 Spiersbridge Way, Glasgow, G46 8NG

NEIL FRASER
1925 – 2001

My father was born and lived all his life in Huddersfield with an enduring interest in all forms of railway transport. He was a magistrate for many years, a long-serving member of the LNWR Society, other organizations and contributor to a large number of publications. His first book, *Hillhouse Immortals – The Story of a London & North Western Railway Engine Shed* was published in 1999 by Oakwood Press.

Shortly after my father's funeral I had discussions with his friend Dr Graham Hardy about the finalization of an incomplete manuscript. I set to work identifying and collating photographs before editing the text and compiling my queries. I had numerous meetings with Graham until we were both satisfied that it was as complete as we could make it. I sent everything to the Oakwood Press during 2002 with their assurances that it was in the pipeline for processing. Unbeknown to me, the owner of Oakwood was considering retirement and the project lay dormant. Eventually I lost hope of it ever being published. However, in 2016, Oakwood was sold, to Stenlake Publishing who found the manuscript with its photographs and revived the project.

Graham died suddenly in June 2017 and I would like to gratefully acknowledge his valuable technical assistance in the following pages.

Rowena Kidger,
June 2019

Published by
The Oakwood Press, 54-58 Mill Square, Catrine, KA5 6RD
Telephone: 01290 551122   Website: www.stenlake.co.uk

Contents

Introduction		5
One	1835 – 1849	7
Two	1850 – 1859	21
Three	1860 – 1869	35
Four	1870 – 1879	65
Five	1880 – 1889	87
Six	1890 –1899	113
Seven	1900 – 1909	129
Eight	1910 – 1913	141
Nine	1914 – 1918	145
Ten	1919 – 1922	149
Eleven	1923 – 1947	153
Twelve	1948 – 1962	163
Thirteen	1963 – 1969	173
Fourteen	1970 – 2000	189

Appendices

One	Copley Hill Engines	203
Two	Assistant Engines	204
Three	Stabling Vehicles	204
Four	Tunnel Names	204
Five	Closures	205
Index		207

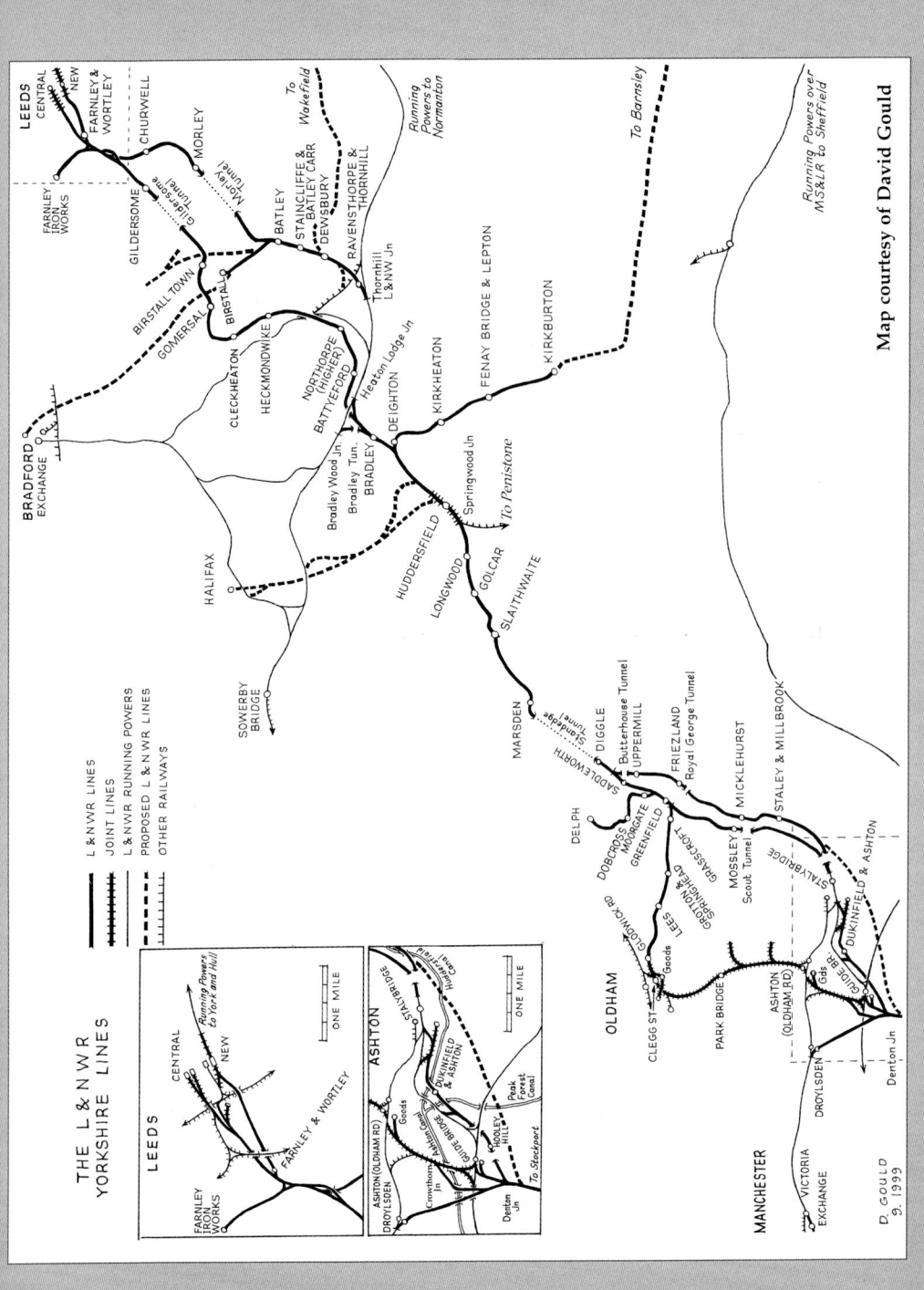

INTRODUCTION

The term 'The Yorkshire Lines' defined the route inherited from the London and North Western Railway's (LNWR) West Riding Constituents, the Huddersfield and Manchester Railway and Canal Company (H&MR&CC), the Leeds, Dewsbury and Manchester Railway (LD&M) and a quarter share in the Leeds Central Station Joint Committee. This was a cross-country artery from the heart of the West Riding to Lancashire and Cheshire but physically separated from the parent network by a two mile section of the Manchester, Sheffield and Lincolnshire Railway (MS&L) between Stalybridge and Guide Bridge. The title 'Yorkshire Lines' was dropped in 1857 when it became part of the LNWR North Eastern Division.

From an architectural standpoint the route offered a diary of architectural refinement: from the classical crossing of the River Aire and Leeds and Liverpool Canal in Leeds to the great example of foundry art where it crossed the Calder and the Calder and Hebble Navigation near Ravensthorpe; to the Elizabethan façade at Dewsbury and Huddersfield's Classical façade – the further travelled the better it became until the train reached Stalybridge – 'a place where all the odds and ends were put when Lancashire was made'.

The operation of 'The Yorkshire Lines' included the most turbulent and bizarre events in railway history with a grand total of 183 accidents between 1850 and 1900. Luckily, the majority were not fatal but notable in causing delay, notwithstanding trains running out of control, derailments, couplings broken, couplings that fractured crank axles, to a disastrous boiler explosion in Standedge tunnel. Until the early 1900s the death of a railwayman at work was a monthly occurrence and routinely described as 'accidental death'. It was one of the first areas to operate Henry Marcus's excursions in 1851. It included many mail train operations as well as newspapers which were printed in both Manchester and Leeds. The route had day trips to view the SS *Great Western* at Liverpool, football specials to Wigan and Wembley and evening excursions to Belle Vue.

To listen to an LNWR goods train during the hours of darkness was a moving experience, whether it be hauled by diminutive 0-6-0 'Coal Engine' or a 'Super D' 0-8-0 which had a deep pitched contralto exhaust note; the indelible shriek of an engine whistle that assailed the ear when heard close to but sounded quite dramatic when heard a mile from the line on a hillside. The smell of steam and hot oil on warm metal as an express stood at the platform end – these were the indelible features of London and North Western Railway operations that would endure to all who ever experienced them.

Other sounds included the mysterious ringing of the station bells, the noise of signal levers being pulled and the satisfying clatter as others were returned. The rails roared on the Leeds New Line and the treadle gong sounding CLANG CLANG, CLANG CLANG, CLANG CLANG which indicated that the end of the tunnel was near. These were the ingredients that made rail travel agreeable at holiday times, monotonously boring to the commuter, with soot on your clothes or a cinder in your eye. Whatever the atmosphere, it was one that has vanished.

Tunnel ventilating shafts in Springwood Street, Huddersfield, 1967.   *Author*

CHAPTER ONE

1835 – 1849

Preliminary

Huddersfield was the fulcrum point of 'The Yorkshire Lines'. It was in 1835 that a link from the town was projected by Frederick Swanwick for the Huddersfield and Leeds Railway (H&L). The route would leave the town via the valley of the Colne and from Heaton Lodge via the Calder Valley to Wakefield, thence to Normanton and through the Aire Valley to terminate at Hunslet Lane, Leeds. The project had much in common with the line projected by the much larger Manchester and Leeds railway (M&L). The local company were invited to withdraw their Bill and give support to the M&L with an undertaking that when complete they would serve Huddersfield with its own branch line.

In 1843 T.L.Gooch prepared a low level branch to serve the town. This was regarded as most unsatisfactory and strong feelings were expressed that Huddersfield should have its own company with a line capable of being extended westwards.

A meeting was called at the Huddersfield Court of Requests on 20th January, 1844 when it was declared 'Huddersfield is in an isolated position …. The M&L want to clap us in a hole and keep us there' (*Leeds Mercury* reporting comments made by John Sutcliffe 27th January, 1844 p5). The meeting was attended by Capt. Laws of the M&L who withdrew when a motion in favour of an independent line was advocated. He returned later (*Leeds Mercury* 2nd March, 1844 p7) and the

The former Court of Requests building, scene of the dramatic meeting in January, 1844.
photograph 1995, Author

occurrence gave rise to an oft quoted but unconfirmed story that Capt Laws stormed from the meeting declaring that 'Huddersfield wasn't worth stopping an engine for.'*

Simultaneously at the Scarborough Hotel in Leeds the Leeds, Dewsbury and Manchester Jn Railway was promoted. A provisional agreement was made with the Huddersfield and Manchester Railway and Canal Company creating a new cross-country link. The route was drawn up by Joseph Locke and Alfred S. Jee for a line between Heaton Lodge to a junction with the Sheffield Ashton-under-Lyne and Manchester Railway at Stalybridge with a branch to Delph. The Leeds, Dewsbury & Manchester Railway was also a member of the Leeds Central Station Joint Committee with the Leeds and Thirsk, Lancashire and Yorkshire Railway (L&Y) and Great Northern Railway (GNR) as partners. Their original scheme would extend from Monkbridge to Infirmary Street, 900 feet long, 400 feet wide and covering 36 acres. On 6th March, 1846 three other plans were examined:

    a Design by Mr Cubitt on south side of Wellington Street raised on arches. Cost £400,000;
    b Design by Mr Grainger on north side of Wellington Street. Cost £285,000;
    c Design by Mr Hawkshaw on north side of Wellington Street. Cost £258,000 (Design chosen).

The Huddersfield and Manchester had absorbed the Huddersfield Canal Company, formed in 1794 which represented a total investment of £558,000. The canal had been completed in 1811 when Standedge Canal tunnel was opened after 17 years in making. Shareholders had received dividends on 13 occasions amounting in total to £19 15s. 0d. per share. Thus the Huddersfield Canal Company was absorbed for £183,730, the railway paying £30 per share then valued at between £7-£8 each. The Sir John Ramsden Canal (a broad navigation) was subsequently purchased on 9th July, 1847 for £45,284 13s. 4d. It cost £11,975 to build and was opened in 1778. Despite an unfavourable report by the Dalhousie Committee, the H&M Act was dated 30th June, 1845. The capital was £830,000 in £30 shares.

At the first AGM of the H&MR&CC an opinion was given that £70,000 would be saved on making a new tunnel by using the canal

---

* This story was printed in an article by the late W.B. Stocks in the *Huddersfield Examiner* of 30th August, 1947 and emanated from a lantern lecture he had presented in a village hall on railways – at the conclusion an elderly gentleman rose to pass vote of thanks and mentioned the story – but that was what it was, and a very good story too!

William Aldam junior, MP for Leeds 1841-47 and Chairman of the Huddersfield and Manchester Railway and Canal Company.

courtesy of J. Goodchild

Huddersfield Guildhall, where Aldam's proposal for a merger with the Sheffield, Ashton-under-Lyne & Manchester Railway was defeated on 15th December, 1845.
Kirklees Local History Collection

tunnel. After some discussion the decision was that a single line railway tunnel would be made.* Director George Loch, however, was quite adamant that a double line tunnel would be better. The Chairman, William Aldam proposed at an Extraordinary General Meeting on 15th December, 1845 to lease the company to the Sheffield Ashton-under-Lyne and Manchester Railway, stating the provisional agreement with the LD&M and Leeds and Thirsk had fallen through, but the benefit of this proposition was they would be merged with an existing railway. However, Joseph Brook, Deputy Chairman championed the earlier cause declaring 'There is an influence on the board conflicting with the best interests of the company' a comment greeted with much enthusiasm and Brook left the Guildhall carried on the shoulders of shareholders. The association with the LD&M was resumed but other matters were to rear their head.

1. The contractor, Messrs Nowell and Hattersley had been prevailed upon to commence work before a contract had been signed.
2. The engineer – Alfred S. Jee had prepared a more extensive schedule and contended that contractors should provide 'extras' without additional payment.

* A cabin was provided at each end of the tunnel, and a telegraph system installed between them, so the tunnel's pilot could signal that the train had reached the other end.

3. Bad workmanship and poor materials caused a stoppage of work with many examples of masonry having to be demolished and a fresh start made. The bridge at Hillhouse Lane developed a bulge and was taken down. The piers of Huddersfield viaduct up to the turnings were inadequate and had to be taken down. Three policemen were employed to prevent theft of tools and materials. Huddersfield station was laid on the wrong gradient and with sub standard sleepers. The skew arch at Paddock was taken down and remade. A bridge at Stalybridge with 'hammer dressed backing' had been built by a mason without reference to plan and was 9 feet out of alignment. The advice was sought of Chancery Council Mr Maling who suggested the company submit to considerable sacrifice rather than be driven into chancery where all sorts of evidence might be admitted to show what were 'extras'.
4. The contractors were dismissed and redress was sought. At York Assizes they were awarded £150,000 in damages. Upon appeal this was reduced to £60,612.
5. In the projected 800 yards Huddersfield tunnel a serious blunder occurred and this was to cost the company £25,000*.

*Premier Business 1996 (LNWR & L&Y Societies).

The uncompleted work was re-let in 17 separate contracts on which much hitherto unknown caution was exercised. Rioting broke out at the British Queen public house, Marsden when 500 navvies, employed by Thomas Nicholson at Standedge were told their wages would not be paid. A large force of police set off to walk by road from Huddersfield to Marsden and unknowingly passed the rioters only a short distance away walking on the canal towing path! What would have been a serious confrontation ended peacefully when wages were drawn at the Warren House Inn, Milnsbridge.

An application was made to Parliament to make a branch from Mossley to Oldham, less than 3 miles long, including a 528 yards tunnel on a one in 25 gradient. A Bill for a line between Bradley and Bradford was estimated at £550,000 and would have crossed the estate of Sir George Armytage 'on a Roman viaduct of an ornamental nature'. An alternative line from Springhead to Manchester by the Medlock Valley was prepared by John Miller and some lines in the Oldham area, but the words of the Deputy Chairman were 'these would be best made by a company of a more local nature'.

The short line from Bradley Junction to Bradley Wood Junction opened in 1850. It was conceived at the same time as diverting the main line at Paddock northwards avoiding Paddock Church to satisfy the

Joseph Kaye (1780-1858) the builder of Huddersfield station.

whim of Isabella Ramsden, mother of Sir John Ramsden, owner of Huddersfield in the 19th century. Here a 40 feet deep cutting produced top quality stone used to make Huddersfield and Longwood viaducts.

The foundation stone of Huddersfield station was laid on 9th October, 1846 but – where was it sited, why was it removed and what happened to it? When asked why his name was not inscribed, its designer J.P. Pritchett replied 'The work itself should be the best record of the builder's name'. A preserved drawing shows Pritchett considered circular windows in the centre block. Pritchett was subject to animosity by Isabella Ramsden but thanks to the ability of George Loch* the station was in the best position for the development of the 'new Huddersfield'.

On 9th July, 1847 the local company became vested in the London and North Western Railway along with the Leeds, Dewsbury and Manchester Railway. The impact of this arrangement was to be felt when Henry Booth, late Liverpool and Manchester Railway, visited the town and observing the Corinthian columns for the station façade lying on the ground, he sarcastically remarked 'Those should be taken to Greenhead and erected there' (at the home of Joseph Brook).

---

* George Loch administrator to Sir John Ramsden was formerly in the same position for the Third Duke of Bridgewater and also a Director of the H&MR&CC. He was known as 'the King of auditors'.

The Fox & Grapes, Northgate, where the contractors gave a dinner for their workers on completion of Huddersfield viaduct. Photograph July 1954. *Author*

The station building at Dewsbury, photographed in 1960. *Author*

Inaugural services began on 2nd August, 1847 between Huddersfield and Heaton Lodge, the Deputy Chairman, Joseph Brook* then naming the engines of the first two trains *Aldam* and *Huddersfield* respectively.

The first meeting of the newly formed Leeds, Dewsbury and Manchester Junction Railway was held at the Scarborough Hotel, Leeds in May 1844. Thomas Grainger and John Miller were appointed engineers. The two men had formed a distinguished Edinburgh partnership in 1825 but this was to be dissolved during the time the LD&M was being built.

The routes ran, a) via Morley, b) via Howden Clough, c) via Birstal and were surveyed by Grainger. Miller surveyed a separate route. That chosen was via Morley to a junction with the Manchester and Leeds at Thornhill. A branch was to be made from Batley to Birstal. The estimate was £288,000 plus £32,000 for land. Before construction began the LD&M embarked on expansion with projected lines from Wortley to Bradford, Churwell to Wakefield, Batley to Gildersome and an extension of the Birstal branch to Birkenshaw. Later ideas envisaged further routes from Churwell to Wakefield where it would end in a three pronged fork; and from Lingwell Nook to Methley and another from Crackenedge to Ossett Green, all of which were dropped or defeated.

The ceremony of laying the foundation stone of Morley tunnel took place at the foot of shaft 18 at the Batley end on 23rd February, 1846 by John Gott, LD&M Chairman. By 6th May all was not well, the two fast converging sections would have passed one above the other and the contractors, Jones, Humphries and Pickering were dismissed.

Contracts for the Leeds viaduct were let to George Thompson for a masonry structure of 254 yards and a timber design leading to a temporary station. The keystone of the viaduct was laid on 4th January, 1848 by Mr Grainger.

Ceremonial opening took place on 31st July, 1848 from a temporary station, a large brick building, formerly occupied by Messrs Schunck and Co. The first train, comprising a 'powerful engine and eight carriages', reached the junction at Dewsbury in 25 minutes and Huddersfield 20 minutes later.

Henry Booth expressed concern at the unsafe state of quantities of rock overlooking the line between Batley and Dewsbury. These were trimmed back while housing built for the company's personnel was modified to give greater comfort for those who were to live there.

---

* Joseph Brook 'the father of Huddersfield' and a man of great insight became Director of the LNWR and mentor to Richard Moon. He is commemorated in Edgerton Cemetery by a 30 feet high granite obelisk.

14 THE YORKSHIRE LINES OF THE LNWR

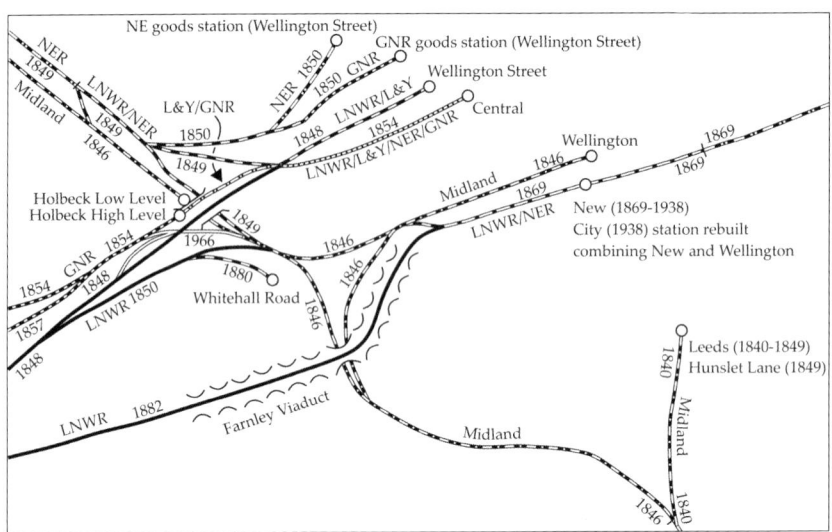

The LNWR's first station was Leeds Wellington Street, a joint station with the L&Y, which opened in 1848, it closed to passengers in 1854 and became a goods station. Wellington Street was sometimes called Leeds Central in advertisements. In 1854, the new larger Leeds Central was opened, adjacent to the site of Wellington Street. Central was a joint station between the LNWR/L&Y/NER and GNR. Leeds New was opened jointly by the LNWR and NER in 1869. The new station allowed through traffic and, in 1938, became Leeds' main station when it was combined with the Midland's Wellington station to form City station. It became the only station in Leeds in 1967 when Central closed.

The Leeds Central Station Act dated 22nd July, 1848 authorized the Hawkshaw design costing £320,000. The LNWR Directors were John Gott and Thomas Benyon. The latter retired in 1849 and was replaced by Henry Booth but LNWR services advertised as from 'the Railway Station, Wellington Street' had hardly begun when the company expressed displeasure in operating arrangements and proposed transfer of operations to the Midland's Wellington station. An L&Y minute of 7th November, 1848, and signed by Henry Booth, records L&Y operation of all LNWR trains until the opening of the Huddersfield to Manchester route brought about by the deplorable condition of LNWR locomotives then available. In addition there was a diversion of some L&Y Manchester – Leeds trains using the Dewsbury route and the practice lasted until 2nd August, 1854, upon opening of the Leeds, Bradford and Halifax Junction line.

A new junction was made at Copley Hill with a 38 chain spur to Whitehall Junction on the Leeds and Bradford Line of the Midland. The LNWR transferred all its passenger operations to the Midland station on

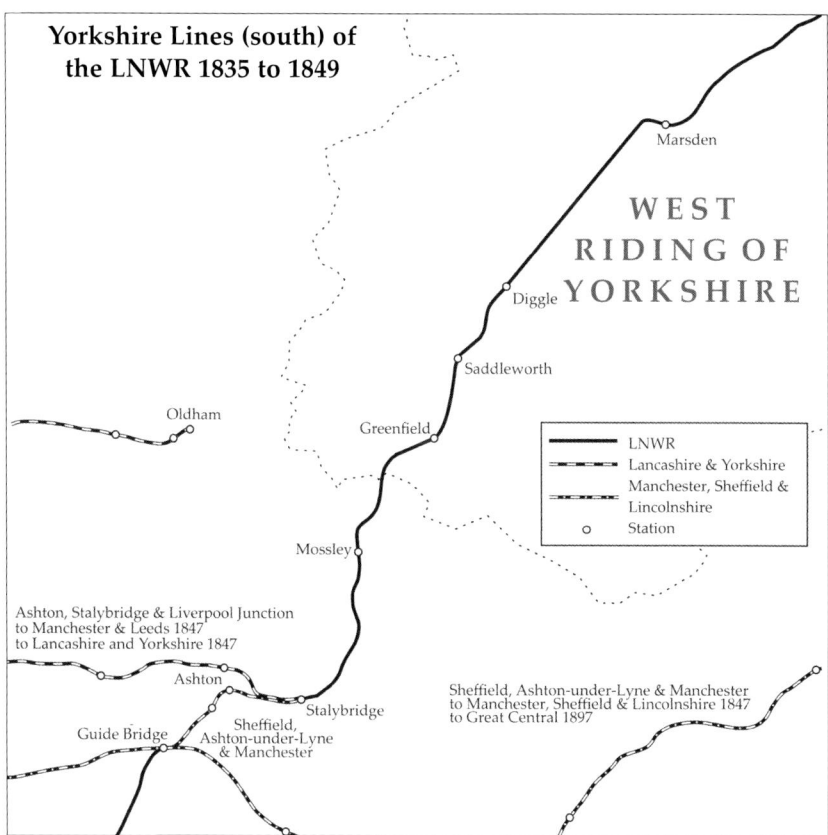

1st October, 1850. LNWR goods services used Leeds Goods High Level station which was built on 13 arches from a junction with the LD&M viaduct line.

In 1852 Joseph Brook replaced John Gott as an LNWR Director of Leeds Central Station. Its date of completion is uncertain except that flagging in front of the station was finished on 1st May, 1852.*

Official opening of the entire main line to Stalybridge and thence to Manchester took place on 13th July, 1849 when a train of 29 carriages drawn by two engines and banked by a third departed from Huddersfield and stopped at Paddock to pick up Wm Leigh Brook, a Director. On return from London Road station a stop was made for a picnic in a lineside field at Diggle. Regular services commenced on 1st

---

* Leeds Central station minute dated May 1852

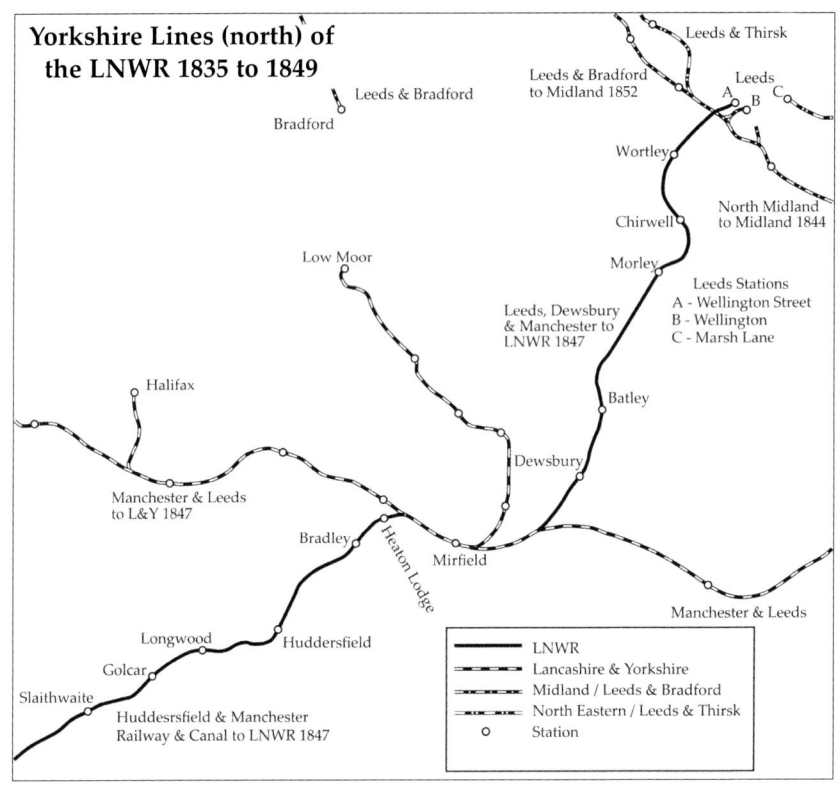

August, 1849 with trains running to and from Manchester Victoria (by agreement with the L&Y who were given powers to use the Bradley Wood curve from Bradley Junction).

The Huddersfield and Manchester line contained 13 major engineering features and 77 bridges. Huddersfield and Saddleworth viaducts were perceived as solid embankments but built after the contractor said they could be made cheaper with a consequent saving in land. Standedge tunnel represented the greatest feature with a 500 yards long deviation of the Huddersfield Canal at Diggle, this first tunnel was later known as the Nicholson tunnel after the contractor.

Stalybridge viaduct comprised seven square segmented arches and three skew arches over streets. The line was carried over Rassbottom Street by two of Fairbairn's patent wrought-iron tubular girders. Huddersfield station stands as one of the great monuments to the optimism which the 19th century placed in railway development: J.P. Pritchett inducing the citizens of Huddersfield to create an architectural

The first station at Bradley, converted into a dwelling house in August 1849.   *Author*

The approach to Leeds Central, with the high level goods station on the left, September 1960.
Author

Morley station in 1958, looking towards Leeds. *Author*

monument rather than a utilitarian structure, a matter that Henry Booth was at pains to point out. Other stations were designed by James Rickaby.

The Leeds, Dewsbury and Manchester line began its route with a 35 feet iron span crossing Lower Queen Street*, Leeds. This was followed by viaduct that comprised 33 stone arches of 30 feet and 20 arches of 35 feet span, the viaduct also had two longer spans, one of 105 feet over the River Aire and a 75 feet span over the Leeds and Liverpool Canal, and twin openings totalling 70 feet over the Leeds and Bradford Railway. Morley tunnel of 3,370 yards length was the greatest feature. The earlier trouble here was the first of many. Little did anyone realize, substantial considerations would be paid to the Earl of Cardigan to leave coal ungotten, for the enabling Act overlooked the prevention of mining beneath the line. In 1920 the LNWR began reconstruction of the tunnel in its entirety. The route thence to Thornhill LNWR Junction was packed with bridges and viaducts that were a delight to contemplate. These epitomized history more vividly than anything else. Dewsbury station, a fine Elizabethan style building designed by John and Henry Paul Child, was constructed at a cost of £5,597 by Simpson and Field who also built the now demolished Dewsbury goods warehouse.

Approaching Ravensthorpe the Calder was crossed by a graceful double span, each of the 100 feet iron segments in the width and five sections in their length inscribed 'Joseph Butler Stanningley – 1848'. Similarly the Calder and Hebble Navigation was crossed by a single span. The entire route had the bearing of great artistry with history

---

* Lower Queen street continued the line of Queen Street south of Wellington Street.

running through a changing landscape of power stations (Leeds and Thornhill), heaps of colliery waste (Ravensthorpe, Haighs, Howley Park, Critchley, West End, Morley Main, Hardings, Churwell Grange and Engine Pit), rows of terraced houses, lamp posts, mill chimneys and groups of Lowry-like people all the way.

At an H&M Board meeting in April 1849 there was said to be a requirement for 35 locomotives for working the whole line at a time when there were three passenger engines, five goods engines, with nine engines at Camden and 15 engines yet to be built. John Ramsbottom expressed the view that Hillhouse shed, Huddersfield was built in the wrong place, it should have been at Copley Hill.

While the affairs of the LD&M were very sound this was in total contrast to the H&MR&CC whose affairs were a jumbled chronicle of good intentions and wishful thinking, where everyone saw the situation differently. The Directors discharged their responsibilities in a sloppy and incompetent manner. They were remiss in the contractual arrangements. Company minutes were open to disingenuousness with newspapers of the day presenting a very critical picture. The standard of engineering supervision was abysmal and the solicitors could not escape criticism. Instead of looking after their clients' best interests they allowed their respective clients to be exposed to dangers that should have been avoided. The heraldic device of the H&MR&CC carried the motto *Devant si je puis* (Forward if I am able) was well chosen. While the company was inefficient, it was not unsuccessful. Its association with the LNWR saw to that.

The H&MR&CC armorial device at Huddersfield station, undergoing restoration in August 1986. *Author*

Ex-LMS 2-6-0 No. 2828 on the Bradley Wood branch with the 4.05 pm from Halifax to Stockport on 9th September, 1948. *Author*

CHAPTER TWO

1850 – 1859

Huddersfield station was completed in October 1850 when a clock was fixed in its centre portion by Mr Heslop, a local clock maker who in 1858 was appointed to repair and maintain all LNWR clocks north of Stafford.

Consolidation of the LNWR 'Yorkshire Lines' began with the opening of the Bradley Wood branch on 26th November, 1850 (1m 15ch) for goods traffic. The earthworks had been finished in 1849 'but no advantage could be made until the West Riding Union Railway between North Dean to Dryclough (Halifax) was complete'. The line had two features: Bradley tunnel 132 yards long and an aqueduct carrying the Lower Cinderfield Dyke. This consisted a long iron channel topped with paving stones and supported by a pair of Tuscan pillars 26 feet 8 inches apart. Passenger services began on 1st January, 1852 when the L&Y inaugurated their service between Huddersfield and Halifax with six trains in each direction. L&Y trains were always more conspicuous than those of the LNWR.

The aqueduct on Tuscan columns that carries the Lower Cinderfield dyke over the Bradley Wood branch, 1948. *Author*

Fowler 2-6-2T No. 57 arrives at Delph with the 4.13 pm from Greenfield on 4th June, 1949.
Author

The terminus and coalyard at Delph, *c.*1910.

Construction of the Delph branch began in April 1850. That short line had two tunnels and a double-span viaduct (all between Dobcross and Measurements). Streethouse tunnel was 81 feet long and Wall Mill tunnel 48 feet long with a 20 feet extension. There were three private sidings: Chattertons serving a quarry; Springbank Mill siding and Mallalieu's. A short line opened, the Copley Hill to Whitehall Junction on 1st October, 1850 which carried all LNWR passenger services to and from Leeds. The Birstal branch was opened on 9th September, 1852 and received scant comment, the death of the Duke of Wellington was accorded precedence.

The first of H.R. Marcus's special excursion trains was run in May 1850 and left the London and North Western station, Leeds at 5.45 am for Liverpool. A similar train on 13th July calling 'at all stations to Stalybridge' saw passengers carried in closed carriages at a fare of 25s.

Two things were synonymous with 'The Yorkshire Lines', rating demands and accidents. At Saddleworth in October 1850 the LNWR obtained a notable victory where instead of the £600 to £700 per mile claimed, the LNWR Director Joseph Brook in company with Mr Watkin, Accountant agreed to pay rates of £250 per mile.

The local authorities regarded the LNWR as being like a milch cow and rating battles to come figured prominently with Marsden and Soothill foremost but other places had much to show in this respect.

Whitehall Junction in 1959, with the LNWR lines from Copley Hill on the right and the Midland route to Bradford on the left. *Author*

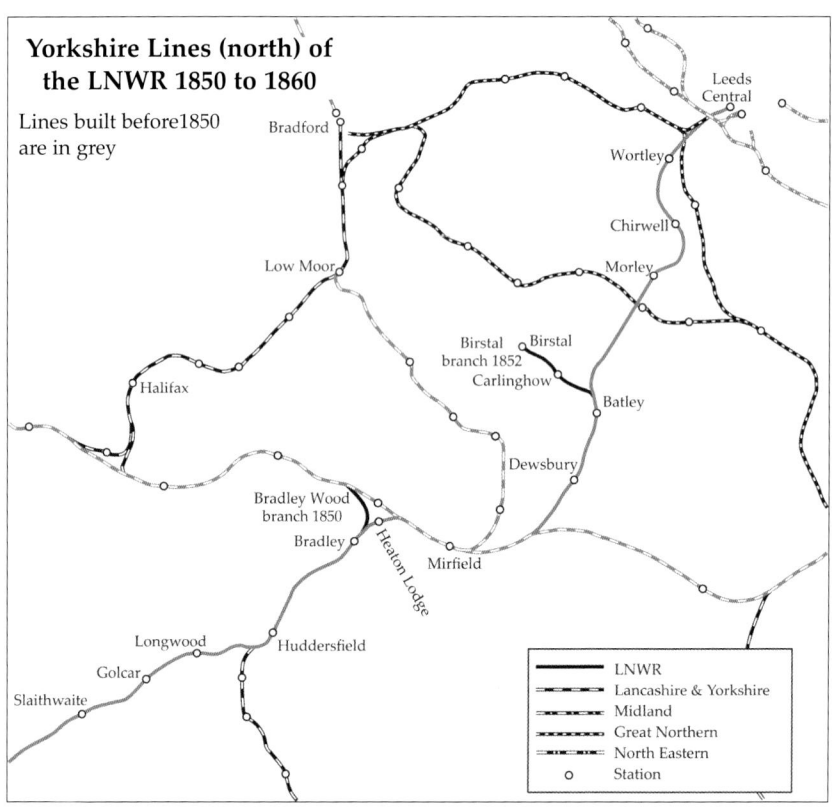

Train services increased from eight to nine daily between Leeds and Manchester while L&Y services over the former LD&M route numbered eight trains, two of which called at all intermediate stations as opposed to three in 1850.

Diggle station was open to passengers as from 1st July, 1850.* The use of local names instead of their designated station names was practised in the 1850s. Mossley was referred to as Mopley Top, Mopley Brow, Trent Top, Edenhole or Hobhole and Saddleworth was known as Brownhill's station. The 1879 Gazetteer however makes no mention of any of these names. At the Wellington Street railway station, as the LNWR described what was to become Leeds Central, a new iron bridge opened over Northern Street inscribed 'Joseph Butler, Stanningley 1852' while flagging in front of the station was completed on 5th May.

---

* First shown in Bradshaw

Birstall station building in 1949, eleven years before demolition.
Author

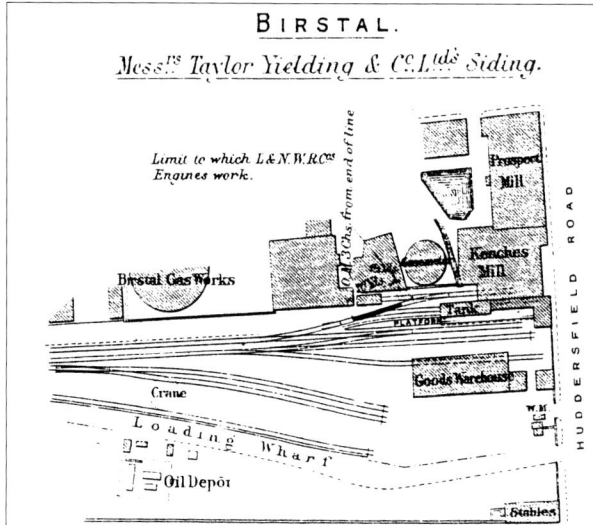

Diagram of Birstall station dated 1915. The engine shed is shown by dotted lines beneath 'Kenches Mill'. The station was renamed in 1907, Birstal gained an 'l' and became Birstall.

Birstall platform and yard from the bufferstops in June 1949.
Author

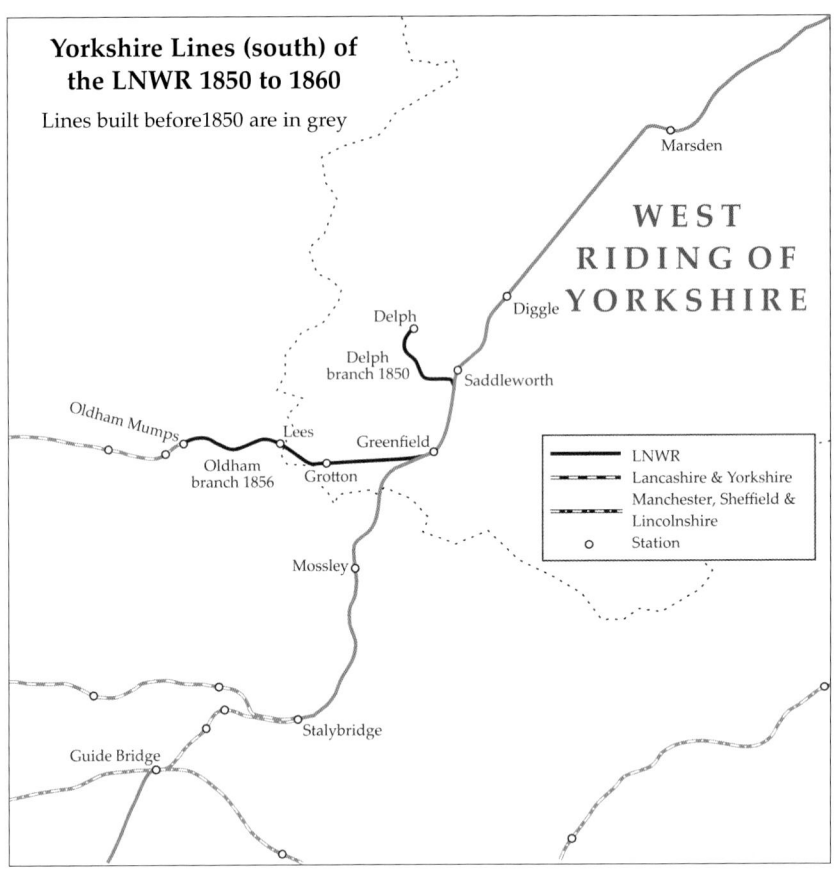

In respect of the projected branch to Oldham from Greenfield, a revized plan was prepared by Joseph Locke and a Bill presented to Parliament. In 1853 the LNWR Oldham Branch Deviation Act allowed another three years for completion of the line.

Excursions blossomed and passenger services improved. A new first and second class service between Euston and Manchester gave a connection in Huddersfield late in 1857:

Euston	9.30 am
Manchester	2.40 pm
Huddersfield	3.50 pm

One of the first private excursions was organized by the Huddersfield Temperance Society on 29th June, 1852 and had to be run in three parts with a total of 3,000 passengers conveyed in 98 carriages with each train hauled by two engines.

1853 was a brisk excursion season, notably to the Saddleworth Exhibition while Henry Marcus, LNWR excursion organizer, was recipient of a public presentation for his valued enterprise. Contract tickets were introduced in December 1853. On Delph Wakes Monday 1855 an excursion took 600 passengers from Delph, Saddleworth and Greenfield to Liverpool. On 11th January, 1854 the lines west of Marsden became blocked in a blizzard. The last train from Leeds to Manchester halted at Marsden station where passengers alighted and sought accommodation for the night. At the Three Tunnels Inn, John Ramsbottom, the LNWR locomotive superintendent became involved in a fracas over the letting of a bed to some ladies, which he took possession of. For Ramsbottom the affair ended better than a similar event some time later at Dudley when he received a black eye!

At Black Rock on 10th April, 1854 the engine of the 4.10 pm Leeds – Manchester express, a Sharp's Yorkshire single, became derailed near Heyrod. The front pair of wheels ran for 386 yards off the track before the engine completely derailed in a cutting and struck the sides of a bridge, overturning to finish up across the down line. The tender, guard's van, horse box and three coaches overturned with three deaths including the engine crew.

Lees station and signal box on the Oldham branch, June 1959. *Author*

Botham Hall siding extended northwards from the Huddersfield & Manchester route near Longwood Goods. It was used for coal traffic until about 1950. Originally 'Bottom Hall' the name was changed late in the 19th century. Photograph 1947. *W.B. Stocks*

A further accident took place at Longwood on 9th August, 1854 when a Leeds to Manchester goods train was reversed onto the down line to allow an express to overtake but a heavy goods train coming from Manchester came into sight. The driver of the latter uncoupled two trucks and ran forward onto the up line. The oncoming goods immediately crashed into the remainder of the train causing damage estimated at £3,000. Subsequently John Ramsbottom complimented the driver, John Luty of Copley Hill shed, for his prompt action in saving the company from a much greater loss.

L&Y operation over the LD&M route via Dewsbury ended on 2nd August, 1854 when their route opened between Bowling Junction and Leeds.

A mail train that began its life in April 1850 lasted until July 1854 leaving Euston at 8.45 pm and arriving in Huddersfield at 6.00 am. In January 1854 the Bangor Mail was introduced, leaving Stockport at 10.25 pm and arriving in Huddersfield at 11.25 pm where it was handed over to the L&Y, concluding its journey at Normanton. Its appearance in the timetable was erratic and regular operation had not become established although by January 1860 it ran between Holyhead and Newcastle.

An agreement dated 23rd July, 1854 saw the Great Northern gain access to Leeds Central High Level by purchasing the moiety of a share of the LNWR/L&Y viaduct from Holbeck to a junction with the Leeds Central station lines.

The end of 1855 saw the expiration of the Gladstone Agreement between LNWR, Midland, MS&L and GNR regarding the division of traffic from the West Riding and the Midlands to London. The Gladstone agreement of August 1851 gave the GNR 63 per cent of West Riding traffic and the end of the Euston Square Confederacy was concluded. On 11th February, 1856 the GNR announced that fares from Leeds and Bradford to King's Cross would be 15s. first class and 10s. second class. From 22nd February the LNWR, Midland and MS&L instituted two new trains from the same places and others to Sheffield Victoria at fares of 5s. first class and 3s. 6d. second class. 'The fares to and from Euston by the above company's route will in no case exceed those charged by any other company', signed Mark Huish, James Alport and Ed Watkin. This was withdrawn on 1st March, 1856 but an advert inscribed 'Derby 20th August, 1856' showed a new service between Halifax, Brighouse, Huddersfield and Sheffield Victoria to Euston with fares from Huddersfield 30s. first class and 20s. second class, leaving Halifax at 12.05 pm with a Euston arrival at 6.00 pm. The arrangement continued until 28th February, 1857 but the train ran in the same times between Huddersfield and Sheffield until 28th November, 1857 without LNWR involvement. The episode was something that Richard Moon disapproved of. A meeting was held at King's Cross on 7th April, 1858 relating to the GNR/MS&L's 5s. fare between Manchester and London. Rates were advanced in June when all companies charged the same, the LNWR at a disadvantage for traffic from Leeds. Settlement on competitive rates was finalized in December 1858.

A major event on 4th July, 1856 was the opening of the Oldham branch from Greenfield. From Manchester Victoria station to Mumps there were nine trains operated each way, two of which were extended to Delph. The horse-drawn train had been provided by Paul Scholes, formerly a local carter from Leeds. Having an obliging personality Scholes frequently operated improvised trains. The absence of these quickly led to discontent by travellers from Delph being expressed in the *Huddersfield Chronicle* and *Huddersfield Examiner*.

The year 1857 saw the replacement of 'The Yorkshire Lines' title, the area incorporated in the North Eastern Division of the LNWR. Locomotives had 400 added to their fleet numbers. Mention should be made of the Oldham, Ashton and Guide Bridge Junction Railway (OA&GB), authorized by an Act dated 10th August, 1857 whereby a partnership between the LNWR and MS&L was established.

A meeting was held at the Coopers Arms, Ossett to consider the LNWR proposal for a line between Dewsbury and Wakefield to a junction with the Midland. Support was wholehearted and the LNWR announced they would finance the project themselves.

Traffic in the mid-1850s was building up in every direction but operational black spots were evident. The decision to make only a single Standedge tunnel caused delays which led to sad observations on the state of the LNWR. Standedge, Huddersfield, Heaton Lodge and Mirfield had become repeatedly prone to mishaps.

The four and seven day excursion ticket had been introduced and a choice of seven trains given from 22nd February, 1857 to those travelling via London, where fares from Huddersfield were 28 day return 37s. first class, covered carriage 17s. and the fares for four and seven day returns at 21s. and 12s. 6d. respectively.

On 26th February, 1857 a Leeds – Manchester express collided on Slaithwaite viaduct with a goods train that was being shunted and this caused 11 passengers to be injured. At Marsden on 30th October, 1857 a truck left on the line during shunting ran back on the wrong line. An engine driven by John Adkins set off in pursuit and overtook the runaway whilst travelling on the down line at Slaithwaite. On reaching Low Westwood Crossing he rejoined the up line and travelling in the direction of Huddersfield allowed the loose wagon to gently catch up, then pushed the offending vehicle back to Marsden.

A new first and second class service between Euston and Manchester gave a connection to Huddersfield at the end of 1857:

Euston	9.30 am
Manchester	2.40 pm
Huddersfield	3.50 pm

In 1858 Bottom (Botham) Hall Siding was in use for coal traffic. This left the line at Longwood and ran northwards with 11 chains of track owned by the LNWR and the remainder by Dale Shaw. Expansion in other places saw a projected line from Batley to Adwalton Junction with lands to be purchased in Bradford. The line would have commenced at Birstal Junction and thence via Howden Clough to join the Leeds

Bradford and Halifax Junction line at Adwalton Junction having a length of 2 miles 6 furlongs and 70 links with a ruling gradient of one in 40. At Bradford a short line of 6 furlongs and 6 links was envisaged near Adolphus Street station. A projected Wakefield line would have commenced at Dewsbury and run to Ossett with a branch from Ossett to Alverthorpe and an Alverthorpe North curve. Lands would be acquired at Wakefield from a junction with the Bradford, Wakefield and Leeds Railway near Piccadilly and to a junction with the L&Y at Ings Road. Here, as in the Bradford plan, the ideas of the Great Northern Railway prevailed. Short lines to serve particular industries all met the same fate, the GNR had the advantage as all its lines ended at King's Cross.

Excursions acquired an established pattern and provided exceptional value for money with destinations at this time chiefly Liverpool, Belle Vue and London. On 5th July, 1858 a Catholic Church outing from Huddersfield to Greenfield carried 1,700 passengers in 34 carriages. A Royal visit to Leeds induced large crowds to travel but in this case at normal fares.

A strong desire to reduce the excessive hours worked by railwaymen was voiced by Joseph Woodhead, owner of the *Huddersfield Examiner* and a great liberal. One example mentioned was of the staff of

Adverts for LNWR excursions to the Isle of Man and for the Royal visit to Leeds

Plan of the site of collision at Springwood Cutting on 13th June, 1858.

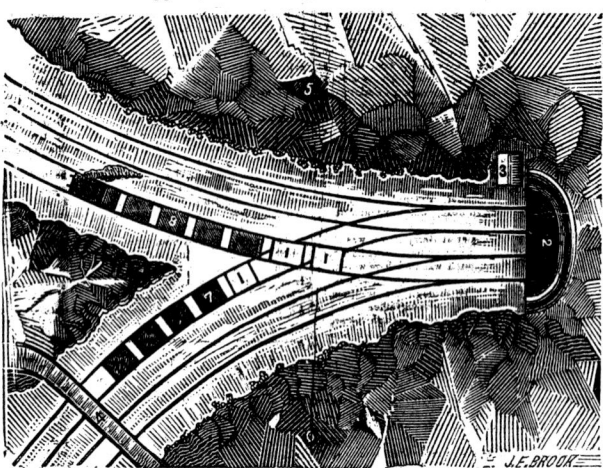

Springwood Junction on 6th July, 1958 with Farnley 'Jubilee' 4-6-0 No. 45695 *Minotaur* on the 3.20 pm Leeds to Liverpool express.
Author

Huddersfield goods warehouse whose hours of work were from 7.00 am until 10.00 pm with half an hour for breakfast, one hour for dinner and half an hour for tea, for a wage of 17*s*. 10*d*. weekly. When traffic was busy work continued until 2 or 3 am!

An unusual mishap occurred on 15th March, 1858 near Marsden when the 2.00 pm from Huddersfield stalled beyond Slaithwaite due to overcrowding, which then caused the coach springs to flatten. The train was ultimately dragged to Marsden.

A serious accident occurred at Springwood Junction, near Huddersfield, on 13th June, 1858 as a consequence of five loaded wagons having escaped from Honley goods yard on the L&Y Penistone branch. The wagons ran back and collided with the two rearmost vehicles of the 1.30 pm Huddersfield to Manchester train, which then caused four persons to lose their lives. The cause of the runaway was never established. There was yet another accident on 20th July, 1858 at Longwood, when a coal train being reversed into Bottom Hall siding was run into by the ill-fated 1.30 pm Huddersfield to Manchester train, the driver of which had overrun signals.

Delph branch services were increased from two to three each way daily as from 25th September, 1859. Heavy rain at the start of 1859 caused delay to the opening of the OA&GB Junction Railway. The foundation stone of Park Bridge viaduct was unveiled by Leigh Richmond Esq, estate manager to the Earl of Stamford, on 1st October, 1859.

Expansion was contemplated to Normanton where property was earmarked and a short line to be made opposite the recently completed Midland engine shed on the east side of the line with a length of 5 chains. A further purchase for a short line, 7 chains, was from a junction with the York and North Midland Railway near Altofts Junction facing Castleford.

The LNWR's growing traffic to the north-east was hampered by Leeds still being a terminus. Running powers were obtained from Heaton Lodge to Bradford, to Halifax via North Dean and between Thornhill and Goose Hill Junction, under clauses contained in the Amalgamation Act between the East Lancashire Railway and the L&Y, dated 13th August, 1859.

The operation of LNWR passenger trains between Leeds and Manchester was divided between two sheds, Copley Hill at Leeds and Ordsall Lane at Salford, with other duties supplied by Hillhouse and Edge Hill. Engine lists dated 1858-59 by J. Wells and George Hinchliffe are given in *Appendix One*.

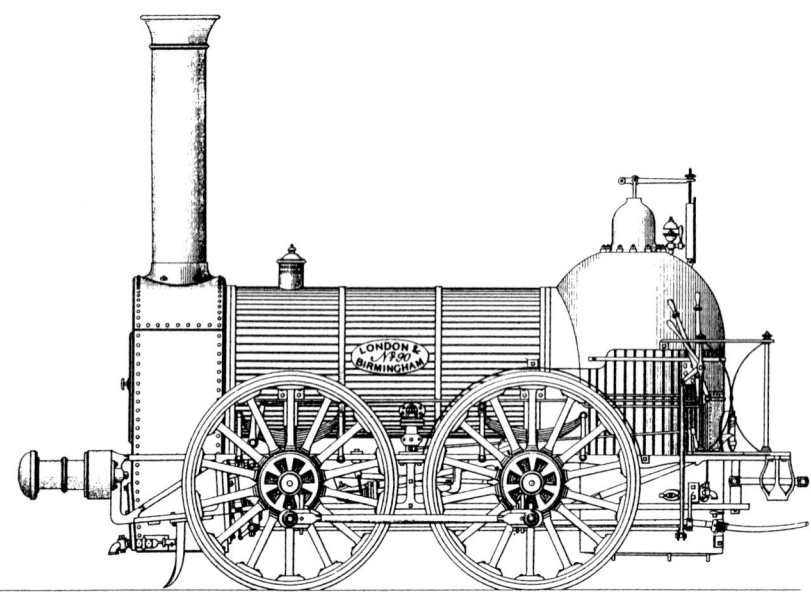

London & Birmingham Bury type 0-4-0 built by Maudsley & Field as used on the Birstal branch in its early years.

'Crewe Goods' 2-4-0 No. 512. Members of this class were allocated to Copley Hill shed in the 1850s and were used on all types of work.

CHAPTER THREE

1860 – 1869

Normanton Joint Station Committee (NJSC) gave full approval to the LNWR joining under terms of its Act of 1860. Two sidings were earmarked for LNWR use with joint use of a warehouse and provision for an engine shed accommodating four engines. The LNWR had an interest in the Dewsbury, Batley, Gomersal and Bradford Railway drawn up by J. E. Errington Barnes from a junction with the Birstal branch and to cross the Bowling Junction and Laisterdyke – Adolphus Street, Bradford. Features included a ruling gradient of 1 in 55, a tunnel 3,115 yards in length on a line of 6 miles $6^{3}/_{4}$ furlongs.

In July 1860 space occupied by a siding at the L&Y end of the Huddersfield station was excavated. At Marsden criticism was made in November about an urgent need for a large goods warehouse and coal chutes. However, the new station at Bradley elicited praise from the *Huddersfield Examiner* on 14th July '…a tasteful station garden laid out by the station master Elisha Binyon'. The principal features were two mottos sown in Virginia Stock: 'May they ever be united – England and France' and 'God Save the Queen'. A drastic overhaul of the timetable was effected on 2nd January, 1860 (Sundays excepted) when the following were inaugurated:

am	*am*	*pm*	*pm*		*am*	*am*	*pm*	*pm*
6.30	9.05	2.20	4.30	LIVERPOOL	12.00	12.25	6.30	11.45
8.50	10.20	3.45	5.25	MANCHESTER VICTORIA	9.40	11.25	5.15	10.25
10.00	11.25	5.15	6.55	HUDDERSFIELD	9.10	10.15	4.04	9.00
10.40	12.05	5.50	7.30	HALIFAX	7.40	9.40	3.30	8.30
10.55	12.15	6.10	7.45	BRADFORD EXCHANGE	7.20	9.30	3.20	8.15
10.50	12.10	5.50	7.45	WAKEFIELD KIRKGATE	7.25	9.35	3.20	8.15

At this time the Bangor Mail was timed:

am		*pm*
7.08	NEWCASTLE	6.01
9.38	YORK	3.35
11.07	HUDDERSFIELD	1.05
12.12	STOCKPORT	12.48

thence via Crewe to Holyhead. Inauguration occurred in September 1860. Another improvement was the introduction of 1st and 2nd Class return tickets from Huddersfield to Manchester, the facility previously available only in the opposite direction. A number of anomalies still

Webb 'Precursor' No. 680 *Gifford*, which was stationed at Farnley Junction shed 1890-91.
Locomotive Publishing Co. - Author's collection

Newspaper notice December 1859

LONDON AND NORTH-WESTERN RAILWAY.

NEW ROUTE BETWEEN LANCASHIRE AND YORKSHIRE.

ON and after Monday, January 2nd, 1860, the London and North-Western Company will run Passenger Trains daily (Sundays excepted;) between BRADFORD, WAKEFIELD, HALIFAX, and LIVERPOOL, MANCHESTER, and intermediate Stations on the London and North-Western Railway, as follows :—

To BRADFORD, WAKEFIELD, and HALIFAX—

	a.m.	a.m.	p.m.	p.m.
Leave Liverpool	6 30	9 5	2 20	4 30
,, Manchester	8 50	10 20	3 45	5 45
Arrive Huddersfield	10 5	11 25	5 15	6 55
,, Halifax	10 40	12 5	5 50	7 30
,, Bradford	10 55	12 15	6 10	7 45
,, Wakefield	10 50	12 10	6 10	7 45

To MANCHESTER, LIVERPOOL, &c.

	a.m.	a.m.	p.m.	p.m.
Leave Bradford	7 20	9 30	3 20	8 10
,, Wakefield	7 25	9 35	3 20	8 15
,, Halifax	7 40	9 40	3 30	8 30
,, Huddersfield	8 10	10 15	4 5	9 0
Arrive Manchester	9 40	11 25	5 15	10 25
,, Liverpool	12 0	12 25	6 30	11 45
,, Stockport	9 37	11 33	5 23	10 30
,, Macclesfield	11 5	12 42	7 35	
,, Crewe	10 17	12 45	6 27	11 55
,, Birmingham	12 20	3 30	8 25	2 26
,, London	2 30	6 25	11 0	5 0

The London and North-Western trains will depart from, and arrive at, the Lancashire and Yorkshire Company's Stations at Bradford, Halifax, and Wakefield.—For particulars, see the London and North-Western Company's Time Bill for January ; or apply to their Booking-Offices, at any of the Stations. By Order.

W. CAWKWELL, General Manager;
Euston Station, December, 1859.

existed, i.e. the cost of an LNWR return between Manchester and Halifax was 5s. 3d. and the cost of two single journeys between Huddersfield and Manchester was 7s. 6d., while the L&Y return from Berry Brow to Manchester was 4s. 3d.

Jonas Brook and Bros of Meltham Mills gave their employees an outing to Scarborough with two trains running from Slaithwaite. Period excursions to coastal resorts were advertised 'Every Saturday from Leeds Wellington station at 1.45 and all stations to Marsden, thence Liverpool for the Isle of Man'. In the opposite direction 'every Wednesday and Saturday from Liverpool Lime Street at 12.05 pm, Manchester Victoria at 2.00 pm and all principal stations to Harrogate and Scarborough'. The route of the Liverpool excursion had hitherto been via Manchester Victoria, but was now altered to run via Guide Bridge and Ordsall Lane. On the other hand the MS&L would have liked more traffic on their route. An advert dated 19th October, 1858, not naming the company, described trains from the MS&L station each Monday and Wednesday.

A special 1st Class express ran for the Liverpool Cotton trade:

AM		PM
9.10	STALYBRIDGE	5.35
9.15	ASHTON	5.31
9.17	DUKINFIELD	5.26
9.20	GUIDE BRIDGE	5.24
9.35	ARDWICK	---
---	MANCHESTER SOUTH JUNCTION	5.05
9.45	OXFORD ROAD	4.50
10.10	WARRINGTON	4.20
10.30	GARSTON	4.00
11.00 / 12.00	NORTH JOHN STREET (Liverpool by special horse bus)	3.16

Prize fighting attracted crowds that arrived by train at Greenfield but when the police became aware stern measures were taken to stop this practice in the early 1860s.

For Slaithwaite Feast on 11th August, 1860 1,100 passengers were taken to Liverpool with special trains also to Rhyl and Belle Vue. Delph Wakes excursions from Leeds to Belle Vue on the day called at all stations to Marsden and were divided into one train of 32 carriages, 'a second of almost equal length', while a third with 20 carriages had to be

No. 535, a Ramsbottom 'DX' 0-6-0. Locomotives of this class were allocated to Copley Hill shed from about 1860. Although built for goods traffic they worked all types of trains, including passenger expresses. Note the absence of brake blocks on the locomotive.
Locomotive Publishing Co.- Author's collection

put on at Huddersfield where 1,899 had booked. The occasion was a hand bell ringing contest!

The annual crop of mishaps began on 25th February, 1860 at Greenfield when the 2.00 pm train from Oldham stopped short of the platform on an incline where the engine was to be detached and the coaches run into the platform by gravity. The guard's brake failed and the coaches hit the buffers like a tidal wave which caused injury to 11 passengers and serious damage to four coaches. On 28th April at Heaton Lodge the engine hauling the 3.15 pm express from Leeds collided at fast speed with two trucks being shunted on the main line. The engine suffered serious damage to its cylinders and after 40 minutes' delay the train continued, hauled by the shunting engine.

On 2nd July at Springwood Junction a Crewe to Leeds goods train collided with the tender of an L&Y goods train which had overshot signals and fouled the main line. The driver of the latter was in the act of reversing his engine and was pushing his train back on to the Penistone line at moment of impact.

A second accident at Heaton Lodge occurred on 1st August when the 3.45 pm Huddersfield to Leeds train approached the station and ran into a goods train emerging from a siding. A similar accident occurred on 1st September involving the 3.40 pm L&Y train from Huddersfield.

At Mossley in November 1860 a goods train caught fire. This was divided, with half run onto the Delph branch and the remainder placed in Saddleworth goods yard where stock and contents were totally consumed and the rails distorted by heat.

A notable agreement made in 1861 was when the North Eastern Railway (NER) concluded for 20 years to accept all traffic except mails for destinations between the Humber and West Hartlepool, later being extended to Newcastle. In reciprocation the LNWR would take all traffic from ports between the Mersey and Port Carlisle. Additional trains were to be run if required by either company and the NER would be allowed to run between Altofts Junction and Heaton Lodge Junction and the Ashton branch of the L&Y to Manchester. This preceded the operation of emigrant specials, a traffic that lasted until the 1920s.

An inaugural run was made over the OA&GB Junction Railway on 1st June when an engine and two coaches ran to Oldham from Guide Bridge. The official opening took place on 31st July when 30 new

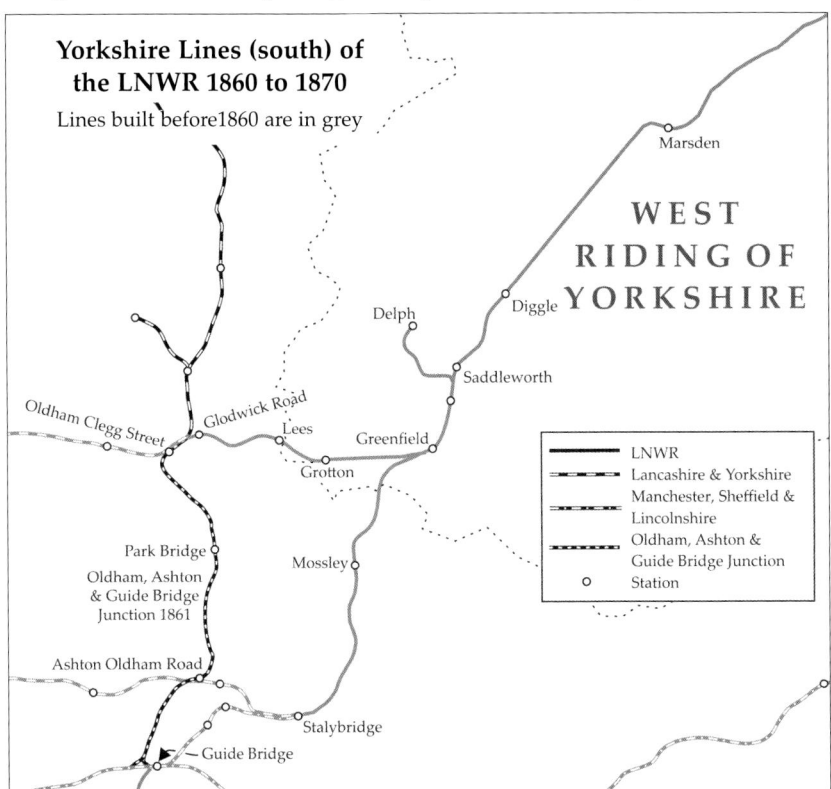

> **Specials of Emigrants—Hull to Liverpool.**
> Specials with Emigrants from Hull will be worked, as occasion requires, between Leeds and Liverpool via Stockport. Mr. Swaine, Leeds, will advise the Line in all such cases, and special steps must be taken to keep a clear road for the running of the Train.
> Mr. Swaine will specially advise Diggle of the composition and time of departure of the Specials, which will stop at Diggle for necessary purposes, and Mr. Arksey will arrange to have a number of Buckets filled with clean water, for drinking, ready on the arrival of the Trains.
> The Trains to be Telegraphed from Huddersfield to Diggle and Guide Bridge; Diggle to Stalybridge, Guide Bridge, and Heaton Norris; Stockport to Arpley, Ditton, and Liverpool.

Notice re emigrant trains.

carriages were hauled from Manchester London Road by a locomotive that had been decorated. On the footplate were Mr Sacré MS&L locomotive superintendent and Colonel Yolland, the Board of Trade inspecting officer. Reversal was made at Guide Bridge and the train passed the site of the incomplete direct junction. A stop was made at Park Bridge to inspect the viaduct made of grey stone and decorated archways at both ends. After a party marched in procession to Oldham Town Hall, one speaker was acclaimed when he said 'they had at last emancipated Oldham from the L&Y'. That portion of line beyond Clegg Street was not yet complete while at Mumps a new warehouse was under construction. It had been intended to have the Clegg Street station located at Rhodes Bank, a move opposed by the L&Y. The line had two notable features, a triangular junction at Guide Bridge and another at Ashton Moss. The OA&GB Rule Book of 1861 included engine whistle codes to be used for routing at the junctions.

Two excursions were run before public services commenced on 26th August when nine trains ran between Oldham and Guide Bridge and two to London Road, but in each case there was one more train in the reverse direction. Sunday trains comprised three to Guide Bridge and two to London Road while four trains arrived from Guide Bridge but only one from London Road.

On 16th September the OA&GB introduced a horse bus between Oldham and Rochdale and run in connection with London trains with three services in each direction. The journey took 60 minutes. From 1st October the direct service between Oldham and Manchester London Road was increased to 13 trains each way with five on Sundays.

On 11th March a new station was opened at Morley, the old one located 'nearer to the tunnel'. Speculation occurred at Longwood concerning a projected new station for both passengers and goods 'to be placed nearer to Huddersfield'. Land was to be purchased near Adolphus Street, Bradford between the stations Wakefield Road and Heaton Street. The length was to be 34 chains and 7 yards, but such aspirations were quashed as the Leeds Bradford and Halifax Junction Railway received powers by an Act dated 7th July, 1861 to make a branch from that railway to join the Birstal branch at Batley. The Bradford Wakefield and Leeds Railway was enabled to make a line from Ossett to join the LNWR at Batley by another Act on the same day. These two lines terminated in a double junction, one located 140 yards south of the LNWR booking office at Batley and the other 260 yards north of the office. Both lines were operated by the Great Northern Railway and later absorbed by it.

In August 1861 the railway telegraph wires, instead of running through the tunnel, were altered to be carried over the top of Standedge where corrosion was less. Subsequently ownership of telegraph poles at Standedge was subject to enquiry and court action and increased payment of rates to Marsden Local Board.

In 1861 there were six operational mishaps. The first concerned a coal train being shunted at Morley, which ran back down the main line. The train engine chased after it but was unable to couple up, whereupon the guard courageously jumped from engine tender to wagon and was able to fasten down brakes, halting the runaway short of Wortley station.

On 29th March as the noon train from Huddersfield was crossing Dewsbury viaduct, the locomotive crank axle broke resulting in one and a half hours' delay before a fresh engine arrived from Leeds. On 17th October at Greenfield a passenger train coming at speed from Manchester ran into the back of a goods train that had stalled. A mishap

Dewsbury viaduct, showing the arch that spans Bradford Road. *Author*

'Jubilee' class No. 45581 *Bihar and Orissa* on the 5.15 pm Leeds to Liverpool passing Batley on 28th July, 1959. Batley West signal box is to right of the locomotive, with the former Birstall bay platform in front of the warehouse. *Author*

A down goods train crossing Union Mill viaduct, Batley on 5th June, 1958 headed by Stanier 2-8-0 No. 48743. *Author*

at Elland on the L&Y main line occurred as the 3.30 pm express from Halifax emerged from Elland tunnel where it collided with an L&Y ballast engine that was shunting and became badly damaged. The LNWR's driver and fireman received a drenching of water but took their train forward – this comprised a tank engine travelling bunker first and two coaches carrying five passengers. Capt Tyler conducted an accident inquiry and concluded by stating that the LNWR train had run past a badly sited distant signal. At Mirfield on 7th December a collision involving an LNWR engine and tender and two carriages travelling to Wakefield 'was due to the inevitable result of the various systems of working in operation on the L&Y'.

Finally, at Batley on 12th December as the last train of the day was coming into the station from Birstal en route to Dewsbury, the engine stopped short of the platform opposite the goods warehouse, where the driver uncoupled two goods vehicles and drew them forward into another part of the station. Meanwhile, the carriages and remaining trucks on the train were being pushed into the station by staff when the engine returned and collided, the driver being unaware of the movement. A number of passengers were bruised. It was the usual practice when vehicles were to be detached for this to be done at the platform.

The year 1862 saw the LNWR (Additional Powers Act dated 7th August) authorize a line from a junction with the LD&M at Wortley to Farnley ironworks and approach the main line by a curve facing Morley.

Trains from Delph and Greenfield began to work through to the new Clegg Street station at Oldham from 1st July. On 21st October the LNWR's station at Mumps was closed and replaced by a new station at Glodwick Road on 1st November which was also used by OA&GB trains that terminated there. 'The station is a beautiful one .... The appointments are good .... The wretched foot approach to Mumps by way of the railway at Rhodes Bank will be done away with'.

The intermediate stations on the OA&GB line were Park Bridge, Ashton and Ashton Moss. Originally a handful of trains called at the latter, but with one exception all trains ceased to call from 1st March, 1862. The solitary exception ceased on 1st June.

Ownership of the OA&GB passed jointly into MS&L and LNWR as provided for by an Act dated 30th June, 1862. The two companies guaranteed a dividend of $4^{3}/_{4}$ per cent on the locally subscribed capital of £40,000. Passengers carried by the OA&GB during 1862 amounted to 326,905.

Complaints about the condition and facilities at Huddersfield station were made during the year. Its platform was raised by 11 inches

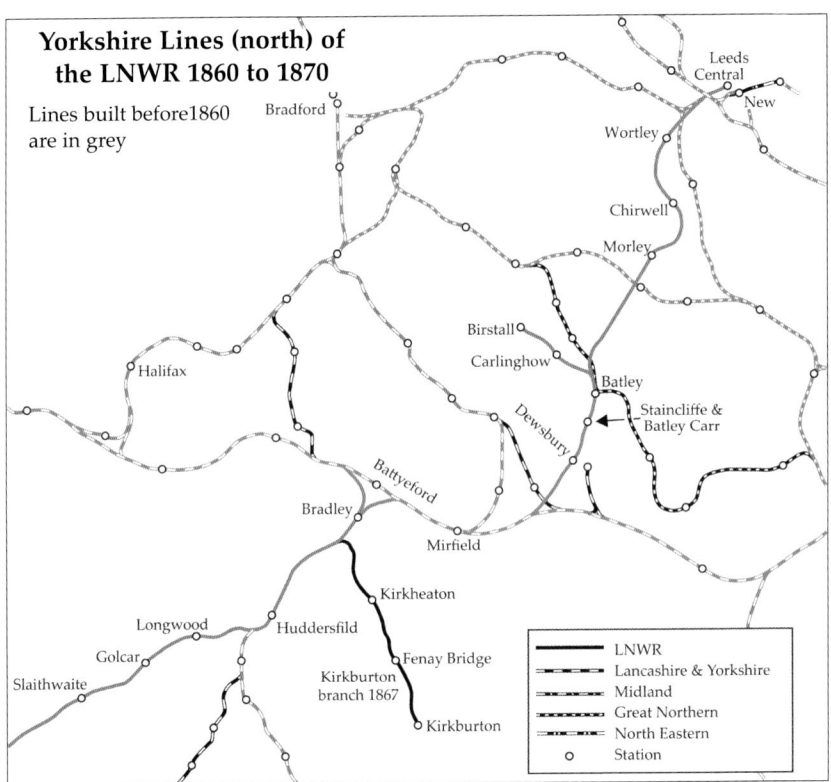

throughout its length. The L&Y waiting room, previously open and facing the platform, became enclosed. The LNWR waiting room was treated in a similar manner, although divided from the passage by a partition. Numerous excursions to both Euston and King's Cross were run in conjunction with the 1862 International Exhibition, the LNWR had a special fare 'for bodies of workmen' from Oldham, Ashton, Huddersfield etc. at 6s. return for parties of 250 and over, and 5s. return for parties of 300 or more. The MS&L/GNR advertised their facilities at the same time but at 5s. return regardless of number.

There were four mishaps. The first involved a locomotive emerging from the goods yard at Slaithwaite on to the viaduct which struck two trucks in a passing down goods, causing derailment before falling over the side of the viaduct on 25th January. On 25th February an LNWR express to Bradford ran past signals and collided with the back of a preceding goods train at Heckmondwike. The LNWR locomotive was severely disabled while the LNWR train was taken forward to its destination by the engine of the L&Y goods train. On 8th May delay was caused at Mirfield by an arriving LNWR train whose locomotive *Una* suffered a broken tender axle. Finally on 4th November as the 5.45 am Manchester to Leeds train was leaving Huddersfield from the platform to the down line, it collided with a double-headed up goods that had overrun signals.

The LNWR (Additional) Powers Act of 28th July, 1863 authorized the making of a line from Hall Wood to Dean Bottom Plantation (Kirkburton). Also promoted in that year was the Halifax, Huddersfield and Keighley Railway, a forerunner of things to come, but in this case not of LNWR conception.

In July 1863 a deputation went to Euston asking for a new station to be made at Batley Carr, one of many signs of exasperation felt throughout the line both in respect of passenger facilities and the movement of goods. However, improvements were being made.

Services on the Manchester to Wakefield route were extended to Normanton on 1st April and by August there were seven trains running in each direction. Goods traffic to Normanton advertised to commence on the same day actually started on 1st May as the lack of facilities at Normanton had resulted in postponement. This had caused speculation

Staincliffe & Batley Carr station after closure, with class '4MT' 2-6-4T No. 42377 on a Huddersfield to Leeds local. The station house is on the left. *Author*

when William Cawkwell disputed the cost and suggested appointing an arbitrator. The NJSC agreed, but the minutes make no further mention, so presumably the matter was settled. The Bangor Mail recommenced (but was unadvertised) on 1st April and ran until 16th April, 1864 when it became publicized:

11.09 pm		Chester		2.15 am
12.04 am		Crewe		12.55 am
12.48 am	↓	Stockport	↑	12.12 am
1.52 am		Huddersfield		11.07 pm
2.34 am		Normanton		

By August 1864 the capacity of the L&Y main line had reached saturation point. The LNWR trains between Huddersfield and Halifax were withdrawn and arrangements were made for the L&Y to run their connections. Excursions and special trains running on specific days to North Wales, Dublin, Windermere, Bangor, Llandudno, Douglas (IoM) etc. were proving immensely popular and ordinary excursion took a larger number of destinations, as exemplified on 25th June:

Leeds Wellington	6.30 am	
Bradford L&Y	5.55 am	change at Mirfield
Batley	6.55 am	
Dewsbury	7.00 am	
Mirfield	7.10 am	Fare 2s. 3d. return
Huddersfield	7.20 am	Buxton arr 10.00 am
Oldham OA&GB	7.45 am	return 6.00 pm
Stalybridge	8.10 am	
Ashton MS&L	8.15 am	
Guide Bridge	8.20 am	

An excursion from Leeds to Bangor later the same month was at a fare of 2s. 8d. – exceptional value.

A further service introduced on 1st April was the 11.45 am Manchester to Leeds for the North Eastern line. The OA&GB route was used exclusively for passenger traffic until 1st February, 1863. A slump in the cotton industry, a period of depression and the knock-on effect of the American Civil War occurred shortly after opening and affected the large number of pits in the area, plus Park Bridge ironworks. Also the MS&L owned the Ashton Canal whose Fairbottom branch also served the area. Goods traffic for the year amounted to 10,218 tons but no mineral traffic was carried, neither was there much through running

Class '5MT' 4-6-0 No. 45015 stopping at Morley with the 8.15 am Leeds–Liverpool on 23rd May, 1959. *Author*

An up goods hauled by ex-LNWR 0-8-0 No. 49323 passes Morley on 23rd May, 1959. *Author*

Top: A York–Liverpool train with class '47' No. 47541 emerges from Morley tunnel on 3rd June, 1981.
Author

Centre: The Leeds portal of Morley tunnel with a class '158', July 1998.
Author

Right: The third shaft from the Leeds end of Morley tunnel. Photographed on 13th November, 1981. *Author*

from the LNWR. The direct passenger service between Oldham and Manchester, London Road dwindled to one train a day and that was discontinued on 1st June, a symbol of the swift and cruel changes in trade and commerce.

The Leeds Central Committee minutes record the LNWR's intention to demolish a glass screen which had been erected by the GNR, who objected. The LNWR required to build offices upon the west wall of the station.

1863 was notable for the number of mishaps, none of which would require investigation by the Board of Trade Railway's inspector. A description is given if only to reveal the extent of the problems caused. On 8th January near Wards Siding, Churwell the 12.00 noon Dewsbury to Leeds passenger train ran into the back of a coal train. On 24th February at Uppermill viaduct where relaying was in progress the 9.40 am Crewe to Leeds goods suffered an axle fracture on its first vehicle. Several trucks were derailed, masonry dislodged and precipitated below. Ten days later during shunting, part of a goods train on the main line was run into by the 4.00 Crewe to Leeds goods. At Stalybridge on 15th August the 2.00 pm ex-Manchester train, having set back into a siding to attach a horse box, resumed its journey but was run into head-on by a train that had overrun signals; two passengers were killed and two coaches wrecked. At Ashton MS&L an MS&L passenger train to Manchester London Road similarly ran past a signal and crashed into the back of an LNWR goods train. On 27th August the engine hauling a Leeds – Huddersfield passenger train broke a crank axle at Thornhill LNWR Junction.

On 5th September an LNWR goods train in thick fog ran through signals at Horbury Bridge and ploughed into an L&Y goods bound for Bradford. On 10th November LNWR No. 308 was derailed at Goose Hill Junction Normanton blocking both L&Y and Midland lines. These accidents caused surprisingly short delays to traffic. While sophisticated breakdown equipment was unheard of, the number of men mustered for such work was very high. Many vehicles made of timber either disintegrated or were reduced to matchwood.

1864 was a year when great ideas were made for expansion, many of which were frustrated. The LNWR participated in the Leeds, North Yorkshire and Durham Railway whose project envisaged a route from Leeds to Scarborough, Stockton and Hartlepool. Commencing at a terminus, facing west alongside Leeds Wellington station on the north side to turn a half circle and thence via Shadwell Wetherby, Tollerton, Easingwold, Ampleforth and Helmsley to Scarborough where it would terminate on the cliff top on the south side of the valley. From Helmsley a line would run via Stokesley and Thornaby to Stockton and from Thornaby to a point near Billingham. At Leeds a connection outside the terminus would be made with the GNR, LNWR and a triangular junction with the Midland thence on a viaduct 200 yards long with a further viaduct 600 yards of 45 arches 35 feet span, followed by a 700 yards long tunnel, then another 500 yards viaduct of 37 arches, 35 feet span at Chapeltown with a maximum grade of one in 100 from Scarcroft to Collingham. At Alne a junction would be made with the North Eastern with a 5 furlong spur leading northwards and a south spur of 4 furlongs, 5.65 chains. A triangular junction was proposed at Helmsley and a tunnel 1,616 yards long 46 miles from Leeds. At Stokesley a spur would lead to the NER 2 furlongs 2.25 chains while from Thornaby $69\frac{1}{2}$ miles from Leeds a branch would lead to South Shore 1 mile 2 furlongs and 4.30 chains. However, the plans came to nothing and the line was never built.

The militia were called in at Rowley on the Kirkburton branch to take possession of some land when surveyors staked out the route, however, were not called upon to use force. The LNWR were willing to allow the harvest to be gathered, which was the object of the dispute, and were happy to avoid paying compensation. This was the first occasion since 1843 the militia had been used in the district. Henceforth Special Constabulary was used when disputes arose and in 1865 this amounted to 865 members in the Huddersfield division.

Class '4' 2-6-4T No. 42377 arriving at Dewsbury with a Leeds–Huddersfield local on 23rd May, 1959. *Author*

The closure of Heaton Lodge station took place from 1st November, 1864 due to declining patronage and although adjacent to Battyeford, no bridge existed over the River Calder. Crossing in bad weather was a dreadful experience, the ferry having on some occasions been swept downstream as far as Mirfield. At the time of closure it was served by four trains to Leeds and three to Huddersfield with the same number on Sundays.

Complaints were made that insufficient expresses called at Slaithwaite, a plea supported by the Earl of Dartmouth who cited a proviso in his agreement with the LNWR which stated the station was a first class one. The sequel was that two semi-fast trains called there additionally, the first of a number of improvements. From 1st May a new service was introduced:

	am		pm
Leeds	8.00 am	Liverpool	4.20 pm
Huddersfield	8.28 am	Manchester	5.25 pm
Manchester	9.35 am	Huddersfield	6.20 pm
Liverpool	10.40 am	Leeds	7.00 pm

The outward journey called at Dewsbury at 8.18 am from 1st December and gave good connections at Stalybridge for Stockport, the Midlands, West of England and Euston.

From 1st June the LNWR inaugurated 'A new route to Blackpool' with an excursion from Leeds. On the same day revised and additional rates for goods, iron and mineral traffic were made while consignments would be accepted for Great Western stations. Later in the month Tourist Tickets commenced. As an antidote, the Huddersfield Chamber of Commerce claimed it was cheaper to send goods to Manchester and then send them on to London, than it was to send them from the West Riding to London via LNW. With pressure applied from other Chambers in the area, a rate reduction came about on 1st November.

On Whit Monday 1864 an excursion ran between Huddersfield and Bangor:

Huddersfield	5.00 am	Bangor	5.00 pm
Bangor	12.00 noon	Huddersfield	1.30 am

Unfortunately it was a trial for all those aboard the train as it failed to make any intermediate stop. The importance of such trains making an intermediate stop to allow a necessary call to be made was emphasized and station masters notified accordingly.

Ravensthorpe goods warehouse 1991, after use as a store by the Electricity Generating Board. *Author*

Dewsbury warehouse on 19th July, 1963. *Author*

For the Leeds Flower Show of 1864 the LNWR advertised 'single fare for return journey' from all stations between Stalybridge and Leeds including Bradford and Wakefield, passengers from those places having to journey to Mirfield and change there. A further attraction by excursion train was to visit Liverpool to see the *Great Western* Steamship and HMS *Majestic*, but in this case stern competition was met from the L&Y whose fare was 3*d*. cheaper.

During July and in connection with the North Staffordshire Railway, excursions were run to Ashbourne and Dovedale. Between 22nd July and 28th September there were excursions each Wednesday and Saturday to Harrogate, Scarborough and Bridlington. A week later the L&Y announced similar facilities but 1*s*. cheaper in each case. The LNWR reduced their fares on 28th August. Two days earlier the LNWR ran a special fast excursion from Manchester Victoria at 6.10 am calling at certain principal stations for the races at York, the return was two days later 'from the goods yard in front of the station'. A similar trip was operated in 1866 but returned from Holgate Bridge. In 1864 excursions to London did not figure in LNWR activities as a monopoly had been established by MS&L and GNR.

On the OA&GB direct services between Oldham and Manchester London Road had restarted. The appointments of James Bancroft of Manchester and William Edwards Hirst of Lascelles Hall, Huddersfield were made to the Leeds Central Station Committee. The former was Chairman of the OA&GB while the latter was subject to great pressure in his home town particularly from the local press and the Chamber of Commerce, of which he was a member. His position as an LNWR Director was one that few would envy.

The station facilities at Normanton were stretched to the limit. To enlarge the platform and buildings contracts to the value of £448 and £900 were awarded to Mr Nowell of Wakefield. Mr Hawkins of Doncaster was also contracted (at a price of £8,214 17*s*. 4*d*.) to perform similar work for an engine shed and retaining walls but he asked to be relieved of this as great trouble was encountered in removing more earth than had been anticipated.

The first of the annual catalogue of accidents occurred in June when, during shunting of an up goods train to the down line in order to be overtaken, a loaded van was left in Huddersfield tunnel and reduced to matchwood when run into by an express. On 9th September at Heaton Lodge Junction the 8.00 am Leeds – Manchester train completely bisected an L&Y coal train. At the same place on 15th September an L&Y goods from Mirfield which had run past signals in thick fog collided with an LNWR shunting engine. The fireman of the former at the time was sitting on the buffer beam dropping sand on to the line. Subsequently all traffic was diverted via Bradley Wood Junction where it had to be reversed.

A letter published in *The Times* of 16th December described a mishap to an L&Y train approaching Huddersfield station running over a turntable that had been left in the reversed position and at right angles to the approaching train. Astonishingly, both engine and train crossed the gap and regained the rails without collision.

Overcrowding at Leeds Wellington station in 1865 was the rule and any advantage gained by connections was negatived by delays from heavy traffic. To alleviate this a new line was considered from a junction with the Midland to Swinegate to form an end-on connection with a new North Eastern line from Marsh Lane. Engineering features comprised:

Canal Basin	1 arch	80 feet span
River Aire	4 arches	45 feet span 30 feet high
Little Neville Street	1 arch	60 feet span 18 feet high
Neville Street	1 arch	60 feet span 18 feet high
Bywash	1 arch	50 feet span 30 feet high

The resultant new station would be jointly owned by LNWR and NER and would be known as Leeds New. The Leeds New Station Act was dated 5th July, 1865. Parliament also gave considerable time to a Bill presented by the Midland for a line from Barnsley to Kirkburton, costed at £407,000, the plan being deposited only two hours before the latest time for acceptance. With a length of 12 miles 3 furlongs and 33 chains from Barnsley Courthouse it would parallel the L&Y Wakefield to Barnsley line and thence via Gawber Hall, Cawthorne, Skelmanthorpe and Shelley with major engineering:

Woodhouse Mill tunnel	814 yards 110 feet deep
Hollin House tunnel	1,294 yards 253 feet deep
Cawthorne viaduct	360 yards long 83 feet high
Silkstone Road viaduct	220 yards 75 feet high

Objectors included landowners, the L&Y and MS&L who argued existing facilities were enough. The L&Y stated that their Crigglestone route was much easier and coal destined for Huddersfield originated in the Thornhill area. The MS&L took a similar line but were not represented. For the Midland it was claimed this was part of a much larger scheme projected as an independent company which had failed on a technical point. The Huddersfield and Halifax project was now taken over by the LNWR under the style The Huddersfield and Halifax Railway, a joint venture with the Midland as partner. Commencing 1,070 yards north of Huddersfield station at Hillhouse, an intermediate station would be sited at Reap Hirst. A tunnel was to pass beneath Fixby and at Elland the line would pass close by the Bethesda New Connection Chapel and Jepson Lane Chapel to terminate at Hope Hall, Clare Hall Road, Halifax. A branch from Bethesda Chapel ran via Little Bradley, Jagger Bridge, Hare Wood and Holywell Green to terminate at Stainland Brookroyd Mills (Shaw Bros).

At a meeting at Derby the Chairman of the Midland stated the LNWR had invited them to join and they were prepared to subscribe £100,000 towards it. It was intended later to extend northwards to Ovenden and Keighley. The plan was drawn up by Messrs Stevenson and Uttley and the Bill came before Parliamentary Committee in February 1865. The L&Y claimed the line was unnecessary as their line although just a little longer was quite able to cope with any future increase in traffic. The Huddersfield Improvement Commission made objections. The projected route had undergone a last minute alteration and left Huddersfield by the west side of Newtown and Bay Hall by an embankment, but the LNWR were willing to substitute a viaduct in its place. When the Bill came before the Lords it was discovered the line

Howley Park signal box in 1952. *H. Gelder*

was wrong in certain aspects due to the fault of the lithographers who were in great demand and had carelessly included wrong measurements that had gone undetected. The Bill, which appeared likely to succeed, was thrown out on 27th February, 1865. The Commission referred to the levels of the viaduct over the Calder and Hebble at Elland. The height of this was 105 feet above water level, the bridge over the road at 72 feet yet the plan indicated the level at the bottom of the navigation.

Lifting of the first sod of the Kirkburton line took place on 7th March, 1865 near the Tandem Inn, Waterloo, followed by a dinner, given by contractors Messrs Eckersley and Bayliss, attended by William Edwards Hirst, the LNWR's local Director. Considerable opposition was encountered and some land seized by force but the line was ready for ballasting at Rowley in September. In November a temporary bridge at Far Dene, installed to allow spoil to be removed, received its girders. Familiar grumbling at Huddersfield concerned waiting rooms, lavatories and platforms often promenaded by ladies of easy virtue. At Dewsbury the Chamber of Commerce protested about bad time keeping

The site of West End signal box with the lines to West End and Critchley pits on the left. Howley Park crossing house is in the background and a shaft of Morley tunnel on the skyline. A class '47' passes with a York–Liverpool train on 13th November, 1981. *Author*

and irregularities of LNWR trains. A petition was made in September 1865 to extend the Farnley Mineral branch. On the LNWR's Ramsden or Huddersfield Broad Canal a notable occurrence was the installation of the locomotive bridge at Turnbridge during the first week in October. Operated by windlass it had a bearing weight of 75 tons and could be raised by 6 feet.

Three accidents marred 1865, notably in August when a train of L&Y excursion coaches broke loose from Lockwood on the L&Y Penistone branch, ran through Huddersfield station to be derailed on Huddersfield viaduct, where some coaches were thrown over the parapet into Viaduct Street.

On 2nd April, 1866 the Farnley Mineral branch was opened to Farnley ironworks. In June a new bridge was opened at Warehouse Hill, Marsden, the LNWR intimating that Marsden Local Board should bear the whole cost of this, but instead received payment only for materials used.

One belated item of Parliamentary business comprised The LNWR (New Lines) Act dated 16th July, 1868 authorizing the making of the second Standedge Railway tunnel with a total length of 3 miles and 9 chains of which the tunnel would be 5,297 yards on a gradient of one in 1,597.

The Huddersfield and Halifax Bill (rejected in 1865) came before Committee on 12th April. The LNWR and Midland Joint Scheme was the work of William Baker and T.L. Crossley and started with a junction immediately outside Huddersfield station at Fitzwilliam Street. Principal features included one in 100 ruling gradient, Fixby tunnel of 1,820 yards, a 225 yards-long viaduct over the Calder at Elland and terminating at New Road above South Parade, Halifax with a branch from Siddal to the L&Y 3 furlongs $2^1/_2$ links and a branch from Storth to a junction with the L&Y at Elland, length 1 mile, 1 furlong, $8^1/_2$ chains. Mr Baker in evidence stated the terminus at Halifax would be on 5 acres of land costing £8,000 with the whole scheme costed at £295,000 but the Bill failed by reason of insufficient estimates.

On the Kirkburton branch a major setback occurred at about 2.15 am on 15th February when the first two arches of Whitacre Mill viaduct collapsed shortly after completion. Damage was estimated at £500. The structure was of 7 arches 64 feet span, 21 feet 4 inches high and built on a 22 chain curve. The sub-contractor Messrs Sigley Miles and Haynes had their plant seized and work on the entire line ceased. The cause was attributed to the removal of staging after being constructed in a dry period. In April, Rowley viaduct of 6 arches 42 feet span and 21 feet high

Lady Anne Crossing box, Batley, in 1950. *W.B. Stocks*

was half complete but poor weather in the summer held up work at the terminus although a contractor's locomotive passed over Far Dene bridge on 15th December.

At Normanton, Messrs Neill accepted a tender for £2,800 to build a new locomotive shed while Hawkins and Verity were contracted to build a sub-structure for £4,500. At Batley, the Soothill Local Board issued a distress warrant upon the LNWR for non-payment of rates amounting to £37 5s. 1d.

Revised fares came into operation between Euston and many places including Oldham. This was followed by a reduction in return fares to London from 1st May from West Riding stations. Changes were made in the tariff of goods traffic between Liverpool and Yorkshire including Bradford and Halifax from 2nd July. The L&Y then did likewise and the LNWR responded by advancing the starting date to 1st June. From that date the LNWR in company with GNR, L&Y, MS&L, Midland and NER agreed to close their warehouse at 6.30 pm (2.00 pm on Saturdays) for the reception of goods. In reality goods traffic was worked by LNWR, L&Y and MS&L locomotives.

1866 was an appalling year in respect of accidents. The first mishap took place at Marsden on 8th January when a down goods train stopped to set down a disabled wagon and was run into from the rear by a passenger train. On 15th January, adjacent to Hillhouse shed, the 9.30 am Leeds – Huddersfield ran into a guard's van, the guard of which was reported to have been asleep. On 5th March at Brooks Siding an up L&Y goods train shunting was run into from behind by an LNWR goods that had overrun signals. On 13th August at Diggle, in the early hours, a train of empty stock from Manchester being set back into a siding was run into by the down Mail which reduced many of the coaches to matchwood. However, the Mail was delayed only by an hour. On 21st August in Stalybridge tunnel, a goods train halted by signals was run into from the rear by another goods completely blocking the tunnel, traffic was not restored until noon the next day. At Mossley on 19th September a Leeds to Manchester train collided at fast speed with a preceding goods being reversed into a siding. The driver of the goods train was aware of what was going to happen and tried to move his train out of the way, but was too late to avoid impact. Five trucks were demolished with severe damage to the passenger engine.

At Marsden on 30th October two up goods trains arrived. One was placed in Tunnel End siding. The other train was set back on to the down line to permit a Leeds – Manchester express to be given precedence but an eastbound goods train overran signals and at a point 80 yards beyond the station crashed head-on at a fast speed. This took place at 8.20 am and the line was cleared and restored to traffic at 11.00 am by which time six passengers and two goods trains had accumulated. The occurrence caused the *Huddersfield Examiner* to comment '… dangers stand thick along the line to drag us to our tomb'.

Between Greenfield and Mossley on 3rd November, a number of goods wagons were in collision with a double-headed goods train coming from Liverpool. The wagons were being shunted at Greenfield on the main line without handbrakes applied and ran backwards.

At Standedge tunnel on 20th November a goods train from Stockport reached a point 400 yards from the Marsden end when it suffered a wagon axle breakage. While the front portion continued, the hindmost portion pushed the disabled wagon laden with chain cable and caused those behind it to pile up. The tunnel was blocked for two and a half hours.

Huddersfield was synonymous with accidents and four took place during the year. In March the 1.10 pm L&Y train to Bradford was fouled by an LNWR goods train causing two coaches to be derailed. The next mishap occurred on 14th July and involved the 9.30 pm train from Leeds which was running 35 minutes late. On arrival at Huddersfield the platform was occupied by three trains – the 9.55 pm to Leeds, a train to

Normanton and an excursion. The 9.30 pm from Leeds arrived at reduced speed and was immediately run into from behind by the up Bangor Mail whose engine and stock were damaged. Thirty passengers were injured and two died. Reports stressed the total inadequacy of the station.

At Marsden in the small hours of 16th August, the driver of a Stockport to Normanton goods stopped to take water and on restarting found that the five rearmost trucks had become uncoupled. A message telegraphed from Slaithwaite to Gledholt stated that the following goods on arrival at Marsden had hit the loose vehicles pushing them forward. The driver of the first train, by now aware of what had occurred, wrongly anticipated the runaways would be travelling at 15-20 mph and if he travelled at a similar speed a mishap might be averted. Unfortunately as the train passed Huddersfield station it was overtaken by the runaways travelling at an estimated 50 mph. A similar event took place on 14th December when seven trucks shunted out of the way of the 1.45 pm passenger train to Halifax ran back, but were overhauled near Heaton Lodge by a light engine despatched for that purpose.

On the previous day at Birstal at 5.00 am a fire broke out in the five-storey mill adjoining the station. The driver of the 'Coddy', Isaac Law, blew his engine whistle to attract assistance. The station staff arrived and evacuated the premises of all stock, traffic and documents.

The third item to come before Parliament concerned the LNWR's opposition to the Huddersfield Waterworks Bill and in that year the LNWR commenced standard charges for water drawn from the canal for manufacturing purposes. The Ramsden Canal had been blocked by the fall of two arches in Whitacre Mill viaduct, although all debris was removed by nightfall.

The year 1867 saw the LNWR (Additional Powers) Act dated 15th July enable the company to purchase lands at Kirkheaton, Kirkburton, Lepton and Marsden and to close certain footpaths.

The Huddersfield and Halifax Joint Committee had its preamble approved on 16th March, 1867. With a length of 6 miles, 1 chain, 79 links the line was to terminate on the south side of Prescott Street at New Road above South Parade, Halifax. A branch was intended to run from Storth, Elland to a junction with the L&Y at the viaduct over the Calder – 1 mile, 1 furlong and 50 links and a branch from Siddal to L&Y at Spring Hall 3 furlongs, $2\frac{1}{2}$ links. The estimated cost was £409,977 with £25,000 for the branch. The station at Halifax would be larger and better than hitherto, while 20 acres of land at Huddersfield had been purchased to enlarge the station.

Evidence was given by the L&Y against the Bill. They ran 16 trains from Huddersfield to Halifax with 17 in the opposite direction, including five expresses which did the journey in 20 minutes. The total passengers in 1866 amounted to 81,809, or an average of eight passengers per train per day who paid £3,940. Goods traffic amounted to 1,255 tons, but many businesses transported their goods by horse and cart owing to the short distance. The Bill was withdrawn before it reached the Lords, Midland shareholders objected to the cost.

At Normanton provision of joint uniforms with cap badges was made. A minute dated 21st October noted 'the engine shed and goods shed shall be moved to make way for a new goods shed'. Fire destroyed the Huddersfield L&Y goods warehouse which measured 180 feet x 90 feet on 3rd March.

Many complaints regarding Huddersfield's station facilities were made. With over 300 trains daily using the station including 140 passenger trains, fortunately, few serious casualties had occurred, but there had been many close shaves. In about 1860, two wooden platforms were erected at the east end of the station to relieve congestion. These were $2\frac{1}{2}$ feet wide and 6 inches above the rails, and used for the Kirkburton services. At the west end, the L&Y services had a similar

Lady Anne Crossing, Batley, in 1959, with class '5MT' 2-6-0 No. 42715 on Sunderland–Manchester train. Former GNR line to Bradford on overbridge. *Author*

Railway staff house in Broomsdale Road Batley, built to John Child's design.   *Author*

erection $5^1/_2$ feet wide and one foot high placed between running rails and reached by crossing on the level. However, frequently the station was blocked with trains on all lines and passengers were exposed to great risks when shunting and other movements took place all around them.

From 1st August free transit of returned empties was discontinued by the LNWR, L&Y, MS&L and GNR while from 1st January the rates and charges by the LNWR, L&Y and Great Western Railway (GWR) would be equal.

Four mishaps occurred during 1867. The first was during shunting on 8th January at Slaithwaite when the 5.30 am goods from Huddersfield allowed a truck to run back down the line. The signalman at Hill Top Crossing Box, sensing something was wrong, diverted the runaway into a siding. On 24th October the driver of the 9.28 am passenger train from Huddersfield observed a portion of a runaway train as he approached Marsden on the same line. Quick thinking enabled him to stop and set off backwards when the runaways ran into him. However, the impact was only slight and after stopping a second time he set off to Marsden, propelling the trucks. Four days later the first mishap occurred on the Kirkburton branch.

As the 8.10 am from Kirkburton approached Whitacre Mill viaduct where the branch changed into double track, it became derailed. Passengers alighted and were allowed to continue their journey to Huddersfield by an L&Y train coming from Normanton, which stopped specially to pick them up from the lineside. Workmen assembled and aided by a contractor's locomotive the engine and coaches were re-railed and the line cleared by 1.00 am. On 23rd December at Thornhill LNWR Junction, in very thick fog, the driver of the 8.05 am Leeds – Liverpool train was given a verbal order which was misunderstood. The train proceeded on to the L&Y main line, but in an attempt to rectify this the driver had reversed his engine when it was in sidelong collision with an LNWR goods train from Normanton, the engine of which overturned. Its driver was a celebrated Yorkshire driver, Joe Secker.

Reconstruction of locks on the Huddersfield Canal began during the year. Lock No. 14W which bore a large date stone inside the chamber was the first of many dealt with in this manner.

1868 saw the LNWR (Additional Powers) Act dated 13th July authorize the closing of footpaths at Kirkheaton and Longwood and gave rights to acquire land at Wortley (opposite Copley Hill shed) while right was given to the public over Green Street, Huddersfield. 'The LNWR and Midland may acquire lands at Huddersfield and to stop up an area from Newtown to St John's Church, while the L&Y may become equal and joint owners'.

Improvements included new coal chutes at Longwood station and alterations at Marsden where accommodation for goods traffic became four times larger. At Huddersfield a warehouse 180 feet x 90 feet was quickly erected and replaced that destroyed by fire in the previous year, but met a like fate on 2nd August. The smouldering lasted a week before being finally extinguished. Goods traffic commenced on the Kirkburton branch on 1st January but the gable end of a new warehouse there blew down in a gale on 7th February. The footbridge spanning the tracks immediately outside Kirkburton station was installed during the first week in February, thus the well-known photograph of 'the first train to Kirkburton' is proved false. The photograph in question was taken on Friday 31st May, 1868 when No. 37 *Hawke* brought empty stock to the terminus for the first excursion next day and was kept in the goods yard overnight. The excursion left Kirkburton at 6.00 am, Fenay Bridge 6.05 am, Kirkheaton 6.10 am and Huddersfield 6.30 am, also calling at Longwood before running via Guide Bridge, Broadheath and Arpley to Liverpool. A passenger boarded the train at Longwood in the mistaken belief that it was a Manchester train and as it emerged from Standedge tunnel he opened a door and jumped out! Another excursion ran on 18th July when over 600 passengers travelled from branch stations departing Kirkburton 5.00 am, fare 3s. 6d. In September a petition was raised for the operation of Sunday trains but was rejected. Before the coming of the railway Kirkburton was served by a horse bus which also operated two Sunday services.

In July it was reported the LNWR were to construct a station at Ravensthorpe located between Brick House and Howgate Hill. A member of Huddersfield Chamber of Commerce secured an interview with Mr Moon and extracted promises that Huddersfield station would be improved.

The entrance to Batley station on the 29th July, 1967, with goods offices in left background.
Author

CHAPTER FOUR

1870 – 1879

The new decade began with the LNWR (Additional Powers) Act dated 4th July, 1870 authorizing the contribution of £50,000 to Leeds New station; £50,000 to the OA&GB and an agreement could be prepared to transfer to the NER, L&Y and GNR the whole or part of the LNWR interests at Leeds Central station, but this was not enacted.

A dispute over costs at Normanton station resulted in Mr George Pownall appointed as arbitrator. The entry of the LNWR there coincided with the greatest expansion of all facilities i.e. station, sidings, warehouse, engine sheds and signalling.

At Huddersfield the overworked accommodation gave great cause for criticism. The Town Council and Huddersfield Chamber of Commerce repeatedly complained. The latter was largely instrumental in every improved facility from the outset. On 1st February at the invitation of Huddersfield Town Council, Colonel Yolland the Board of Trade inspecting officer for railways, visited the town to receive evidence for enlargement of the station. Mr Jones, the Mayor and a Midland Director led with much evidence while Mr R.F. Roberts (LNWR solicitor) and Captain Binstead of the L&Y represented their companies. Evidence was given that the MS&L were permitted to run their Penistone trains into Huddersfield. If the MS&L stopped working them they would have to be worked by the L&Y. The Midland were allowed to use Huddersfield by clauses 51-53 and 54 of the Midland Act of 1868, but the powers had never been exercised and all concerned expressed the view that chaos would reign if the Midland ever did so. Traffic over four Saturdays in August 1869 comprised:

	LNWR	L&Y	Total
Passengers	59	59	118
Expresses	32	14	46
Goods	60	22	82
Total	151	95	246

The station had been opened in 1847 without previous inspection, one single platform was adequate for the traffic of the day. In 1870 there were as many as six passenger trains standing at the platform at once, with heavy goods traffic passing through at the same time and with great danger to passengers standing on the intermediate wooden platform created about 1860.

The report issued following an accident on 14th July, 1866 stated 'additional accommodation is very much overdue and the one sided station should be abolished and the goods warehouse be removed'. Since 1854 there had been 41 casualties in the station. Since 1866 28 acres of land had been purchased by the LNWR and Midland to improve existing conditions, partly for the abortive Halifax scheme. The inspector concluded in his report that the Board of Trade had no powers to enforce any alteration however necessary it may be for public safety on any line of public railway already opened to passenger traffic (report by Colonel Yolland dated 18th February, 1870).

In March 1870 parcel vans were introduced for the collection and delivery of such traffic. However, the Franco-Prussian war was causing a decline in Yorkshire trade.

From February 1870 services arriving at Leeds (New) from Manchester were given improved connections to York and Hull which involved the better spacing out of services. A competitor to the LNWR London service came on 1st May when the Midland introduced their through coach. An excursion was run for the Birmingham Cattle and Poultry Show, with the return journey two days later, fares first class 14s. and 8s. 6d. covered carriage.

The LNWR also operated their own excursion to Doncaster on the occasion of the St Leger, running via Wakefield with fares of first class

LNWR No. 446, originally Huddersfield & Manchester Railway *Brook*, a 2-2-2 tender engine built by sharp Brothers in 1847. Shown as rebuilt 1870s as a tank engine, it was withdrawn in 1874.

7s. and covered carriage 3s. 6d. LNWR running powers in the Doncaster area were granted on 12th October, 1874 between Askern Junction and Bottesford. From 11th July special 'cheap' excursions were run to Yarmouth, Lowestoft and other points in East Anglia and involved using ordinary services and a journey that was something of a circular tour. For the fare charged and distance travelled they offered exceptional value, the passenger going via Stockport, Crewe and Rugby and returning within five days. Excursions and trips were also run on every local holiday, i.e. Kirkheaton Feast, Longwood Thump, Delph Wakes, Halifax Fair Monday, often with a host of private trains.

At the new Standedge tunnel there was a serious mishap at the work face in early May when a charge ignited after being struck by a workman's pick. However, work proceeded at such a pace that the first engine ran through on 21st November, 1870 when 0-4-0 ST *Caldew* passed through, although the finishing touches remained. Nelson's plant and equipment were put on sale at Marsden on 7th to 9th December, but a great blizzard on the 9th brought events to an abrupt end.

Adits from the new tunnel, 21 in total, passed under the Nicholson tunnel (first Standedge tunnel) and allowed spoil from the workings to be removed by canal. The steam boats used burnt coke and in April a number of men had to be rescued from suffocation due to fumes. On 26th August a small boat proceeding to the work face, laden with two half hundred weight lots of gunpowder blew up, killing both boatmen, extinguishing all the candles in the tunnel and with the blast felt more than half a mile away in the new tunnel. A frightened horse bolted, somehow made its way into the Nicholson tunnel and ran almost to Diggle before coming to grief beneath the wheels of an oncoming train.

1870 was one of the worst years for mishaps. The down Bangor Mail was usually double-headed as far as the Marsden end of Standedge tunnel. The pilot engine would be detached there, then crossed on to the up line to return home. On the night of 21st February the Mail was not piloted. A message had been telegraphed but was misunderstood by the Marsden pointsman, William Beresford, an experienced man who was held responsible for the accident. At 1.30 am the Mail emerged from the tunnel and was switched to the up line, running on until it collided with a stationary goods train at Marsden, causing some damage to rolling stock. After clearance the undamaged portion proceeded to Huddersfield where it arrived at 2.30 am and where 'the only person on duty was asleep and showed little inclination to help distraught passengers'.

A further accident occurred at Bradley on 25th February when at 3.00 pm the engine of a goods for Leeds left the rails, taking 14 wagons with it. The up line was left clear but trains to and from Halifax were reversed at Heaton Lodge Junction.

The next mishap was as unusual as it was unexpected. On 29th March in Huddersfield tunnel the roof of a GWR goods van became caught against the tunnel roof as it struck a rail placed there some 20 years earlier as a stiffener. The van body was dislodged from its frame although the prize cow contained therein was unharmed!

On 30th May at Greenfield the 2 pm Delph to Oldham train arrived and, to clear the path for an express, drew forward on to the Oldham branch. A Mossley to Oldham goods train already placed on a refuge siding, due to a misunderstood hand signal reversed and was derailed at trap points. The junction had recently been interlocked.

On 11th June at Hillhouse a goods to Brighouse suffered derailment after its locomotive connecting rod broke loose and struck a sleeper, derailing the tender and part of the train which finished up in a field alongside the line. Miraculously the 7.28 am Dewsbury to Huddersfield passenger train approaching was able to stop with only inches to spare. On 18th August a Leeds to Huddersfield train which had stopped at Batley set back into a siding to attach a van. The train departed and on arriving at Dewsbury was run into from behind by the van which had not been secured. At Copley Hill on 24th August the 5.30 am ex-Manchester passenger train, while planned to travel via Whitehall Junction, had its road set for Leeds Central and after running 70 yards on that line crashed into the rear of a stationary goods. The former, running very late, had been held behind the latter all the way from Mirfield. Captain Tyler, the Board of Trade inspecting officer observed 'this was a mishap which sooner or later, without proper appliances in the form of locking apparatus was almost certain'. At Copley Hill LNWR there were 125 trains daily plus the movement of 1,200 to 1,400 wagons shunting in the yard every 24 hours.

At Johnny Moore's Cabin, Paddock on 25th September a goods train for Leeds was being reversed into the siding when its engine was struck by an oncoming train, causing the latter to be delayed by two and a quarter hours. The line was cleared under the direction of Mr Winby, locomotive superintendent, Hillhouse. At 10.15 pm on 14th November the 5.15 pm salt train from Crewe to Leeds, about one mile in from the Diggle end of Standedge tunnel, suffered a broken axle on one of its trucks. The 21 wagon train continued for two more miles before stalling some 600 yards from the Marsden end. Ten trucks were damaged and some 40-50 tons of salt were heaped inside the tunnel blocking it completely. Seven trucks had been pulled along without wheels, while over 100 yards of track had been ripped up. Both Hillhouse and Longsight breakdown gangs attended, with Mr Winby in charge. The up Mail that had arrived at Marsden was sent back to Huddersfield and thence via the L&Y route to Manchester where it arrived at 2.00 am instead of 12.13 am. Clearance and relaying track in the tunnel was not completed until the following evening. Meanwhile all passenger trains terminated at either end of the tunnel and passengers then walked through the uncompleted new bore before resuming their journey.

On 7th November at Huddersfield during thick fog the 7.00 am Manchester to Leeds passenger train was run into by the 7.50 am express from Leeds to Manchester. The inspecting officer found that the signalman had accepted the latter train but forgotten the one standing at the platform. On 28th November, 1870 between Marsden and Slaithwaite a wagon axle fractured on the 5.15 pm Crewe to Leeds salt train which caused eight wagons to be derailed and damage to the track for half a mile. The final accident of the year occurred at Dewsbury on New Year's Eve when a goods train was run into from behind by the 6.30 pm Marsden to Leeds passenger train. Four passengers were injured.

1871 began with the LNWR (Additional Powers) Act containing a provision to 'sell or exchange or dispose of lands at Aspley formerly part of the canal, but long disused' (this referred to the dock on the Ramsden Canal) and to acquire lands at Ashton OA&GB which later became a goods yard.

The principal improvement of the year was the opening of the second tunnel at Standedge on 12th February, known as the Nelson tunnel after the contractor Thomas Nelson. The new tunnel was examined by Colonel Yolland, the Board of Trade inspecting officer on 5th January. Opening was without ceremony. Completed six months earlier than the time specified, the Nelson tunnel was one yard shorter than the Nicholson tunnel, the first tunnel, of which both ends were pulled down and rebuilt. Its most unusual feature was a cavernous space known as The Cathedral which linked the two tunnels. There the roof was supported by diagonally crossed iron segmented arches. Accounts state that trains passed through the new tunnel with a degree of steadiness unknown in the old tunnel which was then in need of urgent repair. This work was done and it reopened on 30th April. The Standedge pilot was dispensed with after the installation of block telegraph. A new signal box named 'Tunnel End' was opened at the Marsden end and located some 25 yards nearer to the station than the 'Old Indian Cabin' which it replaced.

Deighton station was opened on the Kirkburton branch on 30th August. For many years it was the practice to set back trains which were to be overtaken on the adjacent main line on to the Kirkburton branch. The practice continued for some time after the main line was quadrupled in the early 1880s. Batley Chamber of Commerce protested to both LNWR and GNR over poor passenger accommodation; there was no waiting room on the LNWR side, a booking hall had to be used for every purpose while facilities in the goods yard were also inadequate.

At Paddock a proposal for a new station was made at a meeting held at the Ship Inn on 1st April. William Edwards Hirst, the local Director met a committee formed for that purpose and arranged a visit by the Chairman, Mr Richard Moon, who surprised everyone by arriving half an hour earlier than expected. After listening to the needs of the area, he outlined the cost of the station and startled his hosts by his insight into their requirements. Moon's estimates were:

Cost of station cutting	£500
Maintenance costs	£75 pa
Working expenses	£2 weekly

In September Mr Moon was reported to be considering the matter further, but nearby was the future site of Gledholt Sidings. The LNWR were in dispute with Saddleworth Local Board over their rating obligations, were also in default to the tune of £3,004 for the year, while the goods warehouse at Leeds had a rateable value of £62 1s. 0d. which was regarded as excessive. On 19th July a connection was installed from the Huddersfield Canal at Slaithwaite to Summit Pool, Marsden and connected with a pipe along the lineside to Huddersfield station and beyond. As a consequence the supply of locomotive water became greatly improved. Hitherto the supply of locomotive water had ceased whenever the level of Slaithwaite reservoir fell below the height of the line. Often in summer engines were specially sent to Marsden to take water.

Period excursions were run at special cheap rates to London for the Handel Festival and various exhibitions held there, to the Birmingham Onion Fair, to the West of England, East Anglia etc. The train specified was the 7.50 am from Leeds which called at Batley, Dewsbury, Huddersfield, Stalybridge and Stockport. On 10th July an excursion from Leeds to Belle Vue broke in two near Dewsbury but was recoupled without mishap. Another train from Leeds to Bangor on the same day

LNWR No. 161, one of the 'Prince Ernest' class of saddle tanks rebuilt from 'Crewe Goods' (*see page 34*) 2-4-0 tender engines, as used on Leeds-Huddersfield trains 1870-85.
Author's collection

arrived at Huddersfield on its outward journey at 1.00 am, but on restarting the locomotive burst a tube. Two hours elapsed before a fresh engine could be obtained. Meanwhile the passengers alighted on the platform and seeing a barrel of kippers amused themselves by throwing them at each other!

There were six mishaps during 1871. The first was at Thornhill LNWR Junction where on 3rd January at 2.30 am a Dewsbury to Liverpool goods collided sidelong with an L&Y goods from Wakefield which caused great damage. The wreckage was cleared by 11.00 am when a procession of seven goods trains destined for Leeds went through. The down Bangor Mail was diverted via Mirfield to Heckmondwike where it reversed. On 17th February at Scout tunnel the 5.30 pm Manchester to Leeds passenger train overran signals into the back of a goods causing injury to four passengers. The *Leeds Mercury* observed 'between drunken guards, inefficient signals and tender hearted jurymen, the prospects of the travelling public are certainly growing less and less cheering each day'. The above was to be repeated on 19th March when the 10.30 am Leeds to Manchester train ran into the back of a derailed goods in Scout tunnel. At Copley Hill on 20th February an NER goods being propelled from Leeds stopped behind an L&Y goods which was behind an LNWR goods. Due to darkness and being reversed it struck the latter causing the brake van to be derailed and confusion culminated when the

6.30 pm Manchester – Leeds ran into it. This comprised an engine, tender and seven carriages.

On 28th June at Kirkburton Junction the L&Y 9.30 Halifax to Huddersfield ran into the back of a goods travelling on the same line. In July a locomotive broke an axle close to Riddings Lock. The year concluded when an accident occurred at Marsden where a pick-up goods was set back into Tunnel End siding to allow the 7.50 am Leeds – Manchester express to overtake. At Marsden the latter got a caution signal and reduced speed to 12 mph. As the next signal was at clear, the driver applied steam and a collision was inevitable. The Board of Trade Inquiry revealed the clear signal had not returned to danger due to very severe weather. On 17th January before the second tunnel opened at Standedge, a Manchester – Leeds passenger train ran past adverse signals and collided with a goods train in the tunnel causing injury to four passengers.

In the early 1870s congestion worsened at several places. At Leeds it was freely admitted that no LNWR train ever got past Whitehall Junction without being stopped. At Copley Hill nearby, the presence of the LNWR engine shed, goods yard and exchange sidings made a scene of unremitting activity. Thornhill LNWR Junction had a similar reputation to that of Whitehall Junction. At Mirfield the double line was supplemented by a down goods loop but two lines only over both crossings of the Calder. Like Heaton Lodge it was the scene of much transfer traffic to and from local yards and had a poor reputation for safety and delays, eclipsed only by Huddersfield where, as Ahrons classically declared 'the jointier the worse'. Stalybridge was another place of congestion, the point of divergence of traffic for Stockport or Manchester Victoria, and where MS&L and LNWR were joint owners of the station. Ahrons also remarked that between Manchester and Leeds the faster trains could not be called expresses 'with any approach to truth'.

The LNWR Act dated 18th July, 1872 authorized the Guide Bridge Junction Railway, which extended from Denton Junction to Crowthorn Junction OA&GB to give advantage of reaching Oldham without the necessity of passing through Guide Bridge.

However, the most important business concerned the abortive amalgamation Bill to unite the LNWR and L&Y. There were 13 objectors including many municipalities and the Lancaster and Carlisle, Manchester South Junction & Altrincham and MS&L railways. The matter was long drawn out starting in February and lingering until August, when the Parliamentary Committee presided over by the Rt Hon Chichester Fortescue made the decision that the two proposed partners should iron out the problems. The preamble was approved in December and in February 1873 it was proposed that the new concern should have 30 Directors from the LNWR and 16 from the L&Y, a total to be reduced to 30 by December 1877. Subsequently Huddersfield and Bradford Corporations withdrew their objections and so did Huddersfield Chamber of Commerce. Samuel Pope QC appeared for the promoters and pointed out there were 18 common junctions between the two companies. The proceedings reached the select Committee in May 1873. The Bill failed without objections by other railways being examined.

On 1st April, 1872 third class passengers were carried by all trains except Mails. For the Delph Wakes an excursion to Belle Vue cost 3s. which was regarded as high and patronage was poor, but at the time coal had increased in price by 5s. per ton. Also on 1st April Carlinghow station on the Birstal branch was opened, the result of continuous pressure by Batley Chamber of Commerce, while a contract for a new station at Wortley was let. The annual quota of accidents began on 2nd April.

Following the arrival at Diggle of the 10.20 am train from Manchester, the engine proceeded to run-round its train. The guard forgot to apply the hand brake to the empty coaches which rolled back and collided with a goods at Saddleworth. At the same place on 10th August as the 5.00 pm from Diggle – Longsight goods was shunting, a Leeds to Birmingham goods overshot signals and collided with it.

A mishap occurred at Deighton on 13th November on the Kirkburton branch, when a heavily laden up goods was set back onto the branch. As a result of carelessness an up cattle train was also set back colliding with the former with great force, resulting in cattle and drovers being injured.

A near mishap occurred on 11th January when the 1.10 am Copley Hill – Liverpool goods passed Golcar and half the train ran back due to a fractured coupling. This was quickly diverted to the down line by a pointsman Robert Taylor, and the guard was able to stop the runaway at Longwood without collision.

1873 produced two items of legislation. The LNWR (New Lines) Act dated 21st July, 1873 authorized the Dewsbury Junction Railway from a junction with the Leeds line at West Town to join the L&Y at Ravensthorpe station, length 2 furlongs and 50 links. The LNWR (New Lines and Additional Powers) Act dated 28th July, 1873 authorized the closing of a level crossing at Oldham where the Central Mill Co. Ltd and Star Corn Millers Ltd were compensated each by £2,000. Land at Delph was required for new coal chutes. At Batley land was needed to enlarge sidings and make a new warehouse at Soothill and at Carlinghow where a goods yard was to be built. As a partner in the OA&GB the LNWR was to contribute to the making of new streets at Oldham.

It was during the year that emigrant traffic began running between Hull and Liverpool, worked by NER engines and men. A number of mishaps included one in Lydgate tunnel on the Oldham branch on 3rd February when the 8.58 am Greenfield – Oldham train ran into the back of a goods destined for Liverpool, causing the line to be blocked for two hours.

One Sunday the crew of an Edgeley ballast engine working in Standedge tunnel went out of curiosity into a heading leading to the canal tunnel. Both missed their way and fell in! On the L&Y at Clayton Bridge on 5th August the 11.05 am Leeds – Liverpool express, at full speed and running 30 minutes late, collided with a goods train being shunted causing 19 passengers to be injured.

On 15th November at Bradley a serious accident occurred. The sequence began at Longwood when the 5.15 pm Copley Hill to Crewe goods consisting of an engine, tender, eight trucks and brake prepared to set back to the down line, when the truck immediately behind the tender became uncoupled. The train laden with pig iron ran back on the

Slaithwaite station is in the centre of this picture that dates from the 1870s. A new four-platform station was brought into use in 1888. *courtesy of K. Field*

up line. A telegraph message was sent to Gledholt where the runaways were switched to the down line. The assemblage passed Huddersfield station at an estimated 40 mph and no siding space was available. At Bradley the 6.00 pm Stalybridge to Leeds train stood at the platform. It comprised a tender engine, eight coaches and two brake vans at the rear. After their $4\frac{1}{2}$ mile run, the runaways collided full force, the two brake vans took the main impact. The guard, Higginbottom of Stockport appeared dumbfounded and unable to give an account of what happened, for he had been asleep throughout. A special train with three doctors on board was despatched from Huddersfield by the station master, while the locomotive foreman at Hillhouse shed, Mr Christopher Marshall had charge of breakdown operations. Four days later at 5.30 pm in Crowtrees a Sandbach – Leeds salt train restarted after a signal stop and suffered a broken coupling, which then resulted in half the train being left behind and run into by the following goods.

1874 saw the Leeds New Station (Enlargement) Act dated 16th July. As well as making new streets (notably New Station Street), widening was to be done on the south side to allow more platforms and running lines to be made.

The Huddersfield and Halifax project of the 1860s reappeared but the companies had been reshuffled. The LNWR was in joint promotion with the L&Y for a route extending from the main Leeds line near Hillhouse crossing Bradford Road on the level and climbing at 1 in 60 for one mile into a tunnel 1,914 yards in length, then falling at 1 in 70 to make a junction with the L&Y main line at Saw Smiths Mill Bridge, Elland, length 5 miles, 6 furlongs, 1 chain and 70 links. The plan bore the signatures of Sir John Hawkshaw, William Baker and Sturgess Meek. The LNWR needed to raise £175,000 and borrow £58,000.

The above would run parallel in Parliament with a Midland Bill for a direct line linking Huddersfield from a station at Newtown to Halifax and Bradford – a main line compared with the economy package of their rivals.

Huddersfield Corporation opposed both Bills. Huddersfield Chamber of Commerce favoured the Midland as did all businessmen, with the exception of a Mr Glendenning. The Great Northern opposed the Midland because 'there were enough railways in the district already' and their own Halifax, Bradford and Keighley lines were nearing completion. The LNWR and L&Y project would have cost £334,396 while the Midland was costed at £$1\frac{1}{2}$ million and was not connected with any other railways. Both Bills failed, but had only one been presented it would have been approved.

A large area of land at Whitehall Road, Leeds was acquired, earmarked for development as a goods yard but postponed due to the uncertain state of trade. At Huddersfield station the North Eastern Railway opened their own booking office during February while the LNWR at the request of the NER reduced their rates between Liverpool and Hull as such traffic had been consigned by ship before being despatched to Hamburg and Dutch ports.

New accommodation was opened at Batley in June after many years of pressure from the Batley Chamber of Commerce who declared 'it is a handsome station with airy, well lighted rooms and a broad platform. Better accommodation is still needed on the other side of the line on the GNR'.

The LNWR's legal department had a busy time. The company sought a refund of rates at Marsden and obtained a mandamus against the Local Board.

Excursions were offered to race goers at Epsom. On 14th April a race train was run for the Great Northern Handicap at York, the train calling at all stations from Marsden to Batley. For the Diggle Wakes, Uppermill Co-op ran a trip to Liverpool conveying 700 passengers from Saddleworth station. Blackpool did not figure very much as a holiday destination, but the highlight of the year was that no mishaps occurred!

1875 had a large volume of legal business. The LNWR (New Lines and Additional Powers) Act of 19th July saw the acquisition of lands at Holbeck, in partnership with L&Y (Whitehall Road Goods Depot), at Heaton Lodge, Longwood, Huddersfield and at Copley Hill near the Dragon Inn, the site of the new carriage shed.

In respect of the sale of canal water to industry from the Huddersfield and Ramsden Canals, it was known only to a few that the LNWR had no powers for this, although most of the mills alongside did. A dispute arose between the LNWR and Huddersfield Corporation, even though the latter did not have the capacity to supply. Yet the LNWR had two allies who were former Mayors of the town, of whom one was to say 'the action of the canal authorities has very largely developed the ratepayer's property in the borough and has increased its trade and prosperity'. The proposed Corporation charge of $7\frac{1}{2}$ d. per thousand gallons was eight times that of the LNWR. To anticipate the 1875 Act the latter planned a new reservoir at Redmire Lee. The Parliamentary Committee ruled the company could continue to supply water to those concerns outside the borough, and to those within until the Corporation could meet this demand, but would not be permitted a new reservoir. The reality was the need was never met.

On 16th August an excursion from Kirkburton to Bangor included 200 passengers from the terminus, departure at 1.30 am and return arrival at 4.30 am next day. On 29th August a trip from Delph to Blackpool saw 800 passengers carried with a further 100 joining at Greenfield. Contemporary reports indicated that patronage of this order was quite the usual state of affairs.

In respect of mishaps, on 31st May an L&Y engine and three coaches were standing at Oldham Clegg Street waiting the arrival of a through coach to Rochdale, when an MS&L engine was set back on the same line and collided at speed. Although the handbrake of the L&Y engine was on, the impact caused the coaches to run backwards down the one in 80. The cavalcade passed Ashton Oldham Road at an estimated 55 mph. The L&Y engine actually set off to catch them up. The incident had been telegraphed through and an LNWR train was held at Crowthorn Junction. At Guide Bridge the runaway was diverted onto the MS&L Stalybridge line. At Brookside box a courageous signalman named Greenwood obtained a foothold on a coach and the train came to rest, near Dukinfield unharmed, after a run of about six miles!

On 7th May at Crowtrees a broken drawbar on a Copley Hill – Manchester goods caused the loose wagons to run back and collide with another goods train. On 13th July at Morley after a loose piece of wood hanging from the leading wagon stuck in a set of points, a train of 15 wagons laden with pig iron suffered derailment of nine wagons which damaged the track for 30 yards.

An irate reader of the *Huddersfield Examiner* dated 16th January, 1875 noted the danger occasioned by LNWR trains crossing the Heaton Lodge Junction points at speed, which caused an unpleasant jolting sensation for passengers. He expressed fears of a repetition of the Great Western Shipton disaster of Christmas Eve 1874. He also observed 'L&Y trains reduce speed here' adding 'perhaps if a Bishop or an LNWR director should be killed, then some day LNWR trains will do the same'.

1876

The LNWR (New Lines and Additional Powers) Act of 24th July authorized a replacement footbridge in place of Glodwick footpath. A contribution of £50,000 was to be made to OA&GB and the construction of a branch line at Ashton, length 2 furlongs, 4 chains and 80 links and to purchase lands at Waterloo Road, Oldham. An LNWR Bill that was withdrawn envisaged the enlargement of Huddersfield station.

A significant improvement came about following the opening of the Guide Bridge Junction Railway (Crowthorn Junction to Denton Junction) for goods traffic on 14th February and for passengers on 1st April. Five trains ran daily from Stockport to Oldham and through to Rochdale having made connection with Euston trains at Stockport. Passenger traffic on the OA&GB continued to improve with 930,758 carried during the year. Unhappily the figure dropped to 379,739 in 1879.

Deposited plans envisaged an extension of the arches of Huddersfield viaduct and widening the end of Huddersfield tunnel by 82 yards. Land was to be purchased at Longwood for a goods yard. In March Huddersfield Town Council received a telegram from Mr R.F. Roberts, LNWR solicitor at Euston who said the company had withdrawn all projects relating to Huddersfield station as a result of difficulties created by the Midland Railway. This situation gave rise to the LNWR and L&Y's projected conversion of the Bradford Canal from Bradford to Shipley into a railway.

The Colne Valley service came in for criticism. An irate reader of the *Huddersfield Examiner* dated 2nd December, 1878 said 'Can nothing be done to influence the directors of this line who are recklessly indifferent to public safety and convenience in the matter of punctuality'. Of 17 trains between Marsden and Leeds, three were within minutes of time. The remainder were respectively: 14, 16, 7, 8, 31, 11, 10, 16, 18, 12 and 28 minutes late.

The first mishap of the year occurred at Mirfield L&Y on 30th January when the 8.00 am Leeds – Manchester express was struck by an L&Y goods which had overrun signals in thick fog. The buffers of the goods engine caused only superficial damage to the carriages, but four passengers were injured. On 15th March between Brooks Sidings and Kirkburton Junction a wagon in a Crewe to Leeds salt train was derailed which caused the vehicles behind to pile up. Almost immediately the wreckage was run into by an up goods, the engine of which escaped by a hair's breadth being pitched into the Ramsden Canal and actually finished up overlooking its edge. Clearance was slow and eight hours after the mishap only the down line had been restored.

The theme for the year was expressed at the LNWR half-yearly General Meeting by its Chairman, Richard Moon who said 'any further expansion of traffic is limited only by the company's ability to handle it'. If applied to 'The Yorkshire Lines' the words could be regarded as a masterly understatement, for the line east of Stalybridge was notorious for congestion and accidents.

1877

'The Yorkshire Lines' were not the subject of any Parliamentary proposals during the year but Huddersfield Town Council's Bill compelling the LNWR and L&Y to make improvement at Huddersfield station was not approved. Likewise, the town's Chamber of Commerce at its monthly meetings gave every encouragement, but had opposed the LNWR Bill in the previous year 'as it did not go far enough'. The LNWR were well aware of what was required. A party had inspected Slaithwaite station in June and did the same at Greenfield and Mossley where there was an urgent need for additional goods accommodation. The pressure placed on the local Director, William Edwards Hirst was tremendous, but he explained 'the LNW's hands are tied'. Approval would have to come from not only the L&Y (joint owners) but also the Midland who had running powers but no facilities of their own. As for Colonel Yolland's oft-repeated comments 'Huddersfield station is so inadequate as to endanger safety', Hirst pointed to other examples – Guide Bridge and Preston – one might add for good measure Ahron's words 'the jointier, the worse'.

The Yorkshire Colonial Wool Buyers' Association made acid comments concerning the cost of wool carried from London to Bradford, the LNWR moved about 10,000 tons annually. As a result the LNWR reduced their rate from 40*s*. to 37*s*. 6*d*. per ton. It had been claimed that a ton of wool sent from Paris to Bradford was cheaper than if sent from London. LNWR wool rates were:

London to Scotland	42*s*. 6*d*. per ton
London to Hull	30*s*. per ton
London to Manchester	35*s*. per ton
London to Liverpool	27*s*. 6*d*. per ton (if not for export)

From Slaithwaite third class tickets became obtainable to all stations, but the cost of a second class ticket to Huddersfield went up from 10*d*. to 11*d*. For Marsden Fair of 1877 900 passengers arrived in addition to the 300 passengers each summer weekend to visit a local beauty spot, Blake Lee. For Delph Wakes on 3rd September an excursion ran to Windermere, while a joint works trip on 22nd September for Messrs G. Broom of Haigh Mills and Messrs J. Brierly of Bridge Street Mill, Slaithwaite ran to Scarborough and Southport. It was noticeable that Blackpool still did not feature among the destinations. On the Bradley Wood branch there were 16 L&Y trains daily in both directions with four

View from Red Doles lock on the Huddersfield Broad Canal, looking towards Annesley lock, about 1905. *Author's collection*

on Sundays running between Huddersfield and Halifax. During November a complaint was made about passengers on the down Mail having to obtain their tickets at the barrier owing to the L&Y booking office being closed. Wortley station was renamed Wortley and Farnley, while the LNWR's annual protest over excessive rating levied by Kirkburton Local Board was lost. The Canal Department Engine Bridge at Folly Hall which had an original width of 22 feet was widened by 14 feet, executed by and at the expense of Huddersfield Corporation. The LNWR's canal superintendent Edward Greenwood retired on 20th December. A man of great knowledge and understanding, he should be remembered for his alleviating public mistrust in canal reservoirs when there was widespread concern about safety.

On 1st February the 7.12 pm Huddersfield – Manchester train, by mistake, was turned onto the L&Y Penistone branch at Springwood Junction. The driver was vigilant and stopped before reaching Paddock viaduct to regain his correct route. On 19th May an LNWR engine after shunting near the entrance to Huddersfield tunnel, backed down on to its train. No shunter was present and the engine touching the train caused the trucks to run back and collide with an L&Y train from Bradford and Halifax which caused injury to 11 people. General

Hutchinson in his accident report observed 'as long as Huddersfield station is allowed to remain in its present unsatisfactory state, with shunting on the main line, the recurrence of collisions similar to this can be expected'.

1878

The year was dominated by much legislation.

1. The LNWR (Wortley and Leeds) Act of 17th June allowed the making of a line from Wortley direct to Leeds New station (length 1 mile, 9 chains and 50 links) without the need for LNWR trains to use Midland metals with delay and congestion.
2. The widening of the H&M route between Hillhouse and Heaton Lodge Junction. The River Colne to be crossed by a single span bridge.
3. To allow lands to be purchased at Hillhouse and confirm an agreement made on 9th March, 1878 between the LNWR, L&Y and Midland concerning Huddersfield station which was to be enlarged and done jointly and equally. If an agreement was not made the sections and specifications were to be made by an engineer appointed by the Board of Trade who would settle the matter. The use of running powers by the Midland to reach the station was guaranteed. In the event of any future enlargement the Midland would contribute towards the improvement. The LNWR was to sell land to the Midland for separate goods and mineral accommodation – this purchase to be completed on 23rd March, 1879. To allow Huddersfield viaduct to be widened, the Midland was not to build within 50 feet. All Midland rights to use goods and mineral facilities at Huddersfield to cease. Midland to be at liberty to form a junction with LNWR who were to give powers to Midland from Huddersfield station to that junction.
4. The lands purchased at Hillhouse for use as sidings and goods accommodation to be joint and equal with L&Y, the joint goods station to be worked by a joint staff, but with separate agents. (This removed a threat to the Midland of converting the canal into a railway between Bradford and Shipley.) The canal was causing a public nuisance, had been responsible for two cholera epidemics in Bradford and had been subject to a High Court Order for closure.

Another piece of legislation was the LNWR (Additional Powers) Act of 22nd July authorising:

1. The abandonment of the Dewsbury Junction Railway.
2. The acquisition of land at the north side of and 200 yards west of Glodwick Road and lands north of Lees (for a new locomotive shed).
3. Lands at Gomersal and Slaithwaite.
4. To alter, enlarge or rebuild Stalybridge station where an agreement dated 25th June, 1878 be made between MS&L and L&Y. The L&Y to receive by 1st September, 1879 from LNWR and MS&L £6,250 in respect of their joint interest in Stalybridge station, where the L&Y would give up all their rights.

Important as were the foregoing, undoubtedly the foremost matter was the LNWR Reddish and Leeds Bill which conceived a line running from a junction with the Heaton Norris – Guide Bridge line at Denton Junction to Diggle. It would run north from Denton Junction passing over the MS&L main line near Newton (Hyde Junction) to Stalybridge, passing through the town on its southern side, thence via the Tame

Spinkwell staircase locks on the Bradford Canal. The canal would have been taken over jointly by the LNWR and L&YR, but their parliamentary bill was defeated on 17th February, 1878.

Valley with a length of 10 miles and 2.70 chains. Engineering features would abound: a 60 yards viaduct over the MS&L followed by a 400 yards-long viaduct immediately followed by a 66 yards-long tunnel leading onto a viaduct of 90 yards with a 2 furlong diversion of the Huddersfield Canal near Micklehurst. Subsequently there would be a viaduct of 200 yards at Chew Brook and a tunnel 150 yards long before a junction with the H&M line at Diggle. A connecting line would have led from this to the H&M at a point shown on the plan as Heyrod, which would include a 110 yards-long viaduct over the Tame (length 3 furlongs, 1.55 chains). The route would have had many features similar to the line ultimately made, but the project suffered a number of drawbacks, the greatest being the lack of communication at Stalybridge with existing lines. Objection came from many quarters. The Aire and Calder Navigation claimed the need to deviate the Huddersfield Canal would cause a blockage, an argument refuted as the canal was blocked each year for cleaning and maintenance. Stalybridge Corporation felt it would needlessly divide their town. Samuel Pope QC said 'he hoped he would be forgiven for saying that although Stalybridge was a most important place, it was not the most sightly place one would desire to visit. It was the place where all the odds and ends were thrown when Lancashire was made'. The Bill was, however, rejected. Despite this setback the LNWR were determined to construct a route linking the two places and fresh plans were prepared for the next Parliamentary Session.

Improvements made in the year included work at Leeds New station. When this was completed there were three through platforms and a goods loop, with two bays at the LNWR end and three at the NER end. Staincliffe and Batley Carr station was opened on 1st November after many years of local agitation, led by John Armitage of Dewsbury. At the time there were 22 passenger stations within a three mile radius. Water troughs were added at Standedge tunnels on both lines at the Diggle end where the only level stretch on the whole route was to be found. In August at Huddersfield a speaking tube connected all three station signal cabins in conjunction with a special bell code of signalling. There was a proposal to rebuild Dewsbury station on the site of the goods warehouse, but some years were to elapse before any improvements were made. The station had remained unaltered since it was opened with up and down platforms and a loop platform for trains going out in the direction of Batley. The LNWR intended to purchase land for a new engine shed at Farnley Junction, at Birstal to extend the goods yard and at Slaithwaite for the ultimate widening of Slaithwaite and Crimble viaducts.

A pleasant evening was held at the Greyhound Hotel, Birstal on 24th March when a supper was given in honour of Mr Woods, station master, who was leaving to become station master at Marsden. A speech was given by Mr Billy Bell Senior, the principal driver of the Birstal 'Coddy'.

Enquiries were made by the Normanton Joint Station Committee asking the LNWR to settle their affairs. Agreement was made that the company would pay £28,748 for the period during which they had used the station and henceforth they would be required to pay an annual sum of £250 until such time as they began to use the station again.

On the canals a severe frost caused great disruption of traffic for 14 weeks.

1878 produced three mishaps. On 10th January at Mirfield an LNWR goods from Stockport to Leeds was proceeding on the down loop to allow it to be overtaken by an L&Y express. The goods failed to stop, the driver believing that he was on the main line overran catch points and the engine and 36 wagons plunged down an embankment causing the deaths of driver D. Walker and fireman W. Goodman of Copley Hill shed. On 7th February at Huddersfield station as the 12.20 pm Marsden to Kirkburton arrived, it was set back to collect a van from a siding. The van was struck with so much force that it collided with an oncoming L&Y train from Meltham. On 20th November at Leeds, between Canal Junction and New station, a collision took place between the NER 6.10 am ex-Ilkley and an LNWR light engine which had been overlooked by the signalman.

1879

The LNWR (New Railway) Act of 3rd July authorized lines from Denton Junction to Dukinfield Junction (length 3 miles 3 chains and 50 links) and from Stalybridge to Saddleworth (length 6 miles 4 furlongs, 6 chains and 50 links).

The first named section had a tunnel at Hooley Hill, 170 yards in length which passed beneath the MS&L main line near Guide Bridge by an artificial covered way that was 154 yards long. This was immediately followed by a brick-sided cutting which, in the event of the MS&L widening their line, could have been quickly covered over.

The Micklehurst Line, as the second was known, started with a 290 yards-long viaduct at Stalybridge before plunging into a 315 yards-long tunnel. Later a 66 yards-long tunnel was followed by a 90 yards viaduct and a 2 furlong diversion of the Huddersfield Canal. A 220 yards-long viaduct was required at Chew Brook, then a 150 yards-long tunnel before the junction with the Huddersfield and Manchester line.

The LNWR (Additional Powers) Act dated 21st July allowed widening of the line in Huddersfield to take place, from Gledholt Road to a point 150 yards west of Scar Lane and from Fitzwilliam Street to Hillhouse. As well as the purchase of lands at Huddersfield and Hillhouse on the north side of the engine shed. Two stone arches at John William Street were to be replaced by a new 63 feet span girder bridge of 'ornamental appearance' and four gas lamps to be provided beneath.

The arches at Fitzwilliam Street and Bradford Road were to be widened and their pier abutments set back to 53 feet at the former and 59 feet at the latter, in both cases street lamps were to be provided. The level crossings at Woodhouse Park and Fieldhouse were to be replaced by bridges. The new portion of Leeds New station was fully used as from 5th January. The whole of the premises was constructed on a total of 60 arches and bridges.

From 1st March, after many years of protest and deputations, an extra train was added to the timetable on the Delph branch. Mr Madgewick the station master was subsequently presented with an inscribed gold watch for his service to the community.

During August at Morley a foretaste of things to come occurred when the tunnel was affected by mining subsidence. At Hillhouse, work on the new goods station commenced before any improvement could begin at Huddersfield. In November C.B. King and Co. started work on the west side where a substantial embankment was to be built and the arch at Hillhouse Lane was widened (this bore the date 1880). A new thoroughfare, Alder Street, was made and ran parallel with Huddersfield viaduct and embankment for a distance of 570 yards. New coal chutes with 20 bays, each divided into two were erected by S. Wright and Son of Low Moor. Excavation in the yard proved heavier than anticipated and blasting was necessary. The total excavation amounted to 288,800 cubic yards.

At Dewsbury a new goods station was being erected near Ashworth Road bridge during May. When completed this would occupy much of the station forecourt. At Leeds the foundation stone of the new viaduct was laid on 16th December by Mrs H.C. Findlay, wife of the LNWR's resident engineer. Work was undertaken by Naylor Bros. As planned, the new line would commence with a new Wortley station before passing beneath the Great Northern line and on to a viaduct of 96 arches ending at the Leeds and Liverpool Canal, having crossed 10 roads and the Holbeck.

Mishaps began in July when there was a substantial fall of masonry at Fitzwilliam Street, Huddersfield caused by an L&Y train being roughly shunted on the coal chutes. On 14th November on Huddersfield viaduct overlooking Bradford Road, an L&Y coal train from Horbury to Holmfirth hauled by No. 447 of Mirfield shed, was run into by the 3.50 pm Leeds to Manchester express (driver Joseph Atherton), causing injury to 15 passengers. Atherton had put his engine into reverse but could not avoid the impact. Colonel Yolland in his accident report found the Hillhouse signalman at fault for having given the express 'off' instead of 'caution'. On 2nd December, the 9.25 am Stalybridge to Leeds train, after picking up passengers at Marsden, was set back into a siding to pick up a circus van. On restarting, the third coach was derailed and narrowly avoided striking the buttress of a bridge.

The pair of Leeds, Dewsbury & Manchester Railway houses built adjacent to Copley Hill engine shed. Photograph 16th May, 1959
Author

CHAPTER FIVE

1880 – 89

The LNWR Act dated 6th August, 1880 sanctioned improvements at Hillhouse Yard.

The Delph branch services were increased to six trains daily. At Leeds the jointly owned LNWR/L&Y Whitehall Road goods depot opened on 1st December. All mineral traffic became concentrated there. Hitherto the LNWR's share had been handled at Copley Hill. The new depot had an approach line 40 chains long. (The 1928 *Appendix* showed this reduced to only 23 chains.) Passenger accommodation at Leeds New station was extended. By the end of November a timber footbridge with a ramp at both ends had been built and was far more popular than its British Railways (BR) successor of the 1960s. Refreshment rooms, waiting rooms, toilet facilities and an extended concourse were made by filling in the space formerly used by through lines that were now made into bays at either end.

At Standedge MS&L trains were diverted from the Woodhead route because of flooding, and the Huddersfield area was similarly affected on 14th July when ballast was washed from the track at Bradley causing serious disruption. Furthermore, in December a heavy fall of snow caused more delay and four engines were snowbound, two of which were on the Oldham branch.

Leeds viaduct on 5th November, 1960, with class '5MT' 4-6-0 No. 45075 on the 11.00 am Liverpool to Hull. *Author*

Despite three agreements made previously, the LNWR/L&Y found themselves in dispute with Sir John Ramsden over the purchase of property:

Claimed by Sir John Ramsden	£54,421 2s. 0d.
Offered by LNWR/L&Y	£26,366 4s. 9d.
Court award	£33,800 10s. 0d.

1880 produced five accidents. On 7th August a return excursion from Blackpool to Kirkburton became divided within Stalybridge tunnel and 14 coaches ran back. The guard was asleep and the runaway was halted 2½ miles later, just short of Guide Bridge. On 27th October a goods train from Greenfield ran into a goods train shunting at Saddleworth causing great disruption, clearance took seven hours. Two days later near Johnny Moore's Cabin, Paddock a wagon axle broke causing derailment of a goods train. The following 3.00 am Leeds to Manchester newspaper train due to end its journey at 4.40 am did not arrive until 10.00 am. On 25th November at 5.00 am a non stop Leeds – Liverpool goods struck a Stockport – Bradford goods causing great damage. According to reports, the engine and tender were badly crushed. On 7th December on Huddersfield viaduct at 5.00 pm, an LNWR shunt engine and truck standing in a siding were run into from behind by an L&Y goods, causing the former to be pushed forward on to the main line where it was run into by the 4.10 pm Leeds to Manchester train. Clearance took three hours.

1881

The LNWR (Additional Powers) Act of 18th July authorized purchase of lands at Lees and Deighton while the LNWR (New Railway) Act of the same date permitted:

1. the making of the second Springwood tunnel on the north side of the existing railway, length 2 furlongs and 2 chains, the deposited plan showed this to be 237 yards;
2. Huddersfield second tunnel 580 yards long north of existing line;
3. Farnley North Junction.

In making the new tunnel, the existing arch at Gledholt was to be replaced by a girder bridge and the western abutments of the old arch to be used in making the new but this was not done. A notable departure was that of William Edwards Hirst, the LNWR's Yorkshire Director who retired in April, doubtless worn out by the endless barrage of robust criticism hurled upon him from all quarters, especially from the Huddersfield Chamber of Commerce. 1881 also saw reconstruction at Mossley where a new footbridge was installed complete with glazed cover.

In April work commenced on making the Hooley Hill line with the contractor Walter Scott of Newcastle and J.G. Brickenden as resident engineer. In March work began on widening Huddersfield viaduct by John Wilson & Sons, the same firm widening the line between Gledholt and Scarwood, where stone excavated from Paddock cutting was taken to enlarge the viaduct. Some 35,000 tons of masonry were used. On the south side, 16 arches were extended running from Bradford Road towards Hillhouse, while on the north side 43 arches were widened all the way and ranged from 35 feet to 45 feet in height. One and a half million bricks were used, 1,000 tons of iron work on the bridges, 300 cubic yards of concrete in the foundations and 5,000 tons of dry filling ballast, while the upper surfaces of the arches were covered with a special asphalt half an inch thick to prevent water seepage.

The eastern portal of Hooley Hill tunnel, photographed 18th June, 1960. In the foreground is the site of a station, Hooley Hill (Guide Bridge) opened on 1st November, 1887. The station was closed from 1st January, 1917 until 3rd October, 1921. It was renamed Audenshaw on 2nd October, 1924, finally closing on 25th September, 1950.   *Author*

In September Taylor and Thompson began work on the Micklehurst line, while at Stalybridge the first sod was cut for the new station on 31st January. The girders were marked R.&J. Rankin, Union Foundry, Liverpool. As finished, the layout comprised up and down main lines, up and down platform lines and three west-facing bay lines, two on the down side and one on the up. On the south side of the station were up and down loops and a goods yard at low level with a large warehouse. This was widened on the south side where the premises were supported by a series of arches. At the Stockport end there was a large coal drop, the whole of which had double track and looked almost like a viaduct. To the north of all this was the original L&Y station.

A noteworthy excursion on 22nd August was for the lineside firm of Hutchinson Hollingworth & Co. Ltd which had a works trip to Euston at a fare of 5s. 5d., carrying 250 passengers from Diggle.

1882

The LNWR Act dated 12th July permitted:

1. The deviation of the Denton and Saddleworth Railway No. 2 (1 mile, 6 furlongs, 5 chains) and the abandonment of a portion of that project;
2. the purchase of lands at Wortley and the making of Huddersfield second tunnel (4 furlongs, 4 chains and 40 links) from a junction with the L&Y to form part of the Huddersfield Joint Undertaking. Sections 16 and 41 allowed this to be made on the south side instead of the north, as previously authorized.

Some of the many improvements brought about included the opening of the new Wortley and Farnley station and the Farnley viaduct to Leeds Canal Junction upon which all LNWR passenger services were routed from 1st March. The viaduct consisted 92 spans, 84 of Staffordshire Blue Brick and the remainder of plate girder construction, 1,220 yards long.

Major Marindin examined the line and observed six engines coupled together pass over. The first train to use the new route was the 3.00 am Leeds to Manchester newspaper train. The LNWR refused local requests for an intermediate station at Domestic Street, the only structure there was the Leeds Viaduct signal box, a small cabin controlling only signals

The site of Dukinfield & Ashton station, showing the former entrance at street level. On 18th June, 1960 class '5MT' 4-6-0 No. 44808 passes with a Leeds-Llandudno train. *Author*

and reached by a circular stairway from the street. Opening allowed LNWR trains to enter Leeds without using Midland metals and paying £6,500 per annum for the privilege.

At Copley Hill the old locomotive shed was demolished and reclaimed materials were used on the making of the new Farnley Junction shed. At Hillhouse the new yard opened on 1st June while at Slaithwaite the company gave attention to making new streets. The new Hooley Hill line, which allowed LNWR through trains to avoid Guide Bridge station, was inspected by Major Marindin on 27th September, 1882. Goods traffic began on 2nd October on which day 15 trains passed over the line. Shortly this figure increased to 35 daily. Passenger services commenced on 1st November. The LNWR now had two routes between Stalybridge and Stockport and passenger services were run over both.

At Mossley a new plate girder road bridge was made by the station and bore the name E. Borrows & Sons, Engineers, St Helens Junction, 1882.

Plans for the much overdue improvement at Huddersfield were aired during the year '… of such a character there will be nothing like it in

Yorkshire ...'. With an island platform and road approach from New North Road, work commenced on the hillside at the rear of the station, the cost of which was estimated at:

Huddersfield	Total £152,000	Goods	£76,000
		Pass	£49,000
		Sidings	£15,000
		Land	£12,000
Huddersfield second tunnel	£122,000	Cost	£67,000
		Land	£55,000
Viaduct widening		Cost	£45,000
		Signals	£5,000
Hillhouse to Heaton Lodge widening		Cost	£90,000
Gledholt to Scar Lane widening		Cost	£70,000
		Land	£20,500
		TOTAL	£504,500

The timber footbridge at Springwood Junction was replaced by an iron one on 11th June, 1882. As it was being raised into its final position it slipped and fell on one end.

The Hull and Barnsley Railway's Huddersfield and Halifax Extension Bill contained a clause permitting the making of a junction with the LNWR near Longwood. The LNWR objected to this Bill, in particular to the Longwood clause. Evidence was given by Francis Stevenson (in the absence of Mr Findlay) who pointed out that if a junction were desirable the proper place to make it would be at Fenay Bridge, as Hillhouse Yard was just completed and any traffic should pass through there.

Traffic on the OA&GB was having a lean time, only 36 tons of goods carried and no minerals during the year 1882, a chilling reminder of how traffic fluctuated between places quite close by. On the Bradley Wood branch there were 17 L&Y trains to Halifax with four on Sundays and 16 and four respectively in the opposite direction and eight trains to and from Bradford. (9 Saturdays only and two on Sundays.)

A notable inception from 1st October was the diversion of the 5.45 pm Leeds – Manchester and the 5.52 pm Manchester – Leeds trains to run via Oldham:

	pm		pm
Manchester Victoria	5.52	Leeds New	5.45
Oldham Clegg Street	6.13	Huddersfield	6.29
Greenfield	6.25	Greenfield	6.59
Huddersfield	6.50	Oldham Clegg Street	7.09
Leeds New	7.35	Manchester Victoria	7.30

The former connection to Stockport then started at Greenfield and vice versa. The 5.52 pm ex-Manchester Victoria last ran via Oldham on 23rd October, 1886 while the up train was discontinued after 19th June, 1886. The diversions were necessitated by single line operation over Stalybridge viaduct due to reconstruction and work proceeding on the Micklehurst line.

The LNWR was still concerned with Normanton where the engine shed accommodated only 20 locomotives. A figure of £21,975 was quoted as the cost of a new shed.

Five mishaps occurred in 1882. On 24th January in Huddersfield at 1.00 am an LNWR goods from Leeds to Birmingham was in head-on collision with a goods destined for Halifax at the mouth of Huddersfield tunnel. The locomotive and four wagons of the former received serious damage and the tunnel remained blocked for several hours.

During shunting operations at Huddersfield on 15th April, part of the 7.30 pm Bradford – Stockport goods ran backwards into a Copley Hill – Crewe goods being banked in the rear, which caused five wagons to be damaged.

The *Huddersfield Chronicle* of 3rd June, 1882 observed that a Leeds – Bangor excursion arriving at Huddersfield ran over a turntable left in the reversed position, without a mishap! Shades of the 1864 incident, see page 54.

On 4th October in Stalybridge a MS&L goods train being shunted collided with the back of a stationary LNWR passenger train standing at the platform, which caused a horse box and its occupants to be badly shocked. At the same place on 6th December a MS&L engine became derailed and caused the up Mail to be held at Greenfield while other trains in the vicinity were delayed by six hours. The cutting at Saddleworth became blocked by snow as an 'old fashioned winter had set in' with two engines trapped.

1883

The LNWR (New Railway) Act of 16th July authorized the making of a new line at Diggle from a junction with the Denton and Saddleworth line to a junction with the H&M and the abandonment of an earlier projected alignment near Diggle.

The LNWR (Additional Powers) Act of 2nd August allowed widening between Stockport and Denton and Denton and Dukinfield, Longwood Scar Lane and Golcar and widening at Dewsbury Wellington Road.

View of John William Street, Huddersfield, before the original arch was replaced by a plate girder bridge in 1883.
courtesy of Huddersfield Examiner

Opening included Deighton goods station in February and Stalybridge goods warehouse on 5th March, built by MacGregor and Williams who then turned their attention to the passenger station. Work on the Micklehurst line (authorized in 1879) was proceeding well and Ryfield (or Butterhouse) tunnel was under construction. Due to the scale of the works at Stalybridge, single line operation applied between the station and tunnel. The widening of Huddersfield viaduct was almost complete in January, work had started in March 1881. Widening commenced between Hillhouse and Heaton Lodge by John Wilson and Sons who simultaneously were finishing Paddock cutting and widening on the north side at Longwood viaduct which had started in November 1882. For the rebuilding of the arches at John William Street, Huddersfield, a temporary timber platform was removed on 28th May. The stone arch removal commenced early in June and work on the new girder structure was completed by the end of November. The previous month work started on Huddersfield's second tunnel. The excavation at the back of Huddersfield station was almost complete. The retaining walls were 40 feet high. At this time a new goods warehouse was opened at Longwood while at Marsden the old goods yard crane was replaced in November.

On the L&Y main line widening began in November between Heaton Lodge and Mirfield. Naylor Bros of Denby Dale were the contractors. In spite of all the enormous engineering works progressing, the LNWR introduced an hourly interval service between Huddersfield and Leeds from 1st July, running from 8.30 am until 9.30 pm, while at the same time the 8.30 am and 10.40 am trains from Kirkburton began working through to Marsden. A feature of the Kirkburton service since its inception was the conveyance of mails destined for Clayton West, which were taken forward by a horse-drawn mail cart. This was discontinued from 1st August.

The second appearance of a Royal Train on 'The Yorkshire Lines' was on 13th October when the Duke and Duchess of Albany arrived at Huddersfield from Otley. The train of two saloons and brake was run by the Midland to Leeds Wellington where the LNWR took over following reversal, arriving at Huddersfield at 10.35 am. The occasion was marred when the train overshot the appointed stopping place and had to set back to where the red carpet was laid. G.E. Mawby, the LNWR superintendent, Manchester was in charge. The return train on the following Monday to Sheffield was worked by the L&Y.

The annual quota of mishaps began on 1st February at Hillhouse when an LNWR six-coach train to Kirkburton, driven by George Prestwick, stopped for signals. The following L&Y train from Meltham to Bradford pulled up safely in the rear but was run into by an LNWR Stockport – Leeds train hauled by No. 1515 *Milton* (driver Aaron Sharrett) which was fitted with the patent chain brake. The inquiry conducted by Colonel F.H. Rich found that Sharrett had overrun a signal

The underside of John William Street bridge, 21st June, 1982. *Author*

in thick fog and that the L&Y guard failed to protect his train although he had ample time to do so. The impact caused the Bradford train to be precipitated into the Kirkburton train. Twelve passengers were injured, including Mr W.P. Wallet, the Queen's Jester, 'who was rendered insensible'.

On 27th September at Marsden the 2.00 pm Manchester – Leeds express ran into a goods train being reversed from the up to the down line. The crew of the former, seeing what was about to happen jumped clear but six passengers were injured.

In Huddersfield tunnel on 24th October, the Bradford – Liverpool goods comprising a tender engine and 47 wagons, assisted by a banker in the rear, was in collision. The banker (No. 1950 driver George Mossley) was run into from behind by the 7.55 am Huddersfield – Stockport passenger train hauled by No. 2145 *Precursor* and consisting of 10 coaches (driver Thos Fretter), causing injury to 10 passengers. Major General Hutchinson RE conducted the inquiry and gave six reasons for the accident:

1. The passenger train made too fast an approach to the starting signal in the tunnel, the driver not seeing the signal until 5 yards from it.
2. The speed of 12 mph at point of accident, 43 yards beyond the overrun signal.
3. The signalman at Huddersfield failed to warn the driver that the signal was against him.
4. No red light carried on rear of goods train, the guard was in the act of lighting and wiping the lamp which was covered with mud when the collision occurred.
5. Starter signal 110 yards inside the tunnel and very difficult to see when smoke was present.
6. Goods train despatched only one minute before passenger train due to insufficient accommodation at the station for traffic density.

It was recommended that signals be resited to avoid a similar mishap.

1884

The principal feature of the LNWR Act of 28th July enabled land to be purchased on the south side of Glodwick Road station, Oldham. Manchester Exchange station was opened on 30th June when all LNWR trains were transferred there. Work on the new station, particularly the parcels office was not quite complete. A new station at Bradley came into use on 16th November and had four platforms in contrast to Huddersfield which still had only one! 'The most necessary work left until the last' as reported in the *Huddersfield Chronicle,* 16th August, 1884.

The line from Hillhouse to Heaton Lodge was being widened from two to four tracks and was completed in April. Colne Bridge viaduct comprising two arches and a girder span was built alongside the original line. The L&Y continuation of this widening between Heaton Lodge and Mirfield was completed in July, while from Mirfield to Thornhill was finished in August, except for the crossing of the Calder through Mirfield station which remained a bottleneck until LMS days.

Blasting work in the new Huddersfield tunnel was said to be the cause of a partial collapse of building at South Street. Garbut and Owen were the contractors who used a 0-6-0ST (MW734/81) which was subsequently sold to the Weston, Clevedon & Portishead Railway in Somerset. Longwood viaduct widening ended in February. The four most easterly arches were of irregular size to accommodate the profile of the land below. One arch unusually had four different radii.

In January preliminary work commenced in St Georges's Street for improvements at Huddersfield station. This involved underpinning the LNWR-owned Crown Hotel sited above the tunnel mouth. Work also began at Gledholt in connection with the new Springwood tunnel. Widening commenced in February of the new viaduct at Golcar Brook. There was an 8 feet 2 inches gap between the old and new viaducts. This was followed by widening at Linthwaite and the viaducts at Crimble and Slaithwaite.

An engineer's report on Micklehurst line progress (4th January, 1884) showed that six viaducts were finished and of 627 yards of tunnel, 350 yards were complete.

Proposals for a station at Ravensthorpe were publicized but negotiations were hampered by the Ravensthorpe and the Thornhill Local Boards' unwillingness to contribute £1,000 each towards the cost of making a road bridge over the Calder. The company were in trouble with Huddersfield Chamber of Commerce over the cost of wool storage which amounted to 4*d.* per ton per week for periods of up to six months; thereafter the cost doubled. At this time the North Eastern Railway introduced their notable 'Cotton Buyers' Special' which ran Thursdays only between Hull and Manchester:

```
Hull                   9.15 am    Manchester Exchange  2.53 pm
Manchester Exchange   11.38 am    Hull                 5.23 pm
```

On the Huddersfield Canal traffic was halted due to drought between June and the first week in November.

The annual spate of accidents began on 24th January at Hillhouse when an LNWR light engine (driver John Wm White) coming off shed was placed by the signalman on the wrong line. It was run into by the 6.10 am L&Y Huddersfield – Bradford passenger train. The former was about to haul a goods to Halifax. On 10th April six trucks and a brake van ran back down the gradient from a coal train being shunted at Slaithwaite. The guard was not aboard and the brake was off. At Huddersfield, 4 $\frac{1}{2}$ miles from where it started, the runaway emerged from the tunnel at great speed and struck an engine coming out of the sidings. The implications of this were serious, but considering the scale of engineering works taking place throughout the locality, it must be regarded as an act of divine providence that no one was injured.

At Low Westwood Crossing on 21st July the 10.15 am Leeds – Manchester train was almost stopped by adverse signals, but was called on by the signalman. The engine became derailed and plunged down an embankment. Single line working was in force. Two other engines were obtained with a breakdown crane to put back the coaches that had been derailed. Within three-quarters of an hour they proceeded to Manchester hauled by a fresh engine!

On 5th November at the Fenay Bridge station of the Kirkburton branch, the 3.00 pm ex-Kirkburton was running into the station when it was inexplicably diverted into the goods yard and collided with two loaded gunpowder wagons. The timber wagon was demolished. The van nearest the engine, made of iron, withstood the impact. The train of six coaches, and a 4 feet 6 inches 2-4-2 tank was driven by Tom Clough and fired by H. Shaw.

At Saddleworth on 6th November a stationary goods was run into at fast speed from behind by another goods and a railwayman was injured. Breakdown gangs from Hillhouse and Longsight were summoned and single line operation was resumed three hours later.

1885

At a time when an enormous modernization programme was being undertaken, the year can be regarded as one of quite exceptional nature. The LNWR Act of 16th July extended powers for completing the Micklehurst line for 18 months. It allowed widening of the route between Marsden and Golcar, and the making of a new road at

Ravensthorpe despite the two local authorities' intransigence. It confirmed an agreement between LNWR and L&Y dated 22nd January, 1884 whereby L&Y were granted powers to operate from Manchester Victoria to Stockport via Ashton Branch Junction and from Thornhill to Leeds. The LNWR received powers to run between Mirfield and Bradford, and from Heaton Lodge to Halifax via the North Dean branch.

Of the vast works undertaken, the Micklehurst loop line extending from Diggle to Stalybridge opened for goods traffic on 1st December. Farnley North Curve opened on 15th May (length 15 chains) on which date the South Curve was severed to become used for the purpose of turning locomotives at the new Farnley Junction engine shed. Stalybridge was officially reopened on 21st May. At Huddersfield the scene was transformed when the new goods warehouse 'designed in the poorest style of Lancashire brick architecture with hideous side windows which added to its dismal appearance' was opened on 1st July. It comprized five storeys plus basement. It was 318 feet 8 inches long and 164 feet 10 inches wide; the walls at ground level were 3 feet 6 inches thick. During construction 20 hydraulic cranes were used. The building was equipped with a hydraulic hoist with a capacity of 30 tons capable of lifting a loaded wagon. Hydraulic pumping of water was by a large engine supplied with steam from two ordinary locomotive boilers. On the ground floor there were seven lines of rails and six lines of rails on the second floor. Girder work was by Horsley Iron Co., Tipton and the brickwork was by Samuel Warburton and Co., Manchester. All hydraulic and gas appliances were made at the LNWR Crewe Works 'at a cost of over £400,000'. The hydraulic Tank House accommodated 60,000 gallons of water and served not only the goods department, but also the passenger station. Sixteen hand-cranes were provided on the ground floor with 20 on the second floor, each of 15 cwt capacity. The old warehouse was demolished at once.

At Bradford the LNWR enjoyed facilities at the L&Y's new goods depot in Wakefield Road which opened in May, where grain and wool were handled. New sidings opened at Gledholt in June with coal chutes by John Wilson and Sons.

On 11th January at Huddersfield, a start was made by John Radcliffe and Sons on the new island platform. The first work involved a new subway which was about one-third narrower than the one subsequently used. By July the foundations for the roof pillars were completed on the site of the old warehouse, but a temporary setback occurred when the water pipe from Marsden to Hillhouse burst and flooded the workings.

Roof work for the station was supplied by Samuel Butler and Co., Stanningley. On 10th August at about 10.30 am four complete spans fell down on the tracks. A passenger train to Bradford had just moved clear. The line was cleared at 1.20 pm and the wreckage removed by 2.20 pm with the whole tangled mess placed in the Kirkburton bay. Four persons were killed and five injured as the 50 to 60 tons of roof fell. John Waugh CE of Bradford conducted an inquiry, describing the roof span being 77 feet 8 inches supported by a cast-iron column on one side and the station wall on the other. 'It is difficult to say what caused the roof to fall. I feel satisfied that more support would have prevented the accident'. At the time 16 upright columns had been erected. (Report in *British Architect*.) A temporary roof was fitted in September.

On 9th May the widening of Crimble viaduct was completed by John Wilson and Sons. A dinner at the Lewisham Hotel was given to the workmen. At this time work on the Micklehurst line was virtually complete except at Ryecroft tunnel where 'work was in a shambles' according to press reports because of an ingress of water seeping through from the hillside to the south. Demolition of an old H&M masonry underbridge at Ward Lane, Diggle was only successful after 32 shots had been fired.

The approaches to Marsden station were widened in June while plans for a new station at Golcar indicated this to be nearer to Golcar Brook viaduct than hitherto. The booking office was to be on the down side instead of the up side as before. Scarwood crossing would be abolished.

The collapse of the station roof at Huddersfield on 10th August, 1885.

A number of new roads leading up to and bridging the line by the station were planned and a goods station made at Linthwaite. Work was progressing on Springwood second tunnel. At Longwood construction of the goods warehouse started on 7th July and widening in the vicinity of the station in August. The latter involved new embankments on a sideways extension of the existing route at both ends of Longwood viaduct and the remaking of Lowergate where its gradient was eased. Substantial retaining walls were needed on both sides of Lowergate. In December a contract was given to John Wilson and Sons for the Longwood station, by which time the new Springwood tunnel had been completed.

'The Yorkshire Lines' gave passage to their third Royal Train on 16th July when HRH the Prince of Wales travelled between Leeds and Manchester while en route from Ripon to Preston. The Royal pilot engine passed through Huddersfield at great speed at 11.19 am. Although the station had been temporarily closed 'it soon became filled with passengers for Longwood when the news oozed out'.

The Liverpool – Normanton Mail was operating during 1885. On 1st July it ran:

Liverpool Lime Street	10.45 pm
Warrington Bank Quay Low Level	11.15
Stockport	Arrive 12.15 am
	Depart 12.50
Stalybridge	Arrive 1.08
	Depart 1.13
Huddersfield	Arrive 1.49
	Depart 1.53
Normanton	Arrive 2.28

Connections were made at Warrington with the Up Limited Mail due 11.26, and with a train to Chester at 11.32 pm for the Irish Mail. At Normanton it connected with the Midland travelling post office (TPO) for Newcastle at 2.49 am. There was a comparative absence of excursion trains due to the multiplicity of engineering work extending over much of the route. The GNR, MS&L, L&Y and Midland took all London excursion traffic.

At Dewsbury, after much suffering and great endurance, the station amenities were to be improved. Mr Moon and a party of officers met members of Dewsbury Town Council. Mr Moon explained the new premises would be of four lines. A passenger subway 32 feet wide and the present shunting line were to be abolished. A retaining wall and arching led to Eightlands and the road bridge at Ashworth Road extended over six tracks.

The LNWR's legal department had a busy time. Kirkburton Local Board took the company to court for non payment of rates, 10*d*. in the pound. The Board had seized and detained some property. The LNWR counterclaimed for trespass. The Marsden Local Board made their annual visit to court for the same reason, for the amount of £208 18*s*. 9*d*. The hearing at Leeds Assizes on 6th August was adjourned until 21st December when judgement went in favour of the Local Board with costs to be paid by the LNWR.

During the 1885 General Election, the Liberal candidate for the Colne Valley constituency (extending from Longwood to Greenfield), made repeated claims at public meetings that his Conservative opponent Col Thomas Brooke, the LNWR's Director, 'was the Director of a company that uses intimidation against its workmen'. He cited several instances of workmen opposing LNWR officials for Crewe Town Council seats then finding that they were victimized into leaving the company's service. This accusation was strongly denied, but Mr H.E. Beaumont persisted and ultimately a Conservative reader of the *Huddersfield Chronicle* wrote to the LNWR locomotive superintendent at Crewe asking if the allegations were true. F.W. Webb's reply was emphatic 'there is no truth whatever in the statement to which you refer'. Nonetheless Col Brooke lost the contest. However, the topic would not go away. The LNWR had to contend with it for more than five years. At the LNWR's half-yearly general meeting in February 1890, its Chairman Sir Richard Moon faced a constant barrage of interruption from shareholders; he concluded that 'the people who made the charges stated certain admitted facts and had drawn on their imagination for the reason'. Those wishing to acquaint themselves with this aspect of LNWR history are recommended to read *The Social and Economic History of Crewe* by W.H. Chaloner who deals with it exhaustively.

One of the earliest excursions through Standedge Canal tunnel took place on 10th August when a party of 30 Colne Valley mill owners made the journey aboard the narrow boat *John*. Beforehand, a luncheon had been served under canvas in weather of hurricane force, then bottles of ale enjoyed afterwards. The vessel was equipped with two oil lamps amidships with a candle at either end. Stops were made at intervals to allow members the opportunity to explore the tunnel passages. Four leggers were employed to propel the boat to Diggle, reached in two and a half hours.

Four accidents occurred in 1885. On 25th January at Hillhouse, the 6.00 am L&Y Huddersfield – Bradford train under clear signals was involved in a collision with an LNWR light engine coming off shed. Both engines were extensively damaged. Col Rich in his inquiry report stated he had examined the interlocking at Hillhouse No. 1 box in the previous August when the arrangements were to his satisfaction, but the mishap arose by an omission in the interlocking hitherto undetected.

A notable incident on an unspecified date in April was the use of a vacuum-fitted passenger engine on the 3.45 pm Manchester to Leeds express worked by engines and men of Longsight shed. On that occasion driver Sam Cook pulled up from full speed to an emergency stop in 300 yards at Slaithwaite.

On 18th August at Huddersfield station as the 11.40 am express to Liverpool was leaving the platform, an L&Y train of empty stock moved forward and was involved in a sidelong collision. At Batley on 26th October at 10.30 pm an LNWR perishables train from Hull was diverted into the up platform loop and ran through the buffers, the engine overturning onto the GNR line alongside. Neither driver nor fireman was aware of what had happened, as they were booked to run through Batley station but on this occasion their train was going to be overtaken.

At Heaton Lodge Sidings on 17th November the 9.00 am Leeds – Manchester passenger train ran into the back of a stationary goods train and the fireman of the former was killed. Inquiry revealed the cause to be the signalman's acceptance of the express, overlooking the presence of the goods train.

1886

Express trains began to use the Micklehurst Loop on 3rd May. Local services began on 3rd July when the four intermediate stations, Staley and Millbrook, Micklehurst, Friezland and Uppermill opened. Five trains operated in each direction. A thunderbolt is stated to have landed alongside the track at Uppermill on 20th October.

The new station at Longwood was completed in July. The four platforms were 450 feet in length and the maximum width of the station was 120 feet. The roof was made of iron with ornamental columns and a height of 16 feet 6 inches. The central part of Huddersfield station building had housed the first and second class refreshment rooms and had been known as the Station Hotel, or the Brook's Arms, a

Class '5MT' 4-6-0 No. 45057 passing Friezland station house on 11th July, 1959 with a Saltburn to Manchester Exchange train. *Author*

A Filey to Manchester Exchange train passing Staley & Millbrook on 5th September, 1959. 'Patriot' 4-6-0 No. 45508 carries a stovepipe chimney. *Author*

non-residential establishment specializing in social events. It then became the booking hall with the LNWR section to the right and the L&Y to the left with the entrance through the centre portico. The lamp room had square iron pillars erected in place of the circular ones that had fallen the previous year.

Huddersfield's island platform was first used on 30th May where 'accommodation was commodious'. All rooms were fitted with pipes for heating instead of the usual fireplaces. Work on the roof was not complete. The old signal box in the middle was being demolished when fate took a hand and it collapsed. The island platform refreshment room opened on 10th October on the same day as Huddersfield second tunnel was opened, the 12.23 pm to Manchester being the first train to pass through. The old tunnel then closed for repairs made necessary by subsidence. Completion of the widening of Springwood cutting was in June. At the end of May John Wilson & Sons had been given a contract to widen between Scarwood and Rotcher Hill Top Crossing, where the siding had been made into a loop.

On the OA&GB passenger traffic during the year amounted to 443,019 persons. A weekly workmen's ticket at half the ordinary price came into operation between Slaithwaite and Longwood during July. There were complaints about an excursion organized for B.&J. Whitwam's mill trip to Liverpool. Two hundred passengers had assembled at Longwood station at 6.00 am but their train did not arrive until 8.35 am and a saloon ordered for senior staff was not attached. The staff had to travel later in an ordinary train, 'the return being made in an inferior carriage of another company'. Bookings for the Huddersfield holidays in September amounted to:

Liverpool	971	
Blackpool	1,355	
Scotland	209	
Morecambe	58	
Windermere	17	
Leeds	529	
Longsight	738	(for Belle Vue)
Cross Lane	213	(for Manchester Races)
Douglas	17	
Scarborough	177	

On 16th August two excursions were run from Kirkburton:

Bangor	Depart 12.20 am	Fare 4s. 6d.
Blackpool	Depart 5.00 am	Fare 2s. 9d.

A reminder of the past in Micklehurst goods yard, seen on 20th April, 1962. *Author*

For the International Festival at Liverpool on 3rd November an excursion was run to the Exhibition station. The train called at 10 stations between Leeds (departing 10.20 am) and Ashton, fare 2s. 6d. Excursionists were able to visit many liners in Liverpool free of charge.

At Marsden the company was still in trouble with the Local Board who investigated the ownership of telegraph poles on their land over Standedge. Enquiries revealed these were not the Board's property and the LNWR had a rate of 2s. 6d. per pole per year to pay. By November enforcement proceedings began over non-payment in respect of 75 poles. The Golcar Local Board had a similar action against the company. In the canal department, Edward Greenwood's successor, Mr R.H. Smith was appointed manager of the North Staffordshire Railway Canal (Trent and Mersey) and Francis Goodall, chief inspector of boats was appointed in his place.

The only accident of the year occurred at Huddersfield on 20th July when the driver of the 2.30 pm Leeds – Manchester train missed a signal after stopping, then moved off and converged with an emigrant train on the next line.

1887

The Hull & Barnsley Railway (H&B) Act of 5th July, 1887 sanctioned the abandonment of the Huddersfield and Halifax extension authorized in 1882. This came as no surprise, as it had been predicted in the local press several years before. On the same day that the H&B relinquished its powers, an Act of Parliament permitted the newly formed Hull & North

Western Junction Railway (H&NWJ) to construct a line on the H&B's projected route from Royston to a junction with the LNWR's Kirkburton branch at Fenay Bridge. Since November 1885 there had been correspondence and meetings between George Findlay and Francis Stevenson of the LNWR and James Staats Forbes, joint Managing Director of the H&B. Another H&NWJ Act on 14th August, 1890 permitted a deviation of the route at Flockton Moor, a junction with the L&Y and running powers to Barnsley, where a short branch and a depot were to be constructed with allowance for more time to complete the project. In 1893 however, the LNWR began to use running powers to Hull over the NER. This 'desertion' by the LNWR was a reason given by the H&NWJ for the abandonment of its powers and for the winding up of the company, which was permitted by its Act of 1st June, 1894.

At Leeds New approval was given for improvements to the booking office. On 15th December the original tunnel at Huddersfield was reopened after repairs, the subway leading to Huddersfield island platform was opened, as was the widened line from Springwood to Golcar. This included something not shown on the Parliamentary plan, Paddock tunnel, 43 yards in length, beneath Market Street with a short masonry bridge beneath Branch Street. In November at Slaithwaite new coal chutes opened. The station at Hooley Hill (Guide Bridge) opened on 1st November as well as new LNWR/L&Y goods offices at New North Road, Huddersfield. There was a complaint about workmen's tickets not being available on the Kirkburton branch. A census revealed those passengers who would avail themselves to be:

Kirkburton	117
Fenay Bridge	40
Kirkheaton	40
Deighton	40

The Chairman, Mr Richard Moon paid a visit to Yorkshire on 28th May and, with Colonel Brooke, heard expressed the need for a goods station at Low Westwood.

On the OA&GB line trade improved and a total of 121,392 tons of goods and 234,834 tons of minerals were carried, while passenger numbers rose to 1,377,540, a record!

The only mishap was on 23rd September at Diggle when a passenger train being reversed into a siding was struck by a goods emerging from the tunnel at fast speed. Damage was limited to all the carriage handles being ripped off.

1888

Two main features produced by the LNWR Act dated 7th August were:

1. Making the Stalybridge Junction railway over a distance of 1 mile, 4 furlongs and 50 links from a junction with the Hooley Hill line to Stalybridge.
2. Making a new double line tunnel at Standedge (5232 yards in length) with a new section of line 3 miles, 2 furlongs and 2 chains in length which completed the quadrupling between Heaton Norris at Stockport to Heaton Lodge Junction.

Mr Findlay asked the Normanton Joint Station Committee to reduce the annual fee from £250 to £50, a request that was declined. The LNWR's partnership in the committee ended on 7th October.

The service of 28 trains daily on the OA&GB was equally divided between the LNWR and the MS&L and of the 11 Sunday trains, two ran direct to Manchester, London Road. On the Birstal branch 13 trains plied in each direction while main line improvements directly arising from widening works permitted the following new services from February:

3.19 pm	Stalybridge to Huddersfield	ThO
10.35 am	(ex-Hudds) Leeds to Manchester	ThO
10.43 am	(ex-Hudds) Leeds to Manchester	MO
	From 1st May 5.45 am Huddersfield to Marsden arr 6.04 am	
	From mid-July new services to West of England from Leeds	
1.58 pm	Huddersfield to Shrewsbury, Hereford and Bristol (arr 7.55 pm), Exeter arr 10.30 pm by connection	
1.15 am	Leeds Manchester ran daily from July and from 1st September	
2.38 pm	Huddersfield, Stalybridge (3.11 pm) to Manchester Exchange	SO

ThO - Thursdays only, MO - Mondays only, SO - Saturdays only

Excursion traffic was vastly improved over previous years. Cheap period excursions were available from West Riding stations to Hereford and South Wales, Brighton, St Leonards and Hastings.

On 21st June an excursion for the Handel Festival at Crystal Palace departed from Leeds at 8.20 am with the return available on either 23rd or 30th. For B.&J. Whitwam's annual trip from Golcar to Bridlington via Leeds and Selby, departure was at 5.20 am and arrival at 9.00 am. The return started at 7.50 pm but Golcar was not reached until 12.20 am. The firm subsequently noted 'the LNWR provided some capital carriages, no doubt in penitence for an earlier omission'.

Reconstruction of Huddersfield station was deemed complete on 22nd June when a new 5 feet diameter clock, made by Henry Peace jeweller, New Street, Huddersfield was set in motion. The station handled its heaviest traffic in August when the Yorkshire Show was held. The original platform was now used by up trains and the island platform for down trains, reversible on either face and the inside face of the double bay at the east end used by Kirkburton trains. At the west end of the original platform a bay led directly into its own tunnel. The L&Y installed a turnstile at their end of the station through which all their passengers and luggage had to pass, much to their annoyance. The Chamber of Commerce turned its wrath upon the L&Y from time to time, this was the most blistering yet, but the contrivance was only removed after repeated complaints from that source and by local newspapers. At the east end of the up platform, the bay formerly used for the Kirkburton trains became mainly used for fish, perishable and parcel traffic. Adjacent was the dock complete with short sidings, horse landings and 40 feet turntable. Circus and theatrical specials used this area which had direct access into St George's Square.

Widening work in the Colne Valley was proceeding at a swift pace, nearing completion in May at Slaithwaite, where a new booking office, subway and waiting rooms were brought into use in mid-September. In June the company began a new retaining wall in Meg Lane and in

Uppermill station about 1911 with Mr Charles E. Fry, station master. Mr Fry became station master at Huddersfield in 1931, retiring nine years later. *Author's collection*

August the new coal chutes and warehouse at Low Westwood were opened but underwent a change of identity to Linthwaite Goods. The warehouse was on seven arches made on three levels plus nine coal chutes and the signal box was supported by an elevated gantry. Opening was on 14th August. Simultaneously, Iredales' Siding on the adjacent side of the line was closed. On the Oldham branch a service of 14 trains ran to Greenfield, 18 trains in the opposite direction with three each way on Sundays.

A projected Royal visit by Prince Albert Victor on 9th August to Huddersfield would have seen a special coach attached to an ordinary train between York and Mirfield, then run forward as a special, but the visit was cancelled due to HRH's indisposition with gout.

The only known mishap on the Delph branch occurred on 21st July at 7.30 pm. The engine of a passenger train was required to take some goods wagons to Greenfield. Meanwhile, some young boys playing about the station released the brake on the empty coaches and on a slight incline, these ran back to Tamewater cutting where they were run into head-on by their engine returning light from Greenfield. The driver had no chance to stop the engine. One coach was destroyed and both the engine and the other coaches were damaged.

On 27th September as the 6.30 pm Leeds – Manchester train was passing through Standedge tunnel, a connecting rod broke (2 feet 3 inches from centre of the little end), the loose end flew round and pierced the firebox making a hole $8\,^3/_8$ inches x $1\,^5/_8$ inches. The driver and fireman were both badly scalded and died from their injuries. Mr George Whale attended the inquest where he stated 'it showed considerable courage on the part of the footplate crew to apply the brakes in this condition with the cab full of live steam'. The engine was No. 941 *Blenkinsop* a 6 feet 6 inches Newton built at Crewe (Works No. 1683) in 1873. Following the accident *Blenkinsop* was rebuilt as an 'Improved Precedent' loco.

At the end of the year the Birstal terminus was again threatened when Brookroyd Mill caught fire. The mill was destroyed but the station again escaped serious damage.

Fare anomalies were noted on certain bookings, examples were:

Manchester – Slaithwaite 3rd return	3s. 2d.
Manchester – Huddersfield 3rd return	4s. 6d.
Slaithwaite – Huddersfield 3rd return	$4\,^1/_2 d.$

The lease of the Rochdale Canal began in 1855 and ran until 1876. The agreement lasted until 1888 with the carriage of 688,000 tons of goods.

1889

Commencing on 1st July a new through service began operation between Newcastle and Liverpool, prior to which a change of trains was needed at Leeds.

Newcastle	7.35 am	10.10 am				4.05 pm	ThO
Scarborough		10.50					Hull 8.35 am
York			12.40 pm	2.45 pm	4.20 pm		
Leeds New	10.45	1.00	1.40	3.45	5.15	7.20	10.00
Huddersfield	11.12	1.27	2.07	4.12	5.42	7.58	10.35
Manchester Exchange	11.55	2.15	2.50	4.50	6.25	8.45	11.30
Liverpool Lime Street	12.45	3.00	3.40	5.45	7.10	9.45	
Liverpool Lime Street	8.45 am	11.00 am	11.30 am	2.00 pm	3.30 pm	6.00 pm	NER train via Micklehurst start 5/1/1888
Manchester	9.30	11.45	12.15	3.00	4.15	6.45	3.05 pm
Huddersfield	10.15	12.27	1.02	3.52	4.47	7.27	3.57
Leeds New	10.40	12.27	1.28	4.20	5.23	8.00	4.25
York			2.15		6.15		Hull 6.00
Scarborough		3.00					
Newcastle	1.50			7.15		11.05	

The 7.35 am ex-Newcastle and 11.00 am ex-Liverpool finished on 30th September, 1889. The 2.45 pm and 4.20 pm ex-York and 3.30 pm and 6.00 pm ex-Liverpool were discontinued after 9th March, 1890.

In January the main platform at Huddersfield was heightened. On 14th January a new booking office at Golcar was first used along with the new waiting rooms on No. 1 platform. John Wilson & Sons began the widening between Slaithwaite and Tunnel End in June and a new steam navvy *The Jubilee*, capable of lifting 25 cwts of earth at once did the work of 250 men. Three lines of rail were laid alongside the navvy so as to ensure a constant supply of wagons in which to discharge earth. The trucks were then taken away by two contracted locomotives, *Dryden* at the Slaithwaite end and *Alice* working at Marsden. After reversal the wagons were run onto a spur and up ended on to the 'tips'. By July extensive retaining walls were being made on the north side of the line at Marsden where the new station was being erected. Here in one day the Whittaker's steam navvy removed 600 cubic yards of earth and filled 200 wagons. At the station the level crossing was replaced by a bridge of three spans. The level crossing at Diggle was replaced on 24th November by a new bridge carrying the booking office. However, the old station was not rebuilt until 1894.

At the end of March 1889 the old station at Dewsbury had almost gone. A new booking office, glass roofed portico and a footbridge were opened on 25th March. The old down platform had been removed without interruption of traffic while a new platform and retaining wall were built. The wall incorporated a footpath supported by 10 arches, all of irregular size, leading to Eightlands. The entrance to the judges' chambers at Dewsbury County Court was made from a doorway in the footbridge. Mr J.D. Nowell the contractor completing the task in May.

On 11th December a meeting was held of all LNWR signalmen employed between Copley Hill and Dewsbury at the Valley Hotel, Morley, with regard to the chronic overworking of signalmen, who were required to work 12 hour shifts, seven days a week without a break.

Two mishaps occurred in 1889. On 11th December at Low Moor, an L&Y locomotive was run into from behind by an LNWR engine and brake from Hillhouse in the charge of driver George Owen and fireman B. Sutcliffe. On 19th December at Huddersfield at 5.30 am, three postal sorting vans which had been left in the station by the Mail for an unknown reason ran forward down the viaduct and then were run into by an oncoming train.

The LNWR 'intimidation' allegation was raised again. However, nothing fresh emerged but it kept the topic well alight.

Class '5MT' 4-6-0 No. 45042 heads a stopping train from Leeds at Manchester Exchange in 1955. *K. Field*

CHAPTER SIX

1890 – 1899

1890

The LNWR Act dated 4th August empowered the purchase of lands at Glodwick Road, Diggle, Ward Lane and Dobcross ironworks where a short branch was to bridge the Huddersfield Canal. All this was overshadowed by the LNWR's declaration to make a new line to Leeds and double the track capacity of the entire route.

A meeting was held on 5th August at Heckmondwike between civic heads and a party of LNWR officers. The latter asked to be met at the Heckmondwike L&Y station at 11.00 am but with everyone gathered on the platform, their arrival came unexpectedly by a 'stylish coach' from Dewsbury. The party comprised: Colonel Brooke a Director, Mr George Findlay the General Manager, Francis Stevenson the Engineer and F.W. Webb the locomotive superintendent.

Mr Webb said that despite the gradients envisaged he did not anticipate any problems for locomotives. By choosing this route to duplicate the line between Huddersfield and Leeds they would give the Spen Valley an opportunity to benefit. The population of the locality was:

Heckmondwike	10,000
Liversedge	15,000
Cleckheaton	15,000
Gomersal	10,000
Birstal	7,000
Gildersome	10,000

But the real reason for choosing this route was that to quadruple the existing line via Dewsbury would involve widening at Morley where, in the opinion of the Civil Engineer, such a course would be dangerous because of the state of Morley tunnel. A plan was deposited during the 1891 session but withdrawn. There were a number of differences from the line ultimately made – leaving the H&M near Heaton Lodge, the projected line would rise at one in 90 to cross over the L&Y main line by a 50 feet span bridge 14 feet 6 inches high.

At Standedge the first sod of the new double line tunnel was lifted at the Marsden end on 5th August, the old shafts at Flint and Red Brook were reopened and a new shaft at Brun Clough brought into use. The work was executed by the LNWR who subsequently used 2 feet 6 inches

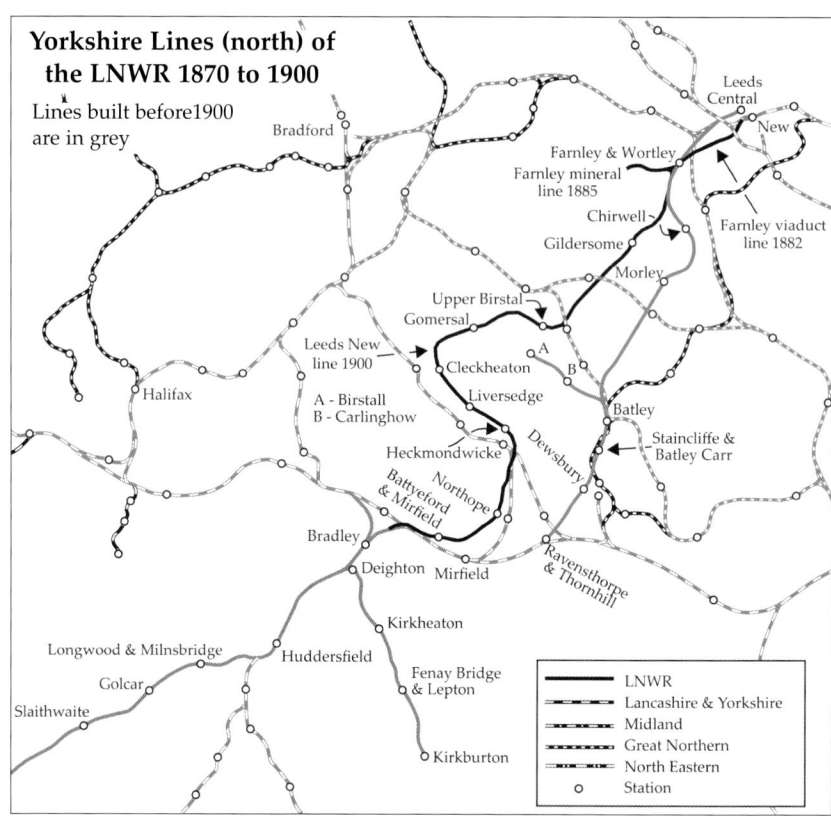

0-4-0WT shunters. On 16th November a pumping engine being placed in position at Red Brook broke loose and crashed 55 feet down the shaft. At Marsden extensive disruption was taking place. In March it was claimed that Wilsons had laid an unauthorized tramway along a road at Smithy Top. The Local Board and others made numerous objections about the 'reckless way' contractors' engines were driven. Their drivers appeared partial to opening their regulators and keeping them open. By June a tramway had been laid in Station Road through Rough Lee Fold to the workings, while in July permission was given to Wilsons to lay a tramway in Plains Road. By August complaints were made about the manner in which locomotives were being driven on the main road to White Syke.

1890 included legal problems from many quarters. The company abortively contested a rate levied on a rateable value of £3,564 whereas the total rate for the whole of Marsden was £6,592. The widening and regrading at Ramsden Mill Lane, Golcar caused action in the High

Court. The LNWR gained support from an unexpected quarter when Golcar Local Board stated the roads improved by the LNWR 'were better than ever before'.

At Marsden work in the station area took place all round the clock, Wilsons had in service a 'Wells Light' with the equivalent of 2,000 candle power. The bridge there was completed in October and the level crossing closed. At Huddersfield the station forecourt was laid out in stone setts, which gained the approval of Huddersfield Chamber of Commerce. Praise indeed!

For the Mossley Wakes 1,467 were booked to Blackpool and 811 to other resorts. In August for the Saddleworth Wakes, the bookings from Diggle, Saddleworth and Greenfield totalled 1,648, while for the September Delph Wakes bookings comprised:

6/9/1890	Saturday	Blackpool	160
	Monday	Blackpool	460
	Monday	Liverpool	150
	Wednesday	Belle Vue	280
The bookings for Longwood Thump were:			
	Saturday	Blackpool	419
	Monday	Blackpool	600
	Monday	Scarborough	900
For Huddersfield's Honley Feast, started 27/9/1890			
	Saturday	Leeds	382
	Saturday	Blackpool	730
	Saturday	Liverpool	170
	Saturday	Isle of Man	134
	Monday	Belle Vue	730
	Monday	Liverpool	931
	Monday	Blackpool	544
From Kirkburton			274

Mishaps started on 18th January when the engine of a Kirkburton train forcefully ran into its coaches at Huddersfield. On 20th January a Manchester – Leeds express due Huddersfield 2.51 pm and running non-stop from Greenfield lost its right-hand leading driving wheel which broke off its axle in Blakestones cutting, Slaithwaite. The train crew had the unusual experience of overtaking part of their own locomotive before the train stopped in safety on Slaithwaite viaduct. The loose wheel was found 300 yards away. The engine was believed to have been a 'Teutonic' class No. 1302 *Pacific* (F.H. Eastwood). Another failure occurred on 16th June. As the 9.50 am Manchester – Leeds train was coming through Standedge tunnel a connecting rod broke loose and caused much damage to the engine before it was able to stop. Two hours elapsed before the coaches could be hauled back to Diggle and then despatched on the up line.

The Crewe intimidation business ended at the half-yearly general meeting when the Chairman, Sir Richard Moon, facing a barrage of continual interruption, denied there was any truth in the allegations.

1891

The LNWR Act of 21st July extended by three years the completion of the Stalybridge Junction Railway. Openings included the Dobcross ironworks branch, extending from Ward Lane Diggle and crossing the Huddersfield Canal by a single-span plate girder skew bridge. After many years of speculation Ravensthorpe station opened on 1st

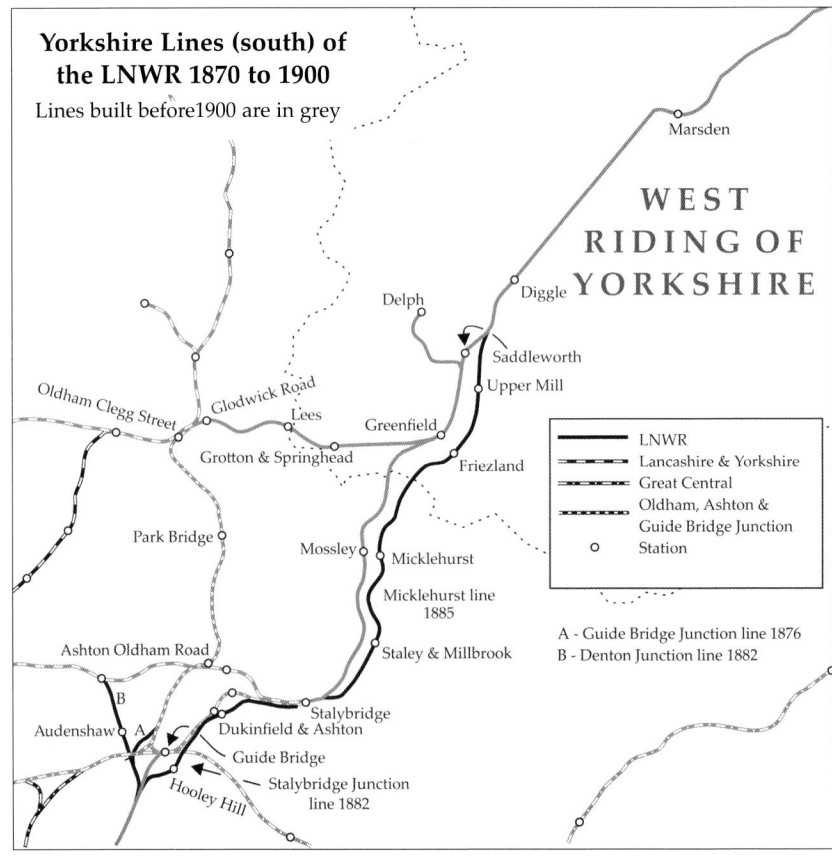

September, sited almost opposite the junction with the L&Y main line. The LNWR was also responsible for the provision of a Warren girder bridge over the Calder nearby. In November the station at Wortley and Farnley altered its name to Farnley and Wortley.

Widening was completed between Slaithwaite and Marsden in July while the *Huddersfield Examiner* of 12th December, 1891 noted the laying of the first brick in the new double line Standedge tunnel at a point 2 miles from Diggle. At Leeds New station, enlargements at both ends were completed in November. During July two new holiday services were introduced:

10.10 am	Leeds - Blackpool	7.15 pm	MFSO
	Blackpool - Leeds	4.00 pm	Non-stop through Huddersfield
10.50 am	Leeds - Llandudno	7.15 pm	
3.20 pm	Llandudno – Leeds	3.10 pm	

MFSO - Mondays Fridays and Saturdays only

The lease of the Rochdale Canal expired during 1891. A mishap on 4th November occurred at Kirkburton when a light engine sent from Hillhouse to work the first train collided with the buffers at a considerable speed. The engine came to rest just short of a 30 feet drop into the road.

1892

The LNWR (Heaton Lodge and Wortley) Act of 27th June enabled the Leeds New line to be built (length 13 miles, 2 furlongs, 7 chains and 51 links with a flying junction of 6 furlongs, 5 chains and 65 links).

It was in this year the LNWR withdrew its support from the Hull and North Western Junction project, agreement was reached in March with the North Eastern Railway for full running powers to Hull.

The greatest single event of the year was a disastrous fire at Leeds New station which started at 4.30 am on 13th January when flames came through air holes in the platform. For 20 hours the fire blazed like a volcano. A 50 yards section of line fell in and one man and a horse were killed. The fire originated in the archway warehouse of Joseph Watson & Sons, Soap Works and is acknowledged as the greatest calamity that Leeds ever experienced. The height of the flames reached above the Midland station and a carriage shed owned by Joseph Watson was destroyed. The NER despatched two fire brigades from York and the Midland sent their brigade from Derby. One fireman was killed when the platform upon which he was standing collapsed. A bridge of 90 feet span and 20 yards wide collapsed and the girders and track work piled up, blocking the Leeds and Liverpool Canal. Disruption caused all LNWR trains to use Leeds Central, while many NER trains started there and later from Holbeck. Wellington station had two platforms put out of action and some LNWR services had to be discontinued. By 23rd January a small number LNWR trains were using the less affected parts of New station. A 30 feet wooden trestle bridge was erected which allowed all LNWR services to resume. LNWR expresses for the NER were diverted via Normanton as was the Hull – Manchester Cotton Buyers' Special which ran until the end of September.

Further traffic alterations included a 10.24 am Birstal to Leeds New which reversed at Batley. Traffic to and from Lancashire was adversely affected from the end of November until the end of March 1893 due to a cotton strike.

In March a reduced fare of $1\frac{1}{2}d.$ instead of $2d.$ was introduced between Longwood and Huddersfield. On the Longwood Thump Saturday traffic from that station amounted to:

Saturday	Blackpool	382
Monday	Blackpool	490
Monday	Liverpool	470
Monday	Scarborough	183

For the Saddleworth Wakes, bookings from the 3 stations were:

Diggle	100
Saddleworth	1,166
Greenfield	1,160

For the Bristol Wool Sales the LNWR ran a special express, via the Severn tunnel, on 13th September. This became a regular feature thereafter. It was never advertised in the timetable but was publicized with similar services operated by the Midland and Great Northern companies:

Bradford Exchange	12.15 pm Tues 13th September, 1892
Halifax	12.29 pm
Huddersfield	12.48 pm

The return departed Bristol 12.55 pm on Thursdays. The train had the reputation of being a crack train, running non-stop between Huddersfield and Stockport, thence non-stop to Shrewsbury where the Great Western took over.

Controversy arose over alleged fare anomalies in regard to travel between Huddersfield and Manchester, initiated by the United

Kingdom Commercial Travellers' Association. The third class return fare was 4s. 6d. but if a traveller booked to Stalybridge and paid an 'excess' a saving of 5d. could be made. Likewise a journey between Huddersfield and Leeds was 2s. 10d. third class return, but if booked to Dewsbury and then rebooked a saving of 3d. was effected. A complainant, Mr Allen Broadbent pointed out the position in a letter to the press. A local solicitor, Mr Wilmhurst, was then instructed to pursue the matter, firstly with the LNWR superintendent at Manchester whose reply was unyielding: 'The official was quite justified in demanding a higher excess fare under bye law three and for reasons already known. I am not prepared to refund the amount asked for', signed G.E. Mawby. Mr Wilmhurst replied that his client would take the matter to the Leeds County Court claiming overcharging on his journey. The letter to Mr Mawby was then passed to G.P. Neele, superintendent of the line who replied and enclosed $1\,^1/_2\,d.$ in stamps, noting 'the company have no wish to put either your client or themselves to the expense of contesting the case in Court'.

At Marsden the upper portion of Station Road was completed in January 1892 with the new station buildings brought into use on 1st May. Again public indignation erupted '…. This great railway …. Enters upon another enterprise (new Tunnel) at Marsden and big or small, it finishes nothing'. In June plans were deposited to purchase land there. A siding was to emerge from the goods yard then run across the canal and along the towpath. Marsden Cricket Club sought an injunction restraining the LNWR from dumping spoil from the new tunnel on the Cricket ground. The company had already taken possession and half the field had been filled up. As a direct consequence, the LNWR purchased land at Fall Lane to compensate the club, having originally offered £250 compensation which was considered a paltry sum.

The LNWR Act dated 17th July empowered purchase of land at Engine Bridge for use by the Canal Dept and extension of the time limit for completion of the new Standedge tunnel by three years. Approval was made for a short line to Springbank Mill, Grotton. The Stalybridge Junction line was opened for goods on 1st October and on 7th October for passenger traffic. It had an intermediate station known as Ashton and Dukinfield, a name that was reversed to remove some of the confusion with three other Ashton stations within three-quarters of a mile distance. Commencing 37 chains east of Hooley Hill station it ran within sight of and parallel to the MS&L line. It first crossed the Tame by three girder spans, then immediately on to a 50-span blue-brick viaduct with curves en route, concluding by crossing the Tame and

Construction gang at Tunnel End box as the third railway tunnel nears completion. The locomotive is 0-4-0ST *Chedworth*, Manning, Wardle No. 1053 built in 1888.

courtesy of M. Swift

Huddersfield Canal by a further 60 feet span, altogether a formidable piece of engineering. Problems with the Standedge workforce saw the company divest itself of construction and from 1st February the principal sub-contractors, Williams, Lee and Thomas took charge with the break observed as a holiday by the workmen. On 28th June Lord Stalbridge, new LNWR Chairman, Sir Thomas Brooke and Mr MacGregor visited the tunnel works.

At Leeds New station an arch was erected over a goit on the north side. By late September alterations at Marsden station were almost complete. A notable development on 1st April was the establishment of a Shrewsbury – Normanton TPO with a Shrewsbury and Crewe sorting coach attached to the Bangor Mail. From 1st June, 1893 daily and weekly workmen's tickets were introduced, but the state of trade affected by the Lancashire Cotton Strike that lasted from November 1892 to March 1893 gave concern.

LNWR operation of services over the North Eastern Railway began on 1st September for goods and 2nd October for passengers when services between Liverpool and Hull commenced with LNWR operation throughout. Spencer Harley, son of the LNWR's late Secretary, was appointed representative at Hull. Goods were centred upon Kingston Street Depot where the LNWR's own staff handled it. LNWR engines went to Dairycoates shed and for many years at least two Farnley locomotives were permanently stationed there. A Hillhouse goods engine worked to Kingston Street and back with express goods. The LNWR working to York began on 1st July and was limited to either an express or through coaches from Leeds.

One accident blighted the year. On 14th November at Greenfield, a 37 wagon goods train standing on the Oldham branch while its engine ran round, ran back into the bay platform and demolished the buffers. The guard had released the brake too quickly.

1894

The LNWR Act dated 20th July permitted an alteration to the course of the New line at Heckmondwike for a distance of 5 furlongs, 7 chains and 82 links and the replacement of the bridge at Heaton Lodge by two segmented brick arches beneath the L&Y line.

The double-line tunnel at Standedge was opened on 5th August. An inspection took place on the 1st by Major Yorke who was accompanied by Mr E.B. Thornhill, the LNWR Chief Engineer and Mr Mawby who arrived in a one-coach special. The tunnel, two bridges and new platforms at Diggle were inspected. A light engine weighing 55 tons ran backwards and forwards through the tunnel to test it, but ran off the line at the Marsden end, turning on its side and sinking into the ballast. The first train to pass through the new tunnel was the 7.23 pm from Diggle, filled to capacity, many sightseers had first walked over from Marsden to Diggle to make the journey. The two single-line tunnels were now closed for repairs for three months. For the building of the new tunnel 13 openings were made from the down-single line tunnel and 1,800 men employed. Among the strata encountered were Yoredale shale and Millstone grit, 25 million Staffordshire blue bricks were used and 4,645 tons of Rugby lime. The three air vents serving the tunnel were respectively 512 feet, 498 feet and 490 feet deep. At Diggle, to allow new station accommodation, the canal tunnel was extended by 200 yards with a covering of steel girders and a new entrance was made dated 1893. A further important work at Marsden was the diversion of the Tunnel End reservoir overflow.

On the Stalybridge Junction line a new goods station, erected by Dransfield and Smith was opened at Dukinfield on 1st January. Mr Hopley, the goods agent at Ashton Oldham Road, was in charge. Situated in Wharf Street, it was supplied with power by Crossley Gas engines. At Leeds a further 124 yards of land was purchased to enlarge New station. An additional train on the Hull – Liverpool service was introduced from 30th June:

	4.05 pm	Hull	2.35 pm
Calls Batley, Dewsbury	5.30	Leeds	1.15
When Liverpool Wool	5.58	Huddersfield	12.49
Sales are on		Stalybridge	12.18
	6.45	Manchester Exchange	12 noon
	7.45	Liverpool Lime Street	11.00 am

A deputation from Huddersfield Town Council journeyed to Manchester Exchange to see Mr Mawby concerning traffic rates. A theft of a quantity of partly finished jewellery from Huddersfield station consigned from Chester to Halifax by an LNWR goods train had occurred on three previous occasions. Five hundred and thirty-six passengers travelled from Delph to Belle Vue for the Wakes. Excursion takings had been £60 less than 1893 due to the depression. In November 9d. market returns on Saturdays between Marsden and Huddersfield were introduced. The company was again in trouble with rating

Diggle station with a Webb 3-cylinder compound locomotive emerging from the double line tunnel. *Courtesy of G.H. Brown*

problems with the Marsden Local Board but an appeal to Quarter Sessions saw judgement in favour of the Board.

A joint committee of both Houses of Parliament heard an LNWR appeal against the Board of Trade's scale of charges for the Huddersfield Canal, which reduced income from that source. The toll for 1891 was £3,441. This would be reduced to £1,498 by the provisional order. It was noted the Leeds and Liverpool Canal rates were reduced by 4 per cent out of a total revenue of £140,000. The Huddersfield Canal working expenses amounted to £4,300. The appeal failed but one concession made was a minimum charge of 5s. on the Ramsden Canal and 2s. 6d. on the Huddersfield Canal.

1895

The LNWR Act dated 6th July allowed yet another change of plans at Heckmondwike on the new line. Work was divided into three contracts with John Wilson & Sons having the Heaton Lodge to Northorpe (Jill Lane) section. They laid a tramway across Wood Lane. The cost of the centre portion of the route was hotly disputed, Mr J.W. Fair of Wigan arbitrated on the issue. Howarth Brook claimed 6,748 yards of excavation, the award was 2,898 yards less than the LNWR had offered! A mid-May progress report indicated that work had commenced in June 1894. Heaton Lodge tunnel was of 53 yards. At the Warren Bridge over the Calder, 300 men, a steam navvy and three locomotives were working. Drub shaft at Gomersal was sunk and there was a deep cutting at Oakwell Wood, one of four thereabouts. Beyond the GNR line a cutting was 17 feet deep, the earth had been tipped into two dams at Howden Clough Mills. A shaft was sunk at Gildersome where 30 to 40 men were at work and temporary rails had been laid to transport materials. The contractors were Baldry and Yerburgh of Westminster.

As from 15th October the Mail began operating from Bristol to Normanton. Fare concessions were piecemeal in their introduction. A market return from Golcar to Huddersfield applied on trains after 1.00 pm, fare 4d.

In July 1895 the first timetabled non-stop service through Huddersfield began on trains introduced in 1894:

Liverpool	11.30 am	York	12.40 pm	2.35 pm
Manchester Exchange	12.15 pm	Leeds New	1.40	3.20
Leeds New	1.16	Manchester Exchange	2.52	4.25
York	1.56	Liverpool	3.43	5.10

The year was a bleak one for accidents. The first involved three trains on 28th March at Mirfield when the 6.25 pm Manchester (London Road) to Leeds goods, placed in the down loop, overran signals, ran through buffers and the engine, tender and 15 wagons crashed down into a roadway. The smoke box of the engine, No. 1580, a Longsight 'DX' was buried in several feet of mud. Both the driver (Wm Glover) and fireman (James Wright) were killed and the engine was scrapped. The wreckage was run into by the 10.45 pm Leeds Whitehall Road Burton beer empties, derailed its locomotive (No. 1807, a 'DX goods' of Farnley Junction shed, with driver Frederick Branston) and 15 wagons out of a train of 38 wagons and brake. The wreckage was also struck by a 'Special DX' No. 1355 of Longsight shed, pilot of the 8.00 pm Liverpool – Leeds goods (driver John Sidebottom and fireman Eldred Parker) attached at Stockport. The train engine was Farnley Junction 'DX goods' No. 1890 (driver William Smith). The train consisted of 35 trucks and brake. The pilot engine was badly damaged as it had been precipitated down an embankment, although the train engine suffered slight damage. Joseph Fisher, an L&Y driver of No. 1120 standing on the Cleckheaton branch gave evidence of sounding his engine whistle as a warning to other traffic.

On 24th August the engine of a passenger train from Stockport was reported to have broken its crank axle and halted at Linthwaite. Eventually the train continued to Huddersfield with the same engine!

On 23rd March 4 feet 6 inches 2-4-2 tank No. 1108 (driver Hudson Parker and fireman Joe Lawton) took the wrong signal at Leeds New station and ran sidelong into the NER 4.05 express from Newcastle to Liverpool hauled by 4-4-0 No. 1531 hauling eight LNWR bogie coaches. While two of the latter were damaged there were no casualties.

The final mishap took place at Cleckheaton Junction, Mirfield on 16th November, 1895 when the 7.45 pm GNR Wakefield – Halifax express (GNR 2-4-0 No. 591) stopped for signals, then took those pulled off for the 7.40 pm Leeds – Liverpool express. The two trains collided at 30 mph and both engines overturned. The LNWR rule that the first three compartments be locked undoubtedly saved many lives as there was no brake van at the front. The GNR driver, F. Bowling, had made this journey only once before and then had been travelling in the opposite direction. The LNWR engine involved was No. 890 *Sir Hardman Earle* of Edge Hill shed with driver Henry Cook, hauling six NER coaches and two vans. Seven passengers were injured. The GNR load was four coaches including a through carriage to Burnley.

1896

Completion of the new line to Leeds was extended by three years under the LNWR Act dated 25th July. Work was proceeding at a feverish pace with 300 men employed between Heaton Lodge and Northorpe together with one steam navvy, four steam cranes, six Scotch cranes and three locomotives. At Heckmondwike, 126 houses were required to be demolished with 80 replacements erected at the top of Church Street.

At Leeds New, dissatisfaction was expressed over the condition of the refreshment room. The tenancy would be passed to the NER from 1st April for five years under a minute dated 26th February, 1896 with the LNWR to receive £720 due in consideration.

At Marsden Tunnel End Sidings a standard gauge line crossed the River Colne and a mill dam before crossing Manchester Road. It was built and owned by Huddersfield Corporation for the making of Blakely and Butterley reservoirs, commencing 1896 and finishing 1906 (length 1 mile, 1 furlong and $\frac{1}{2}$ chain). On the opposite side of the line thereabouts was Hey Green Siding which led from the direction of Marsden to a canal warehouse used for corn and earlier as a magnesium store. In existence from before 1854 until some time after 1890, the siding was taken out by 1894 when the new double line tunnel was finished. In earlier years Hey Green Siding was used at busy times to allow slower trains to be overtaken.

Three mishaps occurred during the year. On 20th March at Heaton Lodge a Copley Hill – London goods was struck by an L&Y engine that pulled out of sidings. On 29th March a Copley Hill – Mold Junction goods caught fire in Morley tunnel and a similar occurrence near Brooks' Sidings resulted in 3,000 gallons of paraffin catching fire.

1897

From the opening of the Stalybridge Junction Railway travellers between Stalybridge and Stockport had enjoyed the luxury of having no less than three LNWR routes:

Trains to Stalybridge	Route	Trains to Stockport
4	Via Guide Bridge	4
5 Sunday		4 Sunday
3	Via Hooley Hill and Ashton Park Parade	5
9	Via Dukinfield and Ashton	10

To the above must be added the MS&L's passenger service between Stalybridge and Guide Bridge. On the Micklehurst route, which got off to a steady start, services were:

Up trains

7.55 am	Huddersfield – Stalybridge	arr 8.51
11.15 am	Huddersfield – Stalybridge	arr 12.12 pm
11.50 am	Leeds (New) – North Wales calls Friezland	1.00 pm
2.20 pm	Huddersfield – Stockport E	arr 3.37
4.10 pm	Huddersfield – Stalybridge	arr 5.07
7.48 pm	Uppermill – Stalybridge	arr 8.05

Down trains

7.30 am	Manchester Exchange – Leeds New calls Uppermill	8.03
9.48 am	Stockport – Huddersfield	arr 11.03
12.20 pm	Stalybridge – Leeds	arr 2.02 pm
2.20 pm	Stockport – Leeds	arr 4.07
6.55 pm	Manchester Exchange – Leeds	arr 8.50

which divided at Stalybridge and called all stations to Uppermill:

7.19 pm	Stalybridge to Uppermill	arr 7.38 pm

In September 1897 the operation of LNWR trains between Leeds and York was:

11.45 am	1.16 pm	5.20 pm	↓	Leeds New	↑ 10.52 am	3.15 pm	5.15 pm
12.25 pm	1.56 pm	6.06 pm	↓	York	↑ 10.15 am	2.35 pm	4.35 pm

The LNWR engine stationed at York worked outward on the 10.15 am, returning from Leeds with the 11.45 am (through coaches (TC) to Scarborough) and left York again at 2.35 pm returning from Leeds at 5.20 pm, the third train being worked by an Edge Hill engine. If the regular York 'Jumbo' was not available to work its train, a 'Special DX' 0-6-0 would deputize.

A deputation at Huddersfield unsuccessfully lodged a reminder for the promised station entrance in New North Road to the island platform.

1898

The LNWR Act of 12th August allowed alterations to a road adjoining the station at Batley, where an additional arch was to be made and a further three years allowed to complete the new line.

Gomersal tunnel under construction in 1896. The 'Shoulder of Mutton' public house above the tunnel was partially demolished during the work. It was partly rebuilt in red brick, contrasting with the original masonry portion.

Many complaints were received in June 1898 at the cessation of cheap train facilities, to which the LNWR replied 'this facility interferes with ordinary traffic'.

1899

By mid-July Gildersome tunnel on the Leeds New line had been completed. The bulk of the work remaining was between Birstal and Heckmondwike and had been delayed by the quantities of rock encountered. Stations were being built at Liversedge and Gomersal. Meanwhile the section between Heckmondwike Junction and Northorpe was opened for goods on 8th September.

James Goulding, Hillhouse locomotive foreman 1894 – 1911 was present some time earlier when a pair of 'Johnny Duggans' (3-cylinder 'A' class 0-8-0s) coupled with a Coal Engine front and rear, tested the great Warren girder bridge over the Calder at Battyeford. This powerful combination started off from Battyeford like an enormous monster unleashed, accelerated fiercely and abruptly halted on the bridge after exploding detonators indicated where brakes were to be applied. With variation, this spectacular performance was repeated four times, much to the delight of a large crowd of spectators who looked on from a safe distance.

At Leeds New a footbridge with a sloping ramp at either end was erected by Joseph Butler of Stanningley Iron Works. At Huddersfield a new subway egress came into use in November. This joined the subway from a flight of steps leading to the main platform.

Services in the year comprised:

KIRKBURTON	11 trains to; 12TO;13SO with the same return		
BIRSTAL	15 trains to; 17SO		
OLDHAM – STOCKPORT	11 trains to; 12SO; 1 Sunday		
	Return 9 trains; 10SO; 1 Sunday		
ROCHDALE – STOCKPORT	3 trains each way:		
	11.30 ex-Rochdale arr Euston 4.15 pm		
	1.10 pm ex-Euston arr Rochdale 9.04 pm		
HULL – LIVERPOOL	9.30 am	12.10 pm	4.10 pm
LIVERPOOL – HULL	9.35 am	11.00 am	4.00 pm

TO - Tuesdays only, SO - Saturdays only

In April, in response to many requests, a new train was inaugurated:

Huddersfield	4.45 am
Manchester Exchange	5.53 am

Mishaps were limited to the breakage of a crank axle on the engine working the 7.40 am Marsden – Leeds in Morley tunnel. One and a half hours passed before the obstruction was removed.

'WD' 2-8-0 No. 90332 shunting at Birstall, 9th April, 1960. *Author*

CHAPTER SEVEN

1900 – 1909

1900

The ultimate shape of 'The Yorkshire Lines' was reached during the year, although a sign of the future came with tramway services which grew rapidly in many places.

   The completion of the New line was unhappily preceded by an accident on 29th June when a regular workmen's train being operated between Cleckheaton and Gomersal consisting of a locomotive, two brake vans and an old coach came into head-on collision near Cleckheaton with a ballast train, causing injury to 12 workmen. The inquiry was conducted by Major General Hutchinson. Dan Haigh, guard of the ballast train related how he usually stopped at Gomersal to allow the workmen's train to pass. On this occasion he was told by the foreman to proceed along the wrong line. LNWR Inspection of the line occurred on 14th June. The official Board of Trade inspection took place on 30th July. Goods traffic commenced using the line on 9th July while the passenger opening took place on 1st October. The first train was the 6.35 am ex-Huddersfield which arrived at Heckmondwike at 6.57 'where the crowds were so dense that 12 minutes elapsed before the train was able to restart'. Similar crowds massed at Liversedge and Cleckheaton and there was brisk traffic from other stations. The first train from Leeds was the 7.35 am and carried an LNWR official party who had journeyed from Euston for the occasion. All the rolling stock used was new. From the outset 12 trains operated in each direction with 13 trains SO. Mr A.R. Bennett, who was a passenger on the first train from Cleckheaton had also travelled on the first train on the L&Y line which opened in 1845.

   Goods stations at Northorpe, Gomersal, Upper Birstal and Gildersome opened on the same day while those at Heckmondwike, Liversedge and Cleckheaton opened on 1st November.

   The New line was a railway of absolute contrasts – severe gradients and sweeping curves, with bridges, tunnels and viaducts in widely varying styles. The unexpected finding of large quantities of stone at Heckmondwike and Birstal resulted in bridges there being of masonry but elsewhere Staffordshire blue brick was the rule. Two viaducts at Battyeford were built of blue brick while one at Heckmondwike and the road approach at Cleckheaton were of girder construction. At Upper Birstal masonry piers supported girder sections as at Farnley Junction,

The twin tunnels carrying the Leeds New line beneath the L&Y main line at Heaton Lodge.
Author

where the up line was carried over the LD&M line by girders. Standard LNWR fencing was found in every form, with extensive use made of the standard 'unclimbable' type, but at Upper Birstal timber railings were seen alongside the other types. Altogether it was a line of great character where everything was made in the grand manner. Engineering featured:

Heaton Lodge tunnel	84 yards
Calder Bridge, Battyeford	270 feet span and 3 brick arches 26 feet 7 inches span
Battyeford viaduct	14 brick arches and one 72 feet girder span
New Scarborough viaduct	10 brick arches 26 feet span, one girder span 58 feet long
Heckmondwike viaduct	5 steel girder spans on the skew of 36 feet span
Heckmondwike tunnel	57 yards
Cleckheaton viaduct	13 steel spans 39 feet 6 inches wide on upright columns carrying road from town to station
Gomersal tunnel	819 yards
Gildersome tunnel	1 mile 571 yards

Oldham Clegg Street station was rebuilt and on one day in the Oldham Wakes handled 35 special trains in addition to its complement of 94 ordinary services. New buildings were made on both platforms and at street level. The OA&GB sold off land surplus to its needs by LNWR Act of 6th August. Grotton station had 'and Springhead' added to its name on 1st April.

At Huddersfield the largest consignment of wool arrived when 500 bales were the first arrival from Liverpool. The new locomotive numbered 4000 and named *La France* was sent to Hull and shipped to France for the Paris exhibition.

1901

From 1st May the company introduced, system wide, a guaranteed delivery offered for goods traffic collected in the West Riding. Delivery was by evening for perishables and livestock with a noon delivery next day in the Dublin area, using a service operated by three fast steamers between Holyhead and North Wall, Dublin. In July the undermentioned services commenced:

5.55 am	Huddersfield to Morecambe	MSO
9.25 am	Huddersfield to Blackpool Central	Arr 12.10 pm
10.00 am	Leeds New to Llandudno	Arr 2.26 pm
10.15 am	Leeds New to Blackpool	Arr 12.25 pm
11.55 am	Huddersfield to Oldham Clegg Street	Arr 12.55 pm
2.10 pm	Leeds to Blackpool	Arr 5.15 pm
4.10 pm	Huddersfield to Oldham and Stockport	
8.25 pm	Huddersfield to Oldham	
10.05 am	Stockport and Oldham to Huddersfield	Arr 10.45 am
11.50 am	Oldham to Huddersfield	Arr 12.28 pm
12.00 noon	Manchester Exch to Scarborough	combined to
11.00 am	Liverpool L St to Hull	Leeds
3.56 pm	Oldham to Huddersfield	Arr 4.29 pm
3.08 pm	Blackpool Cen to Leeds New	Arr 6.32 pm
4.00 pm	Blackpool Cen to Leeds New	Arr 7.00 pm
6.15 pm	Blackpool Cen to Heckmondwike Morecambe to Huddersfield	Arr 9.55 pm MSO

The LNWR Canal department had a bleak time. Drought caused a stoppage on the Huddersfield Canal from September until November 10th when a downpour occurred which lasted 36 hours. March Haigh reservoir which had been empty, filled up in 36 hours and the canal overflowed.

1902

From 1st July the Bangor Mail was diverted to run from Huddersfield via Leeds to York, the NER taking charge at Leeds. It was also known as the Bristol, Shrewsbury and York TPO:

Bristol	7.40 pm	York	9.25 pm
Shrewsbury	10.05 pm	Shrewsbury	2.05 am
York	3.22 am	Bristol	5.49 am

On Sundays the train started and terminated at Shrewsbury

Traffic for Whitsun holidays included:

Oldham Clegg Street	10,000
Oldham Glodwick Road	7,000
Leeds New	20,000

An unusual mishap occurred on 7th February at Heckmondwike Junction when the 5.22 pm Leeds – Manchester Exch express routed via the new line, restarted after a signal stop and sustained a derailed tender which was dragged about 400 yards before the train came to a halt just short of the Colne viaduct.

One of the highlights of the year was yet another fare battle (LNWR v Hinchcliffe). Mr Hinchcliffe had travelled from Huddersfield to Manchester at the fare of 2s. 3d. but he had booked a ticket to Stalybridge which cost 1s. 6d. When his ticket was collected he remained in the carriage and offered to pay a further 7d., which was refused. The fare from Stalybridge to Manchester had been reduced to 7d. to meet competition from the L&Y. The LNWR sued Hinchcliffe for the excess fare of 9d. and the case went to the Court of Appeal. The judgement, in favour of the company, emphasized that the ticket had been issued 'subject to the rules and regulations of the LNWR' and that the rules forbade rebooking at intermediate stations by the same train.

1903

The closure occurred on 1st July of a 27 chain length of line connecting Ashton Junction (LNWR) and Dukinfield Junction (GCR) which had become superfluous.

Whitsun bookings included:

Manchester Exch	48,000
Stockport Edgeley	34,000
Oldham Clegg St	10,000
Oldham Glodwick Rd	7,000
Leeds New	20,000

Belted Will a 'Renewed Precedent' allocated to Farnley Junction shed, but outstationed at York for a time. *Author's ollection*

1904

On 11th December, 1904* the LNWR ceased to operate its own trains to York. Of the men outstationed there, George Hinchliffe was best remembered. Of the locomotives at York a succession included Nos. 1 *Saracen*, 1220 *Belted Will*, 642 *Bee* and 434 *St Patrick*.

The piecemeal introduction of cheap fares saw a workman's ticket introduced from Golcar to Longwood in March at 1*d*. daily and 6*d*. weekly.

A mishap on 29th February at Greenfield occurred when an Oldham train setting back into the bay platform at Greenfield overran buffers. Two coaches were destroyed which dislocated branch services for some time.

The significance of the LNWR canal system was illustrated when a presentation was made to Mr F. Nichols, LNWR wool traffic canvasser who served in that capacity at Engine Bridge, Huddersfield for 25 years. Wool that arrived at ports not served by the LNWR was carried by canal at rates more competitive than those offered by other railways. Wool brought from London to Huddersfield was charged 32*s*. 6*d*. per ton, but if brought by water to Goole and thence by canal, 29*s*. 2*d*. per ton. As

---

* S. Ellingworth stated the date to be 1905, from personal observation.

from 15th February 10s. per ton was slashed from rail-hauled wool with a similar reduction in canal charges.

1905

On 1st January, 1905 an agreement was made with the L&Y giving an improved relationship and better facilities for users. Services comprised:

Kirkburton	11 trains 12TO 13SO in both directions
Oldham	19 18SO 4 Sunday to Greenfield
Oldham	20 19SO 4 Sunday from Greenfield
New Line	13 14SO in both directions plus 1 SO Heckmondwike to Leeds
Birstal branch	6 daily each way

The opening of the New line at Upper Birstal accounted for some of the drop in Birstal branch services but a greater cause of decline was the electrification of Yorkshire Woollen District Tramways which competed all the way from Dewsbury to Batley and Birstal.

From November market tickets became available from Kirkburton branch stations TThSO. Passenger traffic at Easter was:

Huddersfield	12,500
Leeds New	11,000
Oldham Clegg Street	9,500

Thornhill LNWR Junction about 1907, with a Webb 4 cylinder compound 4-4-0 passing through Ravensthorpe & Thornhill station.

On Good Friday 21st April, a serious accident occurred at Huddersfield when the LNWR 4-cylinder compound 4-6-0 No. 610 of Carlisle shed was in collision with L&Y No. 664 a 2-4-2 tank (driver W. Cliffe and fireman C. Luff) in which two people were killed and 13 injured. The L&Y train, the 1.50 pm from Bradford Exchange was entering Huddersfield station under clear signals. The circumstances were that driver Fred Haigh and fireman Arthur Nicholson had arrived back at Hillhouse shed after finishing their duty and were asked to take to Huddersfield a visiting engine too large to use the shed's own turntable. On arriving at Huddersfield it was discovered that the turntable was obstructed by a line of empty vehicles. These had first to be drawn out onto the viaduct and set back onto the main line at the station. The engine was then turned and returned to the coaching stock prior to replacing it. Unfortunately the movement involved No. 610 running eastwards on the up line on Huddersfield viaduct for 45 yards and the collision occurred.

There was a conflict of evidence between the driver and the shunter, the former claiming that the shunter was in charge. After holding their own inquiry the company, later the same afternoon, announced that Fred Haigh was dismissed for negligence. The Associated Society of Railway Servants (ASRS) representative Tom Topping protested that if justice was to be done, it had to be seen to be done. The LNWR decision had been made before either inquest or official inquiry.

An unfortunate accident that occurred in 1905 was at Shrewsbury where the up Mail was derailed outside that station on 5th September. This had earlier run between Leeds and Crewe.

1906

Innovation was the keynote on 'The Yorkshire Lines' in the 20th century. Commencing on 15th January the first sleeping car to appear ran:

Bradford Exchange	9.50 pm	Euston	12.00 midnight
Halifax	10.22	Huddersfield	6.32 am
Huddersfield	11.12	Halifax	7.07
Euston	5.50 am	Bradford Exchange	7.26

Between Bradford and Huddersfield the sleeper was added to an L&Y train and the up service was attached to the up Mail between Huddersfield and Crewe. The service ran Saturday excepted and made its final journey on 29th June as revenue had been insufficient. A further improvement was a connection at Stalybridge from an express leaving Euston at 6.05 pm, though its leisurely 'all stations' progress meant that Huddersfield was not reached until 10.55 pm and Leeds at 11.50 pm.

On 2nd July new services comprised:

9.35 am	Leeds New (con. from Bradford Exch) to Aberystwyth
10.42	Leeds New TC West of England with TC from Bradford Exch to Torquay
10.40 am	Bradford Exch and Halifax via Huddersfield to Llandudno arr 12.50 pm
2.15 pm	Bradford Exch via Halifax and Huddersfield to Bristol arr 8.28 pm
2.20 pm	Bristol (TC Penzance) to Bradford Exch
7.10 am	Gildersome to Blackpool WThx
8.30 am	Leeds New to Blackpool
1.12 pm	Blackpool C to Leeds
6.12 pm	Blackpool C to Leeds
9.25 am	Hull to Liverpool Lime Street
4.05 pm	Hull to Liverpool Lime Street
11.00 am	Liverpool to Hull
4.00 pm	Liverpool to Hull

TC - Through coach, WThx - Wednesday and Thursday excepted

1907

Local traffic over the Micklehurst line was failing to live up to expectations so Micklehurst station was closed to passengers on 1st May.

The summer Hull to Liverpool service comprised three trains in each direction and not two as in 1906. In October a new train was introduced between Leeds and Chester and connected with the Irish Mail.

On 16th September at 3.00 am an 11-wagon goods train laden with newly creosoted telegraph poles caught fire at Marsden en route to Crewe. The efforts of several fire brigades failed to extinguish the flames and the whole train, which was shunted into a siding, was burned out.

Both stations at Birstal had a name change and became Birstall on 1st April, 1907.

1908

The first visit by a member of the Monarchy in 23 years occurred on 6th July when the Prince and Princess of Wales (later King George V and Queen Mary) journeyed from Collingham Bridge NER to Chester. The engines used were *Alaska*, a 'Precursor' and *Princess May*, an 'Experiment'.

The Royal Train at Collingham Bridge (NER) on 6th July, 1908, with 'Precursor' No. 117 *Alaska* piloting 'Experiment' No. 1709 *Princess May*. An NER 'R' class 4-4-0 is in the siding.

courtesy of K. Hoole

The death took place on 16th October of Sir Thomas Brooke, the LNWR's Yorkshire Director since 1882. He had been an unsuccessful election candidate accused of intimidation.

An accident occurred at Hillhouse No. 1 on 13th January when the 1.55 pm Manchester Exch to Leeds express hauled by No. 1957 *Orion* (driver Samuel Haley of Farnley shed) had stopped for a signal, with fireman Unwin reporting to the signal box. On restarting, their train was hit from behind by the L&Y 3.02 pm Huddersfield to Bradford Exch train hauled by No. 790 of Low Moor shed (driver E Garside and fireman J.W. Godfrey). Fourteen passengers were injured. The inspecting officer established that the signalman had overlooked the presence of the first train because of thick fog.

1909

A further Micklehurst line station, Staley and Millbrook was closed to passengers on 1st November. Local services over the line had been reduced from four trains to three in each direction, one of the down trains stopped only at Uppermill. Traffic was no doubt being lost to the electric tram operated by the Staleybridge, Hyde, Mossley & Dunkinfield Tramway and Electricity Joint Board. On the Kirkburton branch services

Battyeford & Mirfield station about 1910, looking towards Huddersfield.
Courtesy of R. Brook

Gomersal station about 1910, looking towards Leeds.

remained at 11 trains each way with 13 SO and the additional Tuesday service discontinued. The Birstall branch service was further reduced to four trains in each direction, two of which were mixed.

Examination of LNWR trains to Hull revealed the following:

1.25 am MO	Copley Hill – Hull	arr 4.10 am express goods
2.30 am MSX	Cleckheaton – Hull	arr 5.21 am express goods
5.05 am SO	Cleckheaton – Hull	arr 7.52 am express goods
7.30 am MSX	Copley Hill – Hull	arr 10.17 am express goods
11.00 am	Liverpool L St – Hull	arr 2.35 pm express
4.00 pm	Liverpool L St – Hull	arr 7.35 pm express
11.40 pm SX	Cleckheaton – Hull	arr 2.32 am express goods
12.20 am Sun	Copley Hill – Hull	arr 2.45 am express goods
12.10 am MSX	Hull – Copley Hill	arr 2.50 am express goods
9.20 am	Hull – Liverpool L St	express
4.30 pm	Hull – Liverpool L St	express
7.00 pm SX	Hull – Birmingham	express goods and fish
9.10 pm MSX	Hull – Liverpool	express goods and fish
9.10 pm MO	Hull – Copley Hill	arr 12.00 midnight express goods and fish
10.50 pm SO	Hull – Copley Hill	arr 1.35 am express goods and fish

MSX - Monday and Saturday excepted

Emigrants from Europe to America were carried from Hull to Liverpool by rail. The trains ran at specified times, usually on Mondays. In October 1909 there were eight departures from Hull if the train was of 12 coaches. If there were between 13 and 17 coaches only six trains would be run. NER engines, used throughout, were either Fletcher '0398' class or 2-cylinder Worsdell-von Borries Compound 0-6-0s. From Leeds the LNWR provided pilotmen and LNWR crews had the rare chance to travel in a decent cab. Engines of luggage trains were exchanged at Leeds. All trains loaded to above 12 coaches were given an LNWR pilot engine between Leeds and Stalybridge. Routing was via Heckmondwike, Micklehurst and Hooley Hill thence via Broadheath, Arpley and Ditton Junction. This traffic ran until the First World War and was resumed afterwards by a smaller scale until the mid-1920s, but with LNWR haulage from Leeds.

The year had two accidents. On 28th January a Manchester to Leeds train due to depart at 10.28 am was reversed into the up north tunnel at Huddersfield to allow it to be overtaken by the 11.08 express to Leeds. On running forward the former was erroneously run into a bay platform, colliding with an L&Y engine and vans standing there. At the time there was dense fog.

On 10th August the 9.00 am Huddersfield to Stockport express, running non-stop to Stalybridge and hauled by 18 inches 0-6-2 tank No. 1608 was derailed at Friezland, killing the driver and fireman. The locomotive turned completely round after running 315 yards with its leading driving wheels derailed, from the end of Friezland platform over Dacres' viaduct. The leading coach finished ahead of the engine. The inquiry held at the King William IV hotel, Greenfield was conducted by Lt Col von Donop RE who found the track at the scene in good order on a 30 chain curve, which since being laid, had moved 18 inches outwards. The train was estimated to have been travelling at between 60 and 70 mph and the mishap was caused by the leading wheels becoming derailed. No. 1608 had done 17,000 miles since its last overhaul at Crewe in February 1909. The inspecting officer concluded that the engine was not a suitable type for use on high speed trains but did not give any reason for this statement.

The accident at Friezland, 10th August, 1909.

CHAPTER EIGHT

1910 – 1913

1910

The Bangor Mail's successor, the Bristol Shrewsbury and York TPO underwent another change on 7th June when it became known as the Cardiff and York TPO Night Mail:

        Cardiff   7.42 pm   York   9.35 pm
        York   3.22 am   Cardiff 5.49 am
        starting and terminating at Shrewsbury on Sundays.

A major court case ensued when the LNWR sought to restrain the Howley Park Coal and Cannel Co. from mining beneath Morley tunnel which was affected by subsidence that had caused a series of problems. The Leeds, Dewsbury and Manchester Railway Act had omitted any safeguard against mining beneath the tunnel. Unhappily the action was lost, as the LNWR's successor was to find to its cost.

On the Oldham – Delph service the LNWR introduced steam railmotor No. 7 (carriage No. 5077) with trailer No. 1777 added specifically at busy times. The railmotor performed well enough on its own but the gradient was too steep when the trailer was hauled. The experiment began on 1st July, 1910 and was concluded in March 1911. However, the whole operation was reorganized from 1st January, 1912 when new halts and motor trains were introduced. A motor train lately used on the Rickmansworth branch took over on that date.

LNWR Rail Motor Carriage No. 7 and trailer No. 1777 were introduced on the Oldham to Delph service on 1st July, 1910, but proved unsuccessful.

Oldham Glodwick Road station about 1910, with a GCR train on the OA&GB service. View looking toward Greenfield.

Hull to Liverpool Lime Street express at Selby in 1912, headed by 'Precursor' 4-4-0 No. 366 *Medusa*, of Edge Hill shed. *S. Ellingworth*

On 18th January a mishap occurred at Hillhouse when the L&Y 7.36 pm Huddersfield to Halifax and Bradford train ran into an LNWR light engine which caused great damage and injured nine passengers.

1911

A railway strike began on 18th August and although it lasted only a few days, it occurred in a busy holiday season. The following schedule was a notable improvement:

8.42 am	Newcastle	9.25 pm
11.07	Leeds New	7.07
12.18 pm	Manchester Exchange	5.45
1.10	Liverpool Lime Street	5.00

The little-used OA&GB west curve at Ashton Moss, shown intact in 1888 and later abandoned, was reopened on 18th December, 1911 by the Great Central. What use was made of it by the LNWR is unknown.

1912

The Oldham route underwent reorganization on 1st November when new halts were introduced at Grasscroft, Moorgate and Dobcross. The Hull service comprised:

9.20 am	2.05 pm	4.13 pm	Hull	2.34 pm	7.35 pm	12.36 am
12.40 pm	5.40	7.45	Liverpool	11.00 am	4.00 pm	7.00 pm
TC to				TC to		
Llandudno				Scarborough		
Arr 2.40 pm				arr 2.58		

Huddersfield was one of the busiest stations for a town of its size:

LNWR	113 arrivals	119 departures
L&Y	113 arrivals	114 departures
Total	459 trains daily	

Second class travel was discontinued from 1st January. In some quarters there was much resentment. It was a severe blow to the OA&GB where an average of 30,000 passengers annually was conveyed by that class in the five years prior to abolition. The OA&GB carried its heaviest traffic yet, with 968,189 tons of minerals and 234,563 tons of goods, in spite of a miners' strike.

The LNWR Act of 1912 authorized the company to appoint Special Constables. This was a sequel to the 1911 strike, enabling the company to protect its property in the event of a recurrence. It augmented the long standing Canal Constables Act, which empowered chosen employees to act as Constables to prevent theft etc on LNWR canals. During 1911 a large number of military personnel had been used for such purposes.

1913

A notable occurrence was the introduction of the 11.15 am from Liverpool Lime Street which conveyed through coaches to Scarborough, hitherto attached to 11.00 am Liverpool – Hull.

On 27th August the 11.45 am Leeds – Llandudno express overran signals in Cocker Hill tunnel at Stalybridge and collided with the back of a goods train. Four people were injured.

Grasscroft halt, between Grotton & Springhead and Greenfield, was opened on 1st January, 1912. This view toward Greenfield was taken 21st May, 1967.   *Author*

CHAPTER NINE

1914 – 1918

Additional traffic arose from the Slaithwaite to Marsden tramway extension built for Huddersfield Corporation. The requirements were for some 5,260 tons of materials to be delivered to Slaithwaite station and 8,240 tons to Marsden. Assurances were given that no difficulty would arise. However, the company intimated they could not in any circumstances accept delivery of rails at either station and these would have to be dealt with at Huddersfield or Longwood which would incur additional cartage charges. The company was able to accept up to 14 wagons at Marsden at any one time but offered facilities at Slaithwaite for up to 10 wagons. Any surplus could be dealt with at Longwood (from 15 to 20 wagons according to the state of the yard) and at Linthwaite where an adjoining field on a steep slope was used for storage.

An office block was built at Deighton on the Kirkburton Branch to serve clerical staff dealing with traffic for British Dyes, 'LNWR 1914' was inscribed above the doorway. A further development was the introduction of road motors at Leeds, where a $2^1/_2$ ton Karrier lorry was used by the goods department.

LNWR goods services to Hull were discontinued on 2nd August as a result of the outbreak of war. Passenger trains continued until February 1915, after which LNWR engines did not work to Hull on a regular basis.

Deighton station before the second platform was added in 1916. The cobbled goods yard is in the foreground.

During 1915 additional accommodation for goods traffic was made at Diggle and Marsden. On the OA&GB, Dean Shut sidings between Clegg Street and Park Bridge were installed but fell into disuse after the war, only to be reinstated during the Second World War.

The foremost consequence of the war was the movement of military personnel and equipment, but gradually the shortages of staff caused economy measures to be taken. Lightly used trains were axed, particularly in 1915, but by 1916 the position was acute and from 1st January, 1917 the following closures were made:

> Micklehurst line – local services, Friezland and Uppermill
> Birstall branch – Birstall and Carlinghow
> LD&M – Churwell and Staincliffe & Batley Carr
> Heckmondwike line – Gildersome
> Hooley Hill line – Hooley Hill (Guide Bridge)

Fares increased by 50 per cent and Sunday services were pruned so as to make a return journey between two nearby places virtually impossible. An estimated 56,000,000 yards of Khaki cloth were despatched from Huddersfield station. At Dewsbury $1\frac{1}{2}$ floors of the goods warehouse were used for the sorting of old uniforms. At Batley $2\frac{1}{2}$ floors were used for similar purposes and traffic in discarded uniforms assisted the shoddy trade. The war record of the Kirkburton branch was most impressive. Fenay Bridge and Lepton goods yard received 10,750,000 hand grenades and after filling at the nearby Lion fireworks factory, were despatched packed 12 to a box. A large traffic in dyestuffs was established from British Dyes Sidings which opened in 1916. Despatch of 1,113,000 tons of acid and explosives were transported in approximately 113,000 wagon loads.

During 1917 public timetables ceased to be issued. The only information available was that displayed on wall boards at railway stations.

On 30th May, 1918 a Royal visit was made to West Yorkshire. The Royal train arrived at Leeds Wellington station, platform 7 from Bolton Abbey. After reversal, departure was made behind 'Princes' No. 479 *Thomas B Macaulay* and No. 2213 *Charles Kingsley*. The train then ran to Dewsbury where King George V and Queen Mary alighted. The empty stock proceeded to Huddersfield, where after a further reversal it departed for Liversedge. Making another reversal, it collected the Royal party at Heckmondwike before travelling to Marsden with the same engines as before. On the return journey the Royal party joined their train at Bradley for a run to Leeds Wellington, hauled by 'Princes'

No. 233 *Suvla Bay* and No. 631 *Thomas Gray*. The Royal train pilot on the outward journey ran to Diggle and was a 6 feet 6 inches 'Jumbo' No. 1177 *Princess Louise*. Empty stock workings were hauled by Hillhouse 19 inches 4-6-0s Nos. 618 and 2587.

On 16th February, 1915 as the 11.07 am Leeds to Liverpool train (from Newcastle) was rounding the acute bend from Canal Junction on to Leeds viaduct, the third coach from the rear became derailed and ran in the four foot way, causing the rearmost vehicles also to leave the rails and travel 100 yards. All the derailed coaches were seriously damaged and 44 passengers were injured. Lt Col Druitt RE established in his report the cause to be a worn wing rail at the junction. The engine hauling the train was No. 1765 with driver John Death and fireman R.H. Jones of Edge Hill shed.

On 9th September, 1918 at Heaton Lodge Junction the down Mail, travelling in thick fog, overran adverse signals and cut in two a 70 truck L&Y goods train from Goole to Brighouse. The engine, 'Claughton' No. 2047 *Charles N Lawrence* ploughed into the ballast up to its driving axles. A relief was run at 6.15 am but other traffic was seriously delayed and an ambulance train destined for Dewsbury travelled via the 'new' line to Farnley Junction where it was reversed.

A notable work performed by the LNW Canal Dept was the dredging of Tunnel End reservoir at Marsden between 1914-18. A 2 feet 6 inches gauge tramway was laid on the canal towpath from Tunnel End to Warehouse Hill where spoil was tipped. Blue clay brought from Micklehurst was taken from Marsden goods yard to Tunnel End.

The accident at Heaton Lodge Junction on 9th September, 1918 when the down TPO from Shrewsbury overran signals in thick fog & cut through a L&Y goods train. There were fortunately no casualties. The LNWR engine was 'Claughton' No. 2047.

Charles N. Lawrence

Lees station on 26th May, 1959, looking east with goods yard and a large warehouse in the background. *Author*

The New North Road entrance to Huddersfield warehouse *c.*1919, showing LNWR/L&Y parcels vans and early motor lorries. *Author's collection*

CHAPTER TEN

1919 – 1922

Few immediate improvements came after the armistice, although the stations at Gildersome, Staincliffe and Batley Carr reopened on 5th May, 1919. Churwell followed on 1st March, 1920 and Hooley Hill (Guide Bridge) on 3rd October, 1921. However, Gildersome closed for the second and final time on 11th June, 1921 after a serious fire completely gutted Northorpe station. The complete Gildersome station was taken down and re-erected at Northorpe on the opposite side of the road from the earlier one. A railway strike took place which lasted from 27th September until 5th October.

Subsidence within Morley tunnel became severe and in November 1920 single line working was introduced between Howley Park and Morley. The tunnel required total reconstruction. The Batley portal was taken down and rebuilt in Staffordshire Blue Brick. Originally estimated to last between three to four years the work was not completed until 1933.

Amalgamation with the L&Y took effect on 1st January, 1922 and one of the first benefits of this was the introduction of a new service on 6th February, 1922:

8.20 am	1.05 pm	3.03 pm	Halifax	↑	3.30 pm	8.07 pm	9.08 pm
8.48	1.32	3.40	Huddersfield		3.00	7.37	8.37
11.56	5.17	6.40	Birmingham N St	11.00 am			
3.56 pm			Brighton		12.25		
4.50			Eastbourne		11.35		
1.45	6.05	8.10	↓ Euston	10.30 am	2.55		4.00 pm
Breakfast and Luncheon car from Halifax						Tea and Dining car to Halifax	

During this period the only mishap occurred on 24th December, 1919 as the 4.45 pm Leeds to Stockport train was leaving Huddersfield. Departing from platform 3 it then crossed to the up main line before being crossed to enter the up north tunnel. It was cut in two by the L&Y 4.45 pm ex-Penistone which had overrun signals and then collided with the third coach of the Stockport train. Major GE Hall RE established that irregular working by signalman Vasey, who first had accepted the L&Y train, which consisted of No. 646, a 2-4-2 tank and seven bogie vehicles was running late. Its driver,

Midwood, had missed a signal at Springwood Junction and another at the tunnel. Driver Merchant with LNWR No. 2304, an 18 inches 0-6-0 'Cauliflower' had a load of nine 6-wheelers with total weight of 114 tons. In spite of the heavy Christmas traffic casualties were light. A recommendation was made that the tunnel signal be repositioned.

In 1920 there came into existence a new powerful body known as the Huddersfield Joint Railway Committee. It comprised senior members of Huddersfield Town Council and the Huddersfield Chamber of Commerce, which for seven years exchanged many suggestions with the company for improved passenger and goods facilities. Delays in deliveries of consignments produced a regular flow of correspondence, but by 1929 a stalemate arose and the committee lapsed. Meanwhile, traffic was gradually lost to the roads. Nonetheless there were some achievements. In 1921 the LNWR began the issue of books of left luggage tickets at 30 for 7s. 6d. for commercial travellers. In 1923 requests were made for a through coach off the 1.30 pm ex-Euston, but this would involve running a train between Crewe and Huddersfield and the London Midland & Scottish Railway (LMS),

Staff at Kirkburton station 1922, poised in their ornamental garden. The station master Mr M. Sykes is second from the left.   *Author's collection*

No. 102 one of two 'Claughton' 4-6-0s allocated to Farnley Junction shed 1921-22. the other was No. 2395 *J.A.F. Aspinall*. *Author's collection*

which had been formed on 1st January, 1923, would not agree to the additional mileage. However, they did add an extra train which departed Huddersfield 9.50 am for Sheffield Midland with a through carriage reaching St Pancras at 2.10 pm. There was a 3.03 pm ex-St Pancras with a through coach to Huddersfield arriving 8.00 pm.

In 1922 there was pressure to reopen Huddersfield island platform booking office but the LNWR were unwilling to comply. However, the west end booking office reopened at this time and in February 1924 the LMS began the issue of tickets to all stations from there. Unfortunately the lack of patronage ultimately caused its closure. Afterwards it was used for excursion bookings at times of heavy pressure.

LNWR Road Motor Transport was inaugurated in the Huddersfield area following the First World War, a number of vehicles were LNWR and L&Y Joint Railways. At Leeds LNWR Road Motors were introduced prior to 1914 but there as in Huddersfield, horse-drawn drays were predominant for the delivery of goods until 1952. Twenty years later, on a damp day, the visitor to Huddersfield goods warehouse could still detect the smell of horses!

The 9.20 am to Stockport and Manchester arriving at Huddersfield from Leeds in 1921, hauled by '5 ft 6in.' 2-4-2T No. 2133 and 'Precursor' 4-4-0 No. 1312 *Ionic*. On the left is an L&Y small boilered 0-8-0. Beyond the elevated signal box another goods train waits to enter Hillhouse yard. *P.F. Cooke*

The first Hillhouse engine to carry LMS livery was '5ft 6in.' 2-4-2T No. 6732, allocated from November 1923 until withdrawal in July 1928. *P.F. Cooke*

CHAPTER ELEVEN

1923 – 1947

Following amalgamation with the L&Y, the LNWR became a constituent of the newly formed London, Midland and Scottish Railway on 1st January, 1923. There was another strike from 21st to 24th January, 1924 which involved Associated Society of Locomotive Engineers and Firemen (ASLEF) members.

In December 1924 Oldham branch services comprised 37 trains on weekdays; 39 Saturday only and 12 Sunday trains but trains to Oldham were one less in each case. 3rd February, 1925 saw the introduction of a tea/dining car on the 11.00 Liverpool – Hull and 4.00 pm ex-Hull. The dining service extended to Liverpool – Newcastle trains on 13th May, 1925.

The General Strike lasted from 4th to 14th May, 1926. A few trains did run, manned by volunteers, including a service between Leeds and Manchester with John and Paddy Hirst (Huddersfield railway enthusiasts) as firemen on a pair of LNWR 19 inch 4-6-0s. Also one train ran to Kirkburton (described in *Hillhouse Immortals*, Oakwood Press 1999). A knock-on effect of the General Strike was the way in which alternative forms of transport were developed. To the bus industry the strike acted as an incentive to make permanent something that had been a short term gain. In many areas the local passenger trains' services were

Ex-LNWR 0-8-0 No. 9087 passing through Huddersfield station on a down goods train.
G.H. Soole

numbered as were the tram routes. They gave way to the all-conquering motor vehicle. A Commer 3 ton motor wagon would be pressed to carry 8 tons so new competition was created, enthusiastically supported by all those whose acquaintance with the motor vehicle had been gained through wartime military service. The spread of bus routes was breathtaking. All formalities were forsaken until the Road Traffic Act of 1930 brought some degree of regulation.

In 1926 the LMS introduced a new service between Huddersfield and St Pancras, a through coach which ran non-stop Huddersfield to Sheffield Midland via Thornhill and Royston.

Huddersfield	7.15 am	St Pancras	1.50 pm
St Pancras	12.10 pm	Huddersfield	6.40 pm

Two new services ran Saturdays only between Huddersfield and Oldham on 2nd October, 1926:

Huddersfield	11.00 pm	Oldham Clegg Street	9.45 pm
Oldham Clegg Street	11.51 pm	Huddersfield	10.41 pm

Football specials were a welcome source of passenger traffic during the 1920s. Matches between Huddersfield Town and north-eastern clubs, such as Middlesbrough, Sunderland and Newcastle United yielded the heaviest traffic. On 15th February, 1928 there were 55,000 spectators who watched Huddersfield play Middlesbrough, with most arriving by train. The supporters were good natured on both the inward and outward journeys. Crowd control at Huddersfield required just two officers of the LMS Police. There were also Rugby League excursions reaching Wigan, Wembley and elsewhere.

In January 1929, in response to ferocious bus competition, a new 2s. day return was issued between Huddersfield and Leeds. On 15th June, 1932 a 'Cafeteria Car' was introduced on two trains, the 8.00 am and 12.15 pm trains from Leeds and the 10.02 am and 4.40 pm from Manchester Exchange, staffed by two women and a boy.

On 2nd June, 1924 station names were altered to avoid confusion for staff and travellers at stations previously owned by different companies:

Cleckheaton became Cleckheaton Spen
Dewsbury became Dewsbury Wellington Road
Heckmondwike became Heckmondwike Spen
Liversedge became Liversedge Spen
Hooley Hill (Guide Bridge) became Audenshaw

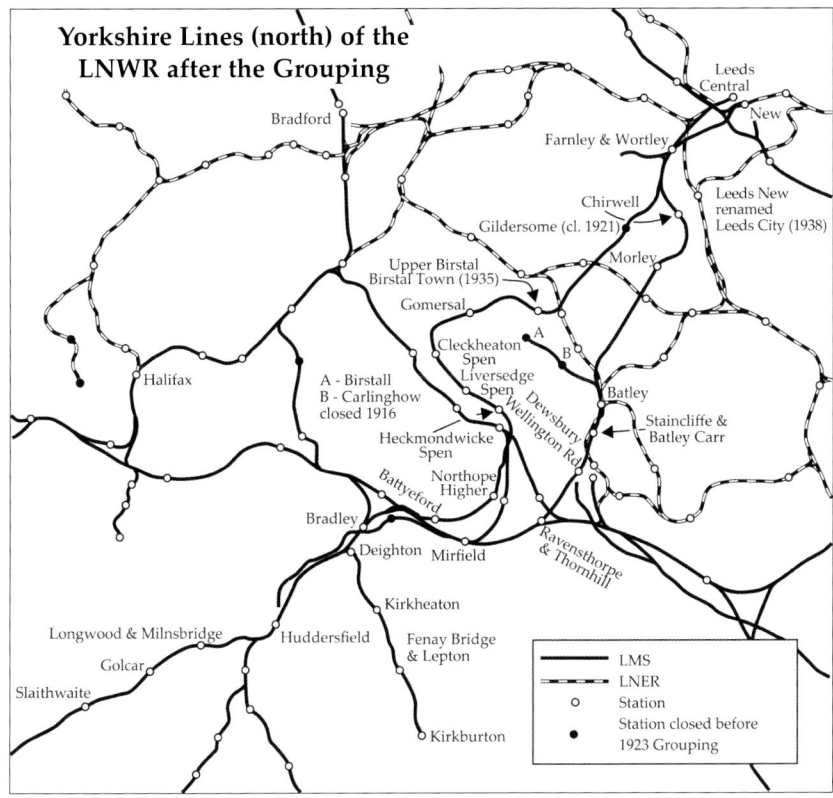

However, this was tinkering with a real problem. The LMS unfortunately became a bureaucracy with rigorous procedures that businesses were not prepared to tolerate. The Huddersfield Chamber of Commerce made the position clear at the time, but the LMS steam roller rolled on regardless.

In 1925 a demand was made for the reopening of the closed stations on the Micklehurst line, but only excursions were restored.

In the spate of passenger closures of the 1928-30 period, the Kirkburton branch closed on 28th July, 1930. Closure was without ceremony and at that time the service comprised 10 trains in each direction with 13 SO. The last train to Kirkburton was worked by Webb Coal Tank No. 7700 in the charge of Herbert Walshaw and W.J.R. Battye. The line suffered intense bus competition and a 5*d*. single fare from Huddersfield. The LMS membership with Huddersfield Corporation in the Huddersfield Joint Omnibus committee dated from 17th May,

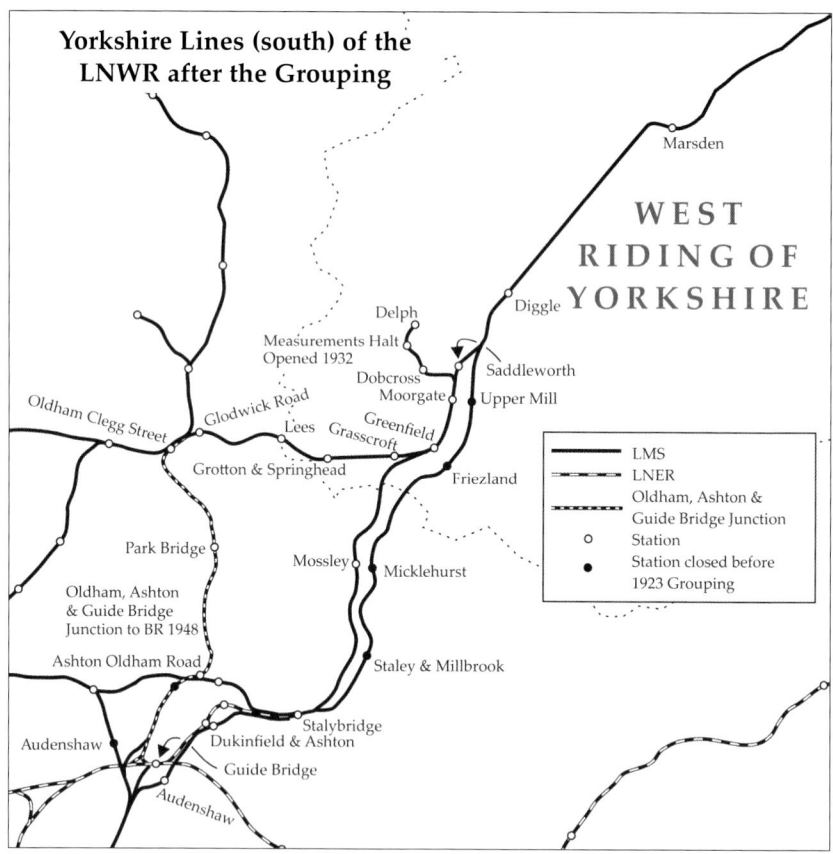

1930. Before this the LMS had begun a local goods service by road motor.

Occasional excursions were run after closure. For Huddersfield holidays a special ran between Kirkburton and Blackpool and Morecambe until the Second World War, with the empty stock taken up to Kirkburton on the previous Friday.

On the Delph branch a new halt called Measurements was opened between Dobcross and Delph on 18th July, 1932. Upper Birstall on the New Line to Leeds became known as Birstall Town on 8th July, 1935. The last station name change was that of Leeds New which became Leeds City under a rationalization scheme, although for operational purposes it was known as Leeds City South.

The first post-war appearance locally of a member of the Royal Family occurred in February 1932 when HRH the Duke of York visited

Huddersfield and returned to Euston on the 4.35 pm Stockport train. A special saloon was added and the train was hauled on this occasion by an L&Y 'Dreadnught' 4-6-0 No. 10405.

The down north line over Crimble viaduct was closed from 8th to 25th February to enable repairs to be carried out. At this time the viaduct was braced with old rail. Following this repair a serious derailment occurred on 11th April when 10 trucks in a down goods train came off the line, ran on the sleepers for 60 yards before five of them rolled down an embankment after dislodging the parapet and coping stones.

1932 saw most significant improvements at Mirfield with the widening of the line over the Calder and at Mirfield station by a huge plate girder bridge added alongside the masonry viaduct on the south side. The new tracks continued over a brick-faced embankment as far as the new Mirfield marshalling yard. A troublesome bottleneck was removed. The widening and the yard came into use on 9th August, 1932, being preceded by the introduction of electric 'speed' signalling on 8th February. The new signals were visible for 1,000 yards and indicated the route and speed of travel.

The mammoth engineering work on Morley tunnel was completed on 9th May, 1933. In 1937 resignalling at Leeds New station was

The old and new signal boxes at Leeds City West in 1937. *W.B. Stocks*

completed. The new concourse at the station proved to be the largest enclosed covered space in the city.

For the Silver Jubilee celebrations at Huddersfield in 1935 the LMS supplied suitable decorations which were illuminated by gas. Much the same was done in 1937 for the Coronation but by then the decorations were electrically lit.

A serious accident occurred at Diggle Junction on 5th July, 1923 when the 9.22 am Leeds to Stockport train hauled by 'Experiment' No. 1406 *George Findlay* with 'Cauliflower' No. 1027 as assistant engine, in the charge of driver R. Holdsworth and fireman J. Whitaker of Hillhouse shed, emerged from the double line Standedge tunnel. In crossing to the Micklehurst line it collided with L&Y 0-6-0 No. 1063 of Low Moor shed. Four persons were killed and many injured.

An inquiry was conducted by Col J.W. Pringle in a saloon coach placed in the short bay on the down north platform at Diggle station. It was established that the express emerged from the tunnel at 40 mph and crossed over at 30 mph, immediately striking the ex-L&Y engine with much force, pushing it forward a considerable distance. There was conflicting evidence between the signalman, the shunter and the driver of the ex-L&Y engine. The signalman had had only 10 days' experience of working the box. The engine shunting pulled out of a

The accident at Diggle on 5th July, 1923, showing derailed 'Experiment' 4-6-0 No. 1406 *George Findlay*.

siding not controlled by a signal but by a flag hung out of the box. The shunter claimed the flag was not exhibited, while the signalman said that it was. Driver Walker of the ex-L&Y 1063 was censured for moving away without permission from the signalman.

On 18th December, 1924 at Stalybridge the 8.15 pm Stockport – Halifax express collided with a light engine detached from a goods train. The latter overturned and blocked the Huddersfield line for several hours.

On 29th December, 1923 a coal train from Grimethorpe destined for Bradford Road Gas Works, Manchester, while approaching Huddersfield sustained a broken drawbar on the 7th wagon. This resulted in 50 wagons rolling back. Due to the alertness of a signalman they were harmlessly diverted into a dead end siding at Hillhouse. On 28th December, 1933 a mishap within Morley tunnel occurred when Hillhouse ex-L&Y 2-4-2 tank No. 10816 lost a connecting rod when half-way through which resulted in a platelayer being injured and 100 passengers trapped for three hours.

A mishap within Standedge tunnel on 26th August occurred when a Crewe to Leeds goods suffered the derailment of four wagons which were dragged along the sleepers for almost three miles. The tunnel was closed for the rest of the day. On the OA&GB a new bridge known as the Jubilee Bridge was opened on 6th May, 1935 to serve the needs of new housing. It was built by Leonard Fairclough & Co. in reinforced concrete. Nearby another bridge was made of red brick and was of unusually narrow width.

Modernization of Leeds New station included a new Queens Hotel, where work commenced on 15th March, 1935 and was completed three years later.

The number of excursions operated reached unprecedented levels. The 1930s saw expansion of excursion facilities for national events and for sporting fixtures. There were evening excursions to Blackpool and Longsight (for Belle Vue) to Leeds (for events in Roundhay Park) and also cheap tickets to Hipperholme (for Sunny Vale), Honley (for Hope Bank) to Rudyard Lake and Alton Towers amongst many others.

Huddersfield station booking hall was modernized in September 1938 in a pleasing LMS house style, replacing two previous offices located on either side of the main entrance.

The closure of Linthwaite Goods for merchandise traffic occurred on 1st July, 1939. In 1939 on the Huddersfield Broad Canal, Fieldhouse lock was rebuilt, the last major canal work undertaken.

The late 1939 passenger timetable came into force when the 1939 winter timetable would normally have been introduced. Wartime goods traffic increased all round. Whole train loads of barbed wire were run daily, as were trains of petrol tanks and troop trains. On 2nd December, 1940 Churwell station was closed.

A great blizzard at the Diggle end of Standedge tunnel lasted from 28th January, 1940 until 1st February, during which time all traffic ran via the L&Y main line. A Sunday train from Leeds City to Manchester Exchange was stuck at Diggle for 12 hours. It was ultimately relieved by three engines and arrived back at Huddersfield at 3.00 am Monday on its way back to Leeds, where it arrived some 14 hours after it had departed.

On 3rd October, 1940, Huddersfield became a closed station where tickets were collected from calling trains instead of the trains making a special stop at either Longwood and Milnsbridge, Bradley or Lockwood.

1941 saw further cuts in timetabled passenger traffic but goods traffic increased. Petrol trains were usually piloted by a 'Cauliflower' 0-6-0 from either Widnes or Edgeley shed. Traffic to British Dyes Sidings and Hollidays Sidings became intense. The twice-daily Liverpool to Newcastle trains and corresponding trains in the

A 'George the Fifth' 4-4-0 standing in platform 3 at Huddersfield with a stopping train for Manchester Exchange. *W.B. Stocks*

opposite direction loaded to 14 or 15 coaches and were hauled between Manchester and Leeds by two engines, usually a 'Jubilee' or 'Patriot' with a Stanier 'Black Five' as pilot, or perhaps a pair of Staniers. The pair of Liverpool – Hull trains in both directions was loaded up to 10 or 11 coaches, but hauled by only one engine. The use of ROD or WD engines was almost unknown. Very occasionally one would make a trial run. The greatest impact was the arrival of the 'S 160' class 2-8-0s of the US Transportation Corps. They were on heavy goods trains in some number, usually from Crewe South, Mold Junction, Birkenhead and Warrington. These locomotives thrived on hard work and little attention.

On 10th January, 1942 the 8.25 pm Manchester Exchange – Leeds City hauled by Farnley 'Jubilee' No. 5708 *Express* running under clear signals ran into the back of a Birkenhead – Copley Hill train, of petrol tank wagons which had stopped and become divided due to a broken coupling, near Farnley railway sheds. The guard of the latter was killed and the inquiry found that he and the signalman who accepted the passenger train were responsible. There was a risk of fire or explosion and, while clearance took place with great care over several days, a shuttle service for passengers was operated between Huddersfield and Morley with passengers being conveyed to Leeds by bus. In 1943 the US 'S160' 2-8-0 No. 2093 was exhibited at Kirkburton in connection with the war effort. The locomotive had been built in February 1943 by the ALCO works, No. 50575.

The end of the war in Europe produced a number of 'Victory' excursions operated for the event but little else. Neither was there any sign of recovery in the number of passenger trains operated or in the speed at which they travelled. Arrears of maintenance had accumulated, speed restrictions were in force and the entire system was run down. The age of austerity was upon Britain and the LMS received more than its fair share of criticism.

On 23rd September, 1946 severe flooding occurred after heavy rain. The spillway from Tunnel End reservoir at Marsden was breached and the flood water washed away the ballast and earth from beneath the up and down south lines. Heavy repairs were needed before the line was restored for traffic and the local unit of the National Fire Service was called upon to pump water clear. That was a forerunner of one of the severest winters for many years. On 12th February, 1947 traffic on the Micklehurst line was suspended after the 3.55 pm Halifax – Stockport train became trapped in a huge snowdrift at the Diggle end of Butterhouse tunnel.

The Royal train came to Stalybridge on 17th July, 1946. It arrived from Lowton in charge of LMS Staniers 'Black Fives' Nos. 4969 and 4970, both of Longsight shed. Afterwards both engines ran light to Crewe.

The LMS Canal Act 1944 empowered the sale of the Huddersfield Broad Canal and a short length of the Huddersfield Narrow Canal up to the third lock to the Calder and Hebble Navigation for £4,000.

During the final year of 'The Yorkshire Lines' under private ownership, it was clear that political rather than commercial considerations were to shape the future.

The LMS was created by the Railways Act of 1921. Notwithstanding some moments of triumph the LMS passed into history run down, shabby and largely unlamented. The LMS was never given a proper chance to show what it might have been capable of – the politicians saw to that.

Huddersfield viaduct under repair in 1947. *Author*

CHAPTER TWELVE

1948 – 1962

A landmark in the first year of public ownership was the fuel crisis when several passenger services were discontinued as economy measures. The new order was very slow to display initiative and services remained in an atmosphere that was austere. One item to enlighten the scene was another visit by the Royal Train which ran from Clayton West Junction after an overnight stop via Huddersfield and the Bradley Wood branch to Halifax.

In 1950 small improvements began to be seen but closure of passenger stations predominated:

    Bradley   4th March, 1950
    Audenshaw, Guide Bridge   30th September, 1950

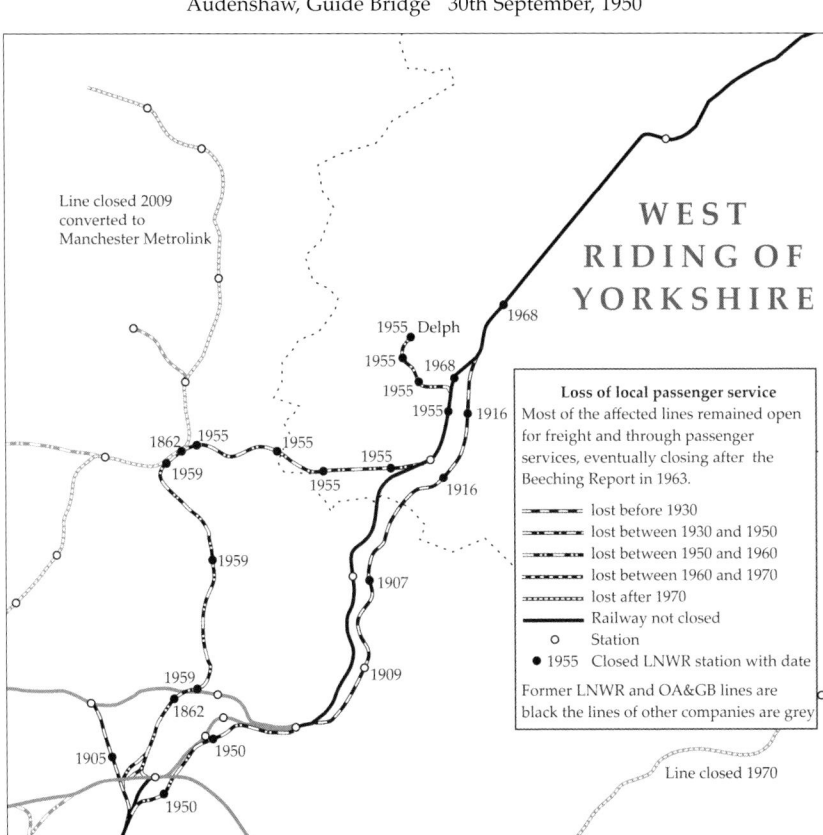

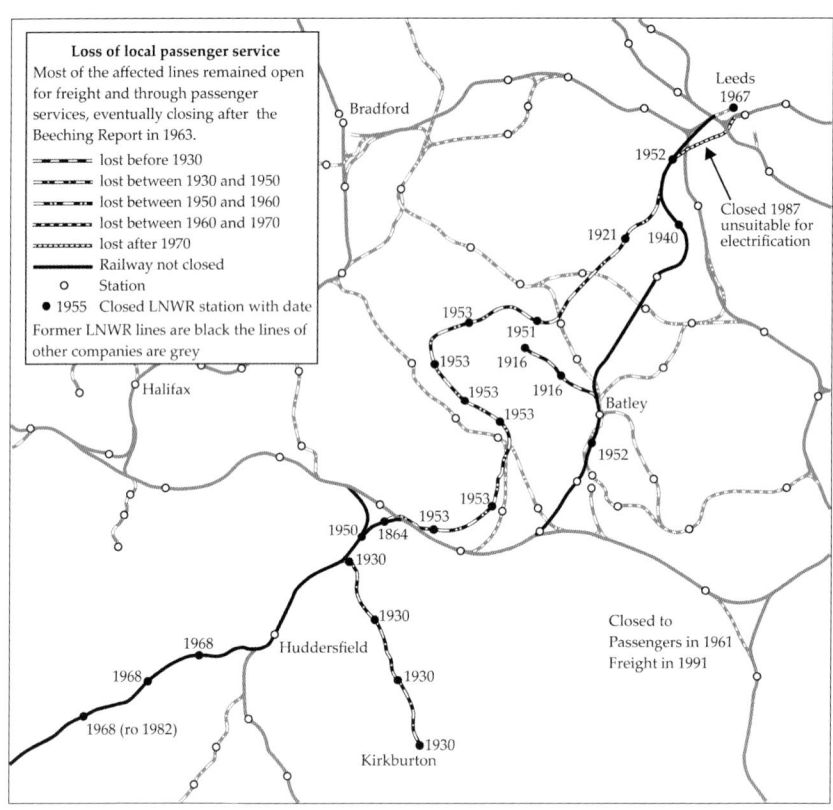

Dukinfield and Ashton	30th September, 1950
Birstall Town	1st August, 1951
Staincliffe & Batley Carr	7th April, 1952
Farnley and Wortley	3rd November, 1952
Cleckheaton Spen	5th January, 1953
Battyeford	5th January, 1953
Northorpe Higher	5th January, 1953
Heckmondwike Spen	5th January, 1953
Liversedge Spen	5th January, 1953
Gomersal	5th January, 1953
Delph	2nd May, 1955
Measurements Halt	2nd May, 1955
Dobcross Halt	2nd May, 1955
Moorgate Halt	2nd May, 1955
Grasscroft Halt	2nd May, 1955
Gotton and Springhead	2nd May, 1955
Lees	2nd May, 1955
Oldham Glodwick Road	2nd May, 1955

Oldham Clegg Street	4th May, 1959
Park Bridge	4th May, 1959
Ashton Oldham Road	4th May, 1959

Traffic on the 'New' line had undergone many changes. It was used as a diversionary route during engineering work in Morley tunnel 1920-33. The Birstall Town cabin register showed:

October 1923	687 trains per week
April 1930	588 trains per week
October 1933	409 trains per week
October 1937	435 trains per week
August 1940	330 trains per week
February 1946	298 trains per week
February 1948	318 trains per week

Patronage of intermediate stations:

1927	88,870
1939	50,686
1946	36,663
1952	18,375

The area involved was well served by bus, especially the Yorkshire Woollen District Transport Ltd of Dewsbury, a BET company of which the LMS had joint ownership with the London & North Eastern Railway (LNER). With the closure of the Delph branch Oldham Clegg Street

The 9.00 am Liverpool to Newcastle entering Huddersfield station in August 1948, hauled by, *Anson*, an LMS 'Jubilee' class 4-6-0.

An ex-L&Y radial tank standing in Huddersfield station on 1st May, 1951, still in LMS livery.

Huddersfield station on 5th July, 1952 with ex-L&Y 2-4-2T No. 50807 at platform 2 (now platform 4).
Author

became the terminus of OA&GB trains to Guide Bridge and Stockport. The decline in OA&GB traffic followed reduction in the train services and their replacement by the buses of the North Western Road Car Co., in which there was a substantial railway holding.

In the Colne Valley the third (south) platforms at Longwood, Golcar, Slaithwaite, Marsden and Diggle had their buildings removed as an economy measure from 20th February, 1953. A new signal box was erected on the Micklehurst line at Staley and Millbrook controlling traffic to Hartshead Power Station.

On 21st September, 1953 a new Huddersfield to Wakefield service provided two trains each way connecting with King's Cross services at Wakefield Westgate. The Stockport – Halifax service declined in importance and ceased at the end of the 1953 timetable. Near Red Doles Junction (for the Huddersfield Midland branch) Black Dyke bridge was filled in.

On 14th September, 1953 Huddersfield platforms and bays were renumbered:

> Platform 1 became Platform 8
> Platform 2 became Platform 4
> Platform 3 became Platform 1
> Bay 1 became Platform 3
> Bay 2 became Platform 5
> Bay 3 became Platform 6
> Bay 4 became Platform 2
> Bay 5 became Platform 7

The major event of 1955 was a disastrous strike by ASLEF members which lasted from 30th May until 12th June. A skeleton service was operated by National Union of Railwaymen crews but much traffic was lost and never returned. 'The Yorkshire Lines' was divided by the BR administration on 4th March, 1957. That portion to the east of Diggle became part of the North Eastern Region.

On 17th August, 1957 work commenced on the building of a new signal box at Huddersfield. This involved shortening Platform 7, thereafter precluding its use for passenger service. The work was completed on 29th October 1958. All semaphores were replaced by colour lights and Huddersfield Nos. 1 and 2 boxes were closed. Both were elevated structures mounted on gantries.

After the OA&GB passenger service ceased on 4th May, 1959 the line remained in use for parcels and goods traffic from Oldham Clegg Street.

The first diesel services of 'The Yorkshire Lines' were those provided

A Newcastle to Liverpool express hauled by 'Jubilee' class 4-6-0 No. 45708 *Resolution* has just crossed the Calder at Battyeford in August 1958. *Author*

between Huddersfield and Wakefield Westgate, with King's Cross connections commencing on 2nd November, 1959.

A light engine on the Oldham branch travelling from Lees shed became derailed at trap points at Greenfield on 23rd November, 1959 when it mounted the former Oldham branch platform. Two name changes made on 1st January, 1960 were:

>Ravensthorpe and Thornhill became Ravensthorpe
>Longwood and Milnsbridge became Longwood

In the same month a new signal box was opened at Morley replacing an early Saxby and Farmer hip-roofed example. At the Birstall branch, terminus buildings were cleared revealing the old locomotive shed that lay behind the station. Still complete with rails, it had been partitioned off and used by an adjoining mill for many years.

At Leeds City track alterations lasted from 19th November until 4th December; the station roof was removed at the west end while work commenced on the erection of a 12-storey office block. Between 19th and 21st July trials took place with a Swindon-built six-car Trans Pennine diesel multiple units (dmu) with a $28\frac{1}{2}$ minute timing to Huddersfield over the Heckmondwike line. Thence, with an unprecedented $9\frac{1}{2}$ minutes for the seven mile climb to Marsden and running via the Micklehurst line, Manchester Exchange was reached in 55 minutes from Leeds. Such a time was never scheduled in the years that followed and a promise made at a public meeting remained unfulfilled. On 2nd January, 1961 the entire 'Yorkshire Lines' timetable was recast with express trains every hour, for which $7\frac{1}{2}$ Swindon sets were supplied. The Liverpool – Newcastle service was given four trains in each direction, each hauled by an English Electric 2,000 hp Type 4 diesel-electric locomotive. The new initiative gained popularity within a month with a 45 per cent increase in passengers shown at Leeds and 30 per cent at Huddersfield. At Leeds a new platform, No. 13, was completed in February while the canal bridge was replaced and all trains between Leeds City and Farnley Junction diverted via Copley Hill from 24th April until 13th May. A temporary connection to the Midland was made by the old Midland turntable until the new structure was complete. The buildings between Platforms 7 and 16 were demolished as well as a large area of roof. At Huddersfield a second stage in resignalling took effect on 8th July and saw the closure of Springwood Junction and Gledholt Junction boxes.

At Diggle on 26th January class '5MT' 4-6-0 No. 45015 (on a Mirfield-Bushbury goods) collided with some empty coaches that were being shunted. Three lines were blocked for the rest of the day.

Completion of work at Leeds City was coupled with an announcement that the plan to merge Leeds City and Leeds Central stations would be postponed for two years. In reply to a query by a local MP, Dr Richard Beeching Chairman of British Railways Board stated '...

Fieldhouse Siding Huddersfield in 1954, showing the remains of track and winding drum for cable haulage. The ground frame hut is on the left and the former Midland Railway route is on the right. *W.B. Stocks*

Warth Mill Siding, Diggle in 1961, with an ex-L&Y 0-6-0 shunting. The hump of the girder bridge over the Huddersfield Narrow Canal is visible in front of the train. *Author*

Wagon turntables at Huddersfield warehouse 1955. *Author*

perhaps the city might consider following the action of some continental cities and offer to contribute towards rebuilding costs'. Local reaction was at first one of bewilderment; later the idea received a measure of support. (Basildon New Town on the Fenchurch Street – Southend Line provided a parallel with Beeching's suggestion.)

Dewsbury station was given a facelift. Redundant buildings on the down platform were demolished while in May 1962 part of the LD&M building on the up side was pulled down, including the only example of the LD&M monogram which had been mounted on gables at the west end.

In July there was a reduction in excursion and special trains operated for the holiday period, while from September 5th the weekday trains between Huddersfield and Manchester ran on Saturdays only. The Birstall branch closed as from 18th June, 1962. The final journey was on 16th when ex-L&Y 0-6-0 No. 52515 hauled the clearance train, at the request of the Wakefield Railway Club. Figures published during the previous year had indicated that closure would make economies of £842 annually.

An ornamental cast-iron spandrel bearing the devices of the LNWR and NER was saved from the demolished roof girders at Leeds New station following representations made by an enthusiast. From 11th November, 1962 Leeds Central was closed on Sundays for the duration of the winter timetable.

Leeds City Modernization

The plan for this was envisaged by the British Transport Act 1960. Preparatory work started in November 1959 and involved reconstructing two bridges spanning the Leeds and Liverpool Canal. Bridge No. 1 spanning four tracks (Midland) had a centre steel plate girder separating two pairs of lines. The wrought-iron bridge No. 11, built by T.W. Panton Sunderland 1869, was on a different level. Both were replaced by a single structure with longitudinal beams of two skew spans 60 feet each. The centre pier was carried on 23 inches diameter bored piles in the canal. When this work was completed the track was remodelled.

In May 1961 work began on the construction of a 12-storey office block which was completed in October 1963. Work on the station involved reconstruction of all facilities, the use of the older Wellington station (Leeds City North) for parcels and mail traffic and provision for parking for over 100 cars. The 'New Station' had been built on a complex system of brick arches and steel girders and this was to accommodate the mechanical and electrical equipment. The new passenger subway was in fact a reconstruction of an earlier one long disused. The station to be replaced had only three through platforms. This was altered to 12 platforms with five through, one of which was built into the south side of the station, while an earlier through platform was made into two bays. The station roof incorporated two high sections of steel portal construction linked by a low level section over the ticket barrier. The larger had a clear span of 150 feet covering an area of 70,000 square feet. At the eastern end the roof was bounded by an overhead barrow-way served by one 5 ton and three $2\frac{1}{2}$ ton lifts. Nearby was a footbridge for passengers. Gelderd Road curve linked the former Copley Hill – Wakefield GNR line with the LNWR Farnley viaduct line. The making of this saw the removal of a redundant bridge near Farnley and Wortley station and repositioning the bridge crossing Gelderd Road. The Farnley viaduct became the route for trains travelling via Wakefield Westgate. The principal contractors involved in the works were Samuel Butler & Co. Ltd, Stanningley who demolished bridge No. 1; and J.W. Tait Ltd, Bradford for the Whitehall curve, Gelderd Road curve and construction of earthworks and bridges.

Belle Vue excursion at Huddersfield on Whit Tuesday 1957, with class '5' 4-6-0 No. 44948.
Author

CHAPTER THIRTEEN

1963 – 1969

'The Reshaping of the Railways' document (the 'Beeching Report') was published on 27th March, 1963. Stalybridge was envisaged as the only intermediate station to remain between Manchester and Huddersfield. In September 1963 the 22.40 Liverpool Lime Street – York TPO commenced to run unadvertised. In 1964 the news was given that only essential maintenance would be carried out between Diggle and Heaton Lodge Junction, as a prelude to the cessation of the Huddersfield – Manchester stopping train service. The future of the two Trans-Pennine routes was under review and consideration was given to using one route for freight and the other for passenger traffic. The 'New' line was closed to passenger traffic from 7th September except the 15.00 Liverpool – Newcastle (as the Transport Users Consultative Committee (TUCC) hearing had not yet taken place). Five Trans-Pennine services now travelled via Dewsbury making additional calls there but on occasion other trains still used the 'New' line. The Micklehurst loop closed to passenger traffic from September. The final trains were the two-car dmu on 5th September on the 14.13 Stockport to Bradford Exchange and class

Tunnel End, Marsden in April 1962. From the left, a PW coach stands in Tunnel End siding, then the two single-line tunnels (Nelson 1871 and Nicholson 1849), next the overflow channel from Tunnel End Reservoir, behind which is the portal of the 1894 double-line tunnel. On the right is the canal with its tunnel entrance and the Tunnel End cottages.

Author's collection

View along the Farnley Mineral branch in May 1958, with Farnley Junction shed and the enginemen's hostel in the background. *Author*

'5MT' 4-6-0 No. 44795 on the 6th hauling the 09.10 Newcastle to Manchester Exchange. In reality other passenger services used this route occasionally afterwards.

A major re-routing of freight traffic took place on 23rd July, 1963 when Healey Mills Yard was opened by Lord Robens. This was preceded by the commissioning of a new signal box there on 16th June. At Copley Hill about 1,000 wagons daily were dealt with previously. On 31st October, 1963 an oil tank train started running to the newly completed Charrington-Hargreaves depot at Liversedge Spen. The implementation of Healey Mills' phase two on 2nd March, 1964 saw a vast reduction in traffic at Hillhouse yard, while goods traffic on the 'New' line was virtually eliminated.

The Oldham – Greenfield line closed on 13th April, 1964 with Delph having gone the previous year. Heaton Lodge Sidings, much reduced since 1932, closed down in October 1964. The last return train to Liversedge from Spen Valley Junction ran on 27th November hauled by class '9F' 2-10-0 No. 92113. The portion between Spen Valley Junction and Heckmondwike closed on 29th November after which the tanks ran via Dewsbury to Farnley Junction, reversing there and travelling via Gildersome to Liversedge. Meanwhile a new spur from the Thornhill to Low Moor L&Y line was made at Heckmondwike to connect to the existing 'New' line on a gradient of 1 in 61.6. This was opened on 11th January, 1966 and the portion between Liversedge and Farnley Junction then closed.

On 25th January, 1964 after an FA Cup Tie at Leeds, an overflow of spectators travelled back to Merseyside aboard the 21.50 Mail ex-York-Hereford/Liverpool. The journey suffered from hooliganism and the train was stopped at Morley and Hillhouse. At Huddersfield ugly scenes amongst the 300 passengers caused the train to be held for an hour. Eventually it left after all doors had been locked and the guard segregated. In September 1964 the Liverpool portion of the Mail began to terminate at Wigan NW.

The 'New' line received attention in 1965 and the TUCC dealt with only four objectors to its closure. An annual saving of £40,800 was envisaged. The planned closure on 14th June was delayed because of a bridge renewal at Dewsbury and the final passenger train was the 15.00 ex-Liverpool on 31st July hauled by class '40' No. D395. Closure was effective from 2nd August, 1965, though a small number of light engine movements were made afterwards to and from Farnley Junction shed. The 23.10 Liverpool Lime Street – York Mail was changed from 4th January, 1966 to run via Warrington Central and Skelton Junction where it regained its former route. On the same day inroads were made in the Trans-Pennine service, the 16.25 Liverpool – Leeds was formed of ordinary dmu stock and buffet car facilities were withdrawn from other services.

The Stockport – Stalybridge route had its TUCC hearing in January 1965 and the line was given a temporary reprieve. The projected withdrawal of the Huddersfield – Manchester stopping train service saw objectors receive a 36 page 'Heads of Information'. Making an estimated loss of £93,700 annually, expenditure of £41,000 would be needed over the next five years if the service was retained. A traffic survey taken week ended 9th February, 1965 produced:

	Joined	Alighted
Monday Friday average ridership	4,557	4,711
Saturday average ridership	4,133	4,056
Sunday average ridership	848	861

If approved, a limited stop bus service at peak hours would be required to serve places between Manchester and Mossley. That entailed the operation of 12 buses, the provision of which was estimated to cost £42,000 annually for which a continuing subsidy would be needed. The amended service with many trains calling at Ashton instead of Stalybridge would commence with the 04.50 ex-Manchester, then hourly from 07.45 until 21.05. The first train from Huddersfield would be at 08.14 and hourly until 20.15 followed by the Mail at 23.25.

There was a TUCC hearing at the George Hotel, Huddersfield on 13th April with a supplementary Heads of Information circulated giving details of a fresh survey made during the week ending 17th March, 1965 when patronage was marginally lower. The proceedings revealed that members of Huddersfield Town Council had been refused permission to enter Huddersfield station on a fact finding mission.

The Micklehurst line, closed officially on 7th September, 1964, was used by four excursion trains and the 17.10 Darlington – Manchester train on Easter Monday 1965.

Beyond British Dyes Sidings the Kirkburton branch was closed as from 5th April, 1965. 'WD' class 2-8-0 No. 90332 was used on the last goods on 2nd April while sister engine No. 90347 ran to the terminus on 9th April to clear all wagons. Hillhouse Yard closed completely on 1st November, while the LMS-built Mirfield Yard closed on 6th September. Apart from the section between Stalybridge and Millbrook Power station the Micklehurst line closed on 29th October, the final trains on the line being the 05.52 Crewe – Healey Mills hauled by class '8F' 2-8-0 No. 48537(55D) on 29th October and class '9F' 2-10-0 No. 92021 hauling the 06.40 Healey Mills – Crewe. By the end of March goods traffic using the Standedge route had been reduced from the former 100 trains daily to 88 and on 2nd October, 1967 these were reduced to 53 daily. It was decided to strengthen the line to take 100 ton oil tankers by fitting a new type of fishplate but by 29th October goods traffic over the Standedge route fell to only 29 trains daily.

Holliday's sidings, Bradley, on 15th June, 1960, with class '5MT' 4-6-0 No. 45401 heading the 18.20 Leeds-Manchester. *Author*

Heckmondwike goods on 25th May, 1961. Excursion stock is stored in the sidings and class '40' No. D245 passes with the 17.05 Liverpool to Newcastle. *Author*

Changes at Leeds saw the closure of the Farnley viaduct from Canal Junction to Farnley Junction to down trains from 11th November and to up trains on 18th November, 1966, services being rerouted via Copley Hill. The winter of 1966 saw dmus used to haul parcels trains. Of those scheduled to work between Huddersfield and Leeds, a 140 ton trailing load was allowed but only 80 tons in the opposite direction.

During November 1966 came the complete withdrawal of the Bradford Exchange – Stockport service, the 15.53 Halifax – Stockport and 19.25 Stockport – Bradford trains, the latter not making the four conditional stops between Marsden and Huddersfield.

Closure proposals for the ending of passenger services at Ravensthorpe, Batley and Morley were heard on 4th May, 1967 at Leeds and the 44 objectors received a 44 page Heads of Information. The stations served a combined population of 87,981 and a survey during the week ending 23rd October, 1966 had daily use by 207 passengers joining and 210 alighting. The combined revenue amounted to £13,349 while annual costs of operation were £9,000.

During the 1967 Whitsun period 16 relief trains were operated on the Leeds – Manchester route, nine of which were steam hauled. The Stalybridge Junction and Hooley Hill lines were closed to all traffic on 1st July and trains hitherto using that route reverted to running via Guide Bridge. A new timetable issued on 7th October featured the closure of seven intermediate stations on the Huddersfield – Manchester route: Longwood, Golcar, Slaithwaite, Diggle, Saddleworth, Droylsden and Clayton Bridge had their last trains on 5th October, 1968. The two final services were the 22.10 Manchester Exchange to Leeds comprising a three-car BRCW dmu Nos. 52075, 59812 and 52086 and the 22.00 Leeds City – Manchester Exchange operated by a like unit Nos. 51815, 59702 and 51835. Few of the usual closure formalities were observed and less than a handful of diehard enthusiasts travelled. The closure eliminated nine weekday services to Manchester and four (five SO) to Leeds, a notable casualty was the 04.50 Manchester Exchange – Huddersfield. Mossley and Greenfield were subject to a much reduced peak hour service. An even greater casualty was the cessation of four of the Liverpool – Newcastle trains to call at Huddersfield, the 08.43 and 16.36 ex-Newcastle and 08.56 and 17.05 ex-Liverpool. In three out of the four cases the running time allowed between Manchester and Leeds was greater than before. Two Sunday trains ran likewise, the 08.50 ex-Newcastle and the 10.00 ex-Liverpool.

On 1st February, 1969 it was announced that Ravensthorpe, Batley and Morley stations had been reprieved from closure. Huddersfield goods yard closed on 4th August, 1969 where D3941 was the last shunter. From 8th December Liner trains began operation on three return services but these proved erratic and never carried much traffic. See *Appendix Five*.

Modernisation of Leeds City station

Platforms 12 and 13 were extended westwards in April 1963 and the first portion of the new roof over platforms 9 to 13 was completed on 9th November, 1963. Phase II of the Leeds modernization neared completion in late 1965 with a new south concourse signal box. Phase III was completed within the next two years, a complete re-signalling and new route linkages including a new connection between Whitehall Junction and Copley Hill which commenced in July 1966. The original section of the LD&M from Three Signal Bridge Junction to Copley Hill was closed in August when the original masonry arch at Copley Hill which had a separate footpath arch, was replaced. The closure of Leeds viaduct in anticipation of its ultimate realignment was followed by remodelling Farnley Junction, the box there closing on 18th December, 1968. Meanwhile Leeds phase II commenced on 13th June and traffic hitherto using platforms 1 to 6 in Wellington station were rerouted into New station. Track was lifted between Farnley Junction and Gelderd Road

A 'WD' 2-8-0 crosses the Huddersfield Canal at Dukinfield with an empty stock train. Whitelands canal tunnel is in the background.
Author

Dukinfield & Ashton signal box on the Stalybridge Junction line, 15th August, 1959.
Author

Bridge where a new curved connection to the GNR lines running to Wakefield was made. This involved the difficult task of making a slight realignment (26th February, 1967) of the bridge which reopened to traffic on 1st May, 1967.

Closure of Leeds Central

The major event of the year 1967 was the closure of Leeds Central station on Saturday 29th April, witnessed by more than a thousand people gathered on platform end, signal box and lineside. The final hours in the life of this station in which the LNWR's influence went back to its earliest days were filled with powerful images.

Stanier 'Black Five' No. 44662 came and went to Bradford Exchange with the 11.50 ex-St Pancras. Class '45' No. D23 stood for some time on the line leading to the Leeds high level goods depot before moving to take charge of an engineers' train at Holbeck where work on completing the new connection from the GNR lines to the LNWR at Whitehall Road commenced at 18.00. In the half-hour before closure class '4MT' 2-6-4T No. 42235(56F) arrived on the 17.20 ex-Bradford Exchange which was added to the 17.50 departure to King's Cross, an 11-coach formation

The 14.45 Leeds to Liverpool Trans-Pennine train passing the site of Heckmondwike station on 23rd May, 1964. *G.H. Brown.*

hauled by 'Deltic' D9015 *The Duke of Wellington's Regiment*. Next a four-car Metro Cammell dmu set out on the 17.56 slow train to Doncaster followed by a three-car BRCW dmu on the 18.05 to Liverpool Exchange. Finally a well-filled eight--car Metro Cammell dmu worked the 18.10 to Harrogate on the final departure. Its exit was accompanied in the traditional manner by exploding detonators. Closure was complete when Class '4MT' 2-6-4T No. 42145(55A) cleared the few remaining vans.

The concentration of all passenger services at Leeds City station was preceded by numerous diversions, out of course stops at fringe stations, substitute bus services and some inconvenience. All routes converging upon Leeds were affected and the platforms at Leeds City North (the old Wellington station) were again used from 27th April. A handful of trains from Manchester Exchange were cancelled beyond Huddersfield or Batley. On Sunday 30th April services to Manchester Exchange and the Newcastle – Liverpool services either commenced their journey or ran via Wakefield Kirkgate while certain stopping trains started from Dewsbury.

Leeds City station was by no means ready to receive the diverted services and temporary arrangements scheduled to finish on 4th May were extended for a few days. Leeds City station was ceremonially opened on 17th May, 1967 by the Lord Mayor of Leeds. Demolition of Leeds City West signal box began the next day and lasted three weeks, frustrated by a collapse that blocked platform 8.

At Huddersfield an exploratory meeting was held between Railway Sites Ltd and various local bodies over the commercial development of the station. Shops, offices, a bus terminal and heliport were envisaged – an imaginative concept in every way! The germ of the Beeching theory had spread and the idea of a car for everyone and door to door freight transport became accepted.

The station's need of urgent attention was advanced by some as reason for demolition on the grounds of safety. In June 1967 Huddersfield Corporation called for tenders for exterior cleaning of the station, an act preceding the transfer to the Corporation of the façade, platform one and a length of track alongside for a distance of 213 feet. A public meeting was convened to discuss future use. An agreement was concluded between the Corporation and British Railways whereby the former would pay £63,174 and BR would pay a rent of £2,350 for 10 years, increasing to £3,000 afterwards. Preliminary work on restoration began on 24th February, 1970. Cleaning of the structure was done with acid and completed at the end of June with the two crests over the end porticos skilfully picked out in colour.

No. 45428 shunting in the Whitehall Road goods depot, Leeds, on 5th November, 1960. Whitehall Junction signal box is on the left. *Author*

The 09.28 Marsden to Leeds passes through Farnley & Wortley station on 10th September, 1967. The wooden warehouse & adjoining building were part of the earlier station on the Leeds, Dewsbury & Manchester route. *Author*

At Dewsbury track economies saw the two central through lines abolished. Likewise at Stalybridge the down through line was lifted and the up through line made into a siding. In December 1964 the Huddersfield station turntable was removed. On the Delph branch there was an enthusiasts' special on 17th April, 1964. Track lifting took place there in September, followed by demolition of the Greenfield – Oldham branch which had lasted until the end of 1964. The Heckmondwike line was kept open to allow renewal of the old LD&M bridge at Webster Hill, Dewsbury built by Samuel Butler of Stanningley in 1848. It was replaced on 14th July, 1965 by a double-span concrete bridge made by Austins of Dewsbury over a widened road and dual carriageway.

On the Micklehurst line track was lifted from Micklehurst goods yard, Friezland Gas Works Sidings and Stalybridge and Millbrook goods. 1965 saw lifting of sidings at Tunnel End, Linthwaite and Heaton Lodge. The original station at Bradley was also demolished but some traces remained. One of the last LNWR semaphore signals disappeared when Hillhouse No. 1 down home was renewed. Signal boxes at Heaton Lodge and Hillhouse No. 4 were demolished in mid-1965. Demolition of the 'New' line north of Liversedge had reached the west end of Gomersal tunnel by 12th June, 1966 and Gildersome by July. On 11th September the demolition train ran back out of control coming to grief at Farnley Junction. At Birstall Town the double-span bridge over the A62 was taken down on 21st September but the site had then become an eyesore as isolated masonry abutments remained. On the section west of Heckmondwike 'WD' class 2-8-0 No. 90680(55G) was used on the first demolition train on 26th September, 1966 and on 15th April, 1967 '8F' class 2-8-0 No. 48522 was so used on the New Scarborough viaduct. Track lifting ended at a point parallel with ex-L&Y main line which became Heaton Lodge East Junction. Dismantling of the Kirkburton branch began on 25th July, 1966 and ended when it reached British Dyes Siding on 1st September when 'WD' class 2-8-0 No. 90649 worked the last demolition train. The skew bridge over Wakefield Road at Tandem was taken down on 14th August.

Track re-modelling took place at Batley when, on 17th April, 1966, Birstall Junction, Batley West and Dewsbury No. 2 boxes were closed. Lady Anne Crossing box was renamed Batley and Batley Loop was abolished. A new spur, 220 yards in length on a one in 80 gradient was opened on the same day linking the LNWR line facing Dewsbury with the GNR Chickenley Heath branch. On the GNR line from Batley to Adwalton Junction which crossed over the LNWR at Lady Anne Crossing, the huge Warren span was taken down on 27th February, 1966.

At Diggle Junction the box had its frame reduced from 81 levers to just 13, the down loop was the only refuge accommodation remaining, while the buildings on the down north platform were demolished and all sidings lifted. At Stalybridge, platforms 1 and 2 (both bays) and the entire L&Y yard were lifted. Only one refuge siding remained at Mossley. Stalybridge re-signalling was completed on 6th November, 1966 when the LNWR No. 1 and No. 4 boxes were closed and No. 2 (GCR) modernized. No. 1 was sited adjacent to the Pointsman Inn near Clarence Street. Stalybridge No. 3 (L&Y) had been taken down some years earlier and was on an elevated gantry between the platforms.

In June 1967 Linthwaite box, a modern structure erected in 1955 to replace an elevated LNWR box, was demolished. At Springwood Junction the connection from the north lines to the Penistone branch was removed in April. The down platform buildings were cleared from Greenfield during the summer of 1967 and the down north platform at Diggle shortened. On the Heckmondwike line, the bridge over Huddersfield Road at Battyeford was taken down in July, the nearby Warren span over the Calder was lowered on jacks and in October was at a height of 6 feet above water level.

At Farnley Junction the signal box, locomotive shed, barracks and ash plant were cleared in October 1967. By September 1967 the demolition of Leeds Central station and LNWR/L&Y joint goods was in hand. At Marsden clearance occurred of an original H&MR&CC building on the up south platform. Latterly used as a 'Gents' it survived the construction of newer buildings in 1894 and their demolition in 1953. A major reconstruction at Huddersfield during 1968 was to the bridge carrying the A642 over Huddersfield tunnel, repaired under Operation Bridgeguard. Demolition of Hillhouse Shed commenced on 1st January, 1968 and was completed by 24th May. The box at Spen Valley Junction was cleared on 11th March, 1968. At Stalybridge half of the roof and some buildings were demolished. At Greenfield there was the removal of a water tank on the north platform. At Mirfield the bay platforms were disconnected at the end of 1968. Hillhouse No. 2 and Red Doles Junction boxes were taken out of use on 30th December after a period of partial use and Slaithwaite box also closed.

At Hillhouse shed demolition included: the water tower cleared on 18th June; plant on 19th June and the coaling plant on 7th July leaving only the footbridge that led to the shed. In 1969 a fresh start was made on cutting up the Warren bridge at Battyeford and piecemeal demolition of the Mickhlehurst line. The line was intact west of Butterhouse tunnel.

Hillhouse No. 1 signal box, 4th June, 1969.   *Author*

Longwood station went in September as did the station buildings at Golcar. The down platform buildings went at Morley and Dewsbury was repainted.

Amidst an atmosphere of wholesale destruction, there was one exception. Work commenced on 17th October, 1969 of the Heaton Lodge underpass connecting the stub of the Heckmondwike line with the L&Y main line, entailing a short length of track being laid.

In April 1969 the timber buildings on the up platform at Batley were cleared. Huddersfield refreshment room closed on 20th April and the down fast line between Marsden and Gledholt Junction was abolished on 5th April. Meanwhile, on the same day Manchester Exchange station closed to passenger traffic, although its island platforms Nos. 4 and 5 remained in use for newspaper trains. All passenger service now transferred to Manchester Victoria thus eliminating one of the longest platforms, or to be more exact, platform 11 at Victoria and platform 3 at Exchange, whose combined length amounted to 2,194 feet and had been opened by the Railway Queen on 16th April, 1929. Pending new legislation to be introduced, most platform hoists were taken out of service with that at Huddersfield (passenger) ending on 23rd May and a replacement costed at £18,000.

On the Kirkburton branch one side of a huge cutting near Tandem was removed and the cleared site became an extension of Kirkheaton Ballast tip. At Huddersfield a new narrow crossing was erected at the east end of the station in November 1969, platforms 4 and 5 had their lengths reduced by 75 feet and platform 1 by 15 feet. At Farnley Junction the former New Line bridge over the A62 was removed on 13th October while Slaithwaite station was cleared in November 1969.

Events at Standedge could never be taken for granted. On 30th May, 1964 a torrential rain storm flooded the tunnels to a depth of 5 feet and the 19.45 Trans-Pennine dmu Leeds to Liverpool became stranded midway. Passengers were eventually rescued after walking over duck boards to a relief train. Another flood on 13th July, 1965 caused much dislocation and diversion of traffic. Under the auspices of the Channel Tunnel Company, a special eight-car test train hauled by D1996 was given complete possession of both single line tunnels on 13th June, 1966 for obtaining measurements of air pressure and wind speed to assist determining the size of locomotives required for Chunnel use. Thirty-one ventilating ducts were sealed off and the trains passed through at speeds between 35 and 55 mph. No. D1766 was used on further tests which lasted until 16th June.

Both single line tunnels closed to traffic on Saturday 29th October, 1966, the last trains to use them were:

>   17.40   Manchester Victoria – Leeds dmu
>   15.15   Crewe – Healey Mills goods hauled by 70015 *Apollo*
>   21.50   Hereford / Wigan TPO hauled by D6790
>   21.45   Leeds – Stockport Parcels hauled by 73139 (9H)

The next day a new connection was made at Marsden from the up fast to the up slow. Closure of the Micklehurst line and the Standedge single line tunnels commonly caused delays of up to 30 minutes but by Christmas the matter had been resolved. Following closure, a connection from what was now the up loop was left in position leading to the original 1849 tunnel to act as a trap for any train which overran signals. This did happen to an up goods which entered the down line tunnel. It reversed a short while later without mishap, although the curve leading to the tunnel slewed to a new alignment and was almost devoid of ballast at one point. The train concerned and those who bore responsibility for this occurrence were not identified!

In January, 1969 the water troughs at Standedge were removed when major repairs were undertaken and continuous welded rail installed. In respect of accidents a down goods passing Longwood on 23rd November, 1964 hauled by 'WD' 2-8-0 No. 90581 got out of control and was diverted into Hillhouse Yard where it collided with the back of a stationary goods and caused damage to eight wagons.

On 1st August, 1967 a dmu forming the 15.51 Greenfield to Stockport was derailed at Greenfield which delayed all services. After this had

Denton Junction with a Swindon-built Stanier 2-8-0 No. 48428 on a Llandudno excursion that has travelled via Guide Bridge. The tracks on the left lead to Droylsden and Crowthorn Junction, while those on the right are the Hooley Hill route to Stalybridge.

Author

been cleared the breakdown train was itself derailed at the same place but not before the 00.15 Manchester – Newcastle Newspaper train entered the same block section. The latter returned to Manchester, then took the L&Y route. On 17th November, 29 vehicles ran back out of control and came to grief near Hillhouse No. 2. Two tank wagons loaded with liquefied ammonia overturned.

On 12th January, 1969 a derailed parcels van fractured the main compressed air pipe controlling all points at Leeds City. Between 50 and 60 services were cancelled, the 09.50 to Manchester was the first to get away when a restricted service started. Trans-Pennine services were diverted via Normanton. A further mishap was on 2nd July when a freak storm blocked the line in several places between Mossley and Diggle, at Droylsden and at OA&GB Junction where earth was washed down embankments to block the line. It was during this year that welded track was first used on 'The Yorkshire Lines' between Greenfield and Mossley. The line between Oldham and OA&GB Junction was closed to all traffic on 1st May, 1967, one of the last trains being hauled by class '5MT' 4-6-0 No. 44924(9F) on the 20.25 Oldham-Stockport parcels.

Filming of the television production 'Inheritance' (Phyllis Bentley) took place on 3rd July at Park Bridge and featured a railway collision. Two replica 1838 coaches were constructed, while the locomotive was an enlarged photograph of No. 3020 *Cornwall* mounted on block board and propped up on the track.

An unusual visitor to 'The Yorkshire Lines' was the erstwhile Midland Pullman on a journey from Reddish to Leeds. The first of the three locomotive sheds to serve the route, Lees closed on 13th April, 1964 and Farnley Junction shed followed on 26th November, 1966. Hillhouse shed closed to steam on 2nd January, 1967 when it became a signing-on point for drivers using diesel locomotives. This ended on 5th November, 1967.

With the closure of the shed at Normanton on 1st January, 1968 steam workings became much reduced and all originated from the London Midland Region with arriving engines being promptly returned to their home sheds. However, during the first three months of 1968 some 15 steam-hauled goods trains were seen, the final one thought to have been class '8F' 2-8-0 No. 48678 noted at Slaithwaite on 24th June. The 'Farewell to Steam' rail tour took place on 4th August when class '5MT' 4-6-0s Nos. 44871 and 44894 ran between Stalybridge and Bradley Wood Junction followed by Nos. 44874 and 45017 with a second train. Dewsbury (Wellington Road) changed its name to Dewsbury on 20th February, 1969.

Another notable event on 29th September, 1969 was the abolition of the Huddersfield Joint Omnibus Committee. Of its fleet of 96 vehicles, those displaying odd numbers bore the name of railway ownership. Operating throughout the Huddersfield area, they provided frequent services, cheap fares and a safety record that was second to none. Locally managed, its operations elicited some criticism but little praise.

The end-on junction of the Hooley Hill line (in the foreground) and the Stalybridge Junction line. This is the site of the former connection from the Hooley Hill line and the MS&LR at Dukinfield Junction, used by LNWR traffic before the Stalybridge Junction line was opened. *Author*

CHAPTER FOURTEEN

1970 – 2000

The demolition of former LNWR property continued. Removal of surplus track allowed easing of curves by using the increased space provided. Constructive measures were few and far between. At Copley Hill the Carriage and Wagon long shed, the up yard and the down yard – always known as 'loco yard' were demolished. From 16th April, 1970 Gledholt Sidings reopened to allow delivery of some 100,000 tons of stone from Tunstead in connection with making the M62 Motorway. This involved the train running past its delivery point onto Huddersfield viaduct where the engine ran round. The final train ran on 1st October, 1970. The demolition of Deighton goods offices took place in 1970. The line into Leeds Central HL goods from Three Signal Bridge Junction was closed on 2nd March, 1970. As from 1st February, 1970 station masters were renamed area managers.

At Mirfield platforms were reduced in length and a new high speed crossover introduced which utilized signalling from the 1932 scheme. The Bradley Wood branch was signalled at the same time. At Dewsbury the down platform was shortened at its east end causing the Birstall bay

A five-car Trans-Pennine dmu forming the 15.35 Hull to Liverpool near Heaton Lodge. The trackbed of the Leeds New line curves away in front of the train. The photograph was taken on 15th May, 1970. Later remodelling saw the curve, on which the train is travelling, reduced to single track. *Author*

Interior view of the former gents' urinal on platform 1 at Huddersfield station on 7th June, 1972.
Author

LNWR cast-iron signs still attached to a platform pillar at Huddersfield, photographed in 1975.
Author

to vanish, as did the huge goods warehouse opposite. The up and down fast lines from Hillhouse to Bradley and Hollidays Sidings closed on 4th October, 1971, with the latter signal box and those at Bradley Junction and Kirkburton Junction abolished. At Hillhouse Sidings 72 concrete girders arrived for the M62 Motorway. The last train from Kirkburton Junction to British Dyes Sidings was on 25th February, 1971. The empty tanks were returned to Deighton instead of British Dyes Sidings by ICI No. 2, a Sentinel diesel shunter. On 31st March, 1971 the Heckmondwike Chemical Co's Siding closed, a short line that ran from Heckmondwike Goods on the Leeds New line.

An accident occurred at Standedge on 8th November, 1970 when two hopper wagons in a ballast train were derailed. The Holbeck steam crane arrived but was also derailed. Re-railing was accomplished in a foul atmosphere of diesel fumes from locomotives and from contractor's plant used to dig foundations for a new trackbed.

On 21st February, 1971 a three-car dmu struck the buffers in a bay platform at Huddersfield, reported to be at a speed of 35 mph. Fortunately the train was empty. On 9th April, 1971 a dmu overran a Huddersfield bay platform causing injury to three people.

In May 1971 goods traffic through Standedge was down to 16 trains daily. A year later outward ash traffic was despatched from Hillhouse Sidings, having been brought from the former L&Y tip at Greetland. In 1973 inwards cement wagons began to use Hillhouse although in neither case was the traffic sustained.

The first ever visit by rail of a reigning monarch took place on 4th October, 1971 when the Royal Train conveying HM The Queen arrived from Euston via Stockport (where fresh motive power had taken over). The route was via Ashton Moss North Junction, Ashton Branch Siding and the L&Y main line to Bradley Wood Junction, to arrive in Huddersfield without the need for shunting. The train overshot the red carpet before setting back into the correct position! The locomotives were class '40s' Nos. D216 *Campania* and D225 *Lusitania*. Her Majesty made a further appearance on 6th May, 1974 en route non stop from Scunthorpe to Lowton with the Royal train hauled by class '25s' Nos. 25068 and 25069.

The remodelled Heaton Lodge Junction became operational on 26th April, 1970 while the Bradley Wood branch was resignalled on 31st May. The most bizarre scheme ever foisted on 'The Yorkshire Lines' ended in May 1970 when the Liverpool – Newcastle services resumed calling at Huddersfield after an absence of 18 months. However, there was a general desire to discontinue unremunerative passenger services. A meeting arranged between the West Yorkshire local authorities and South

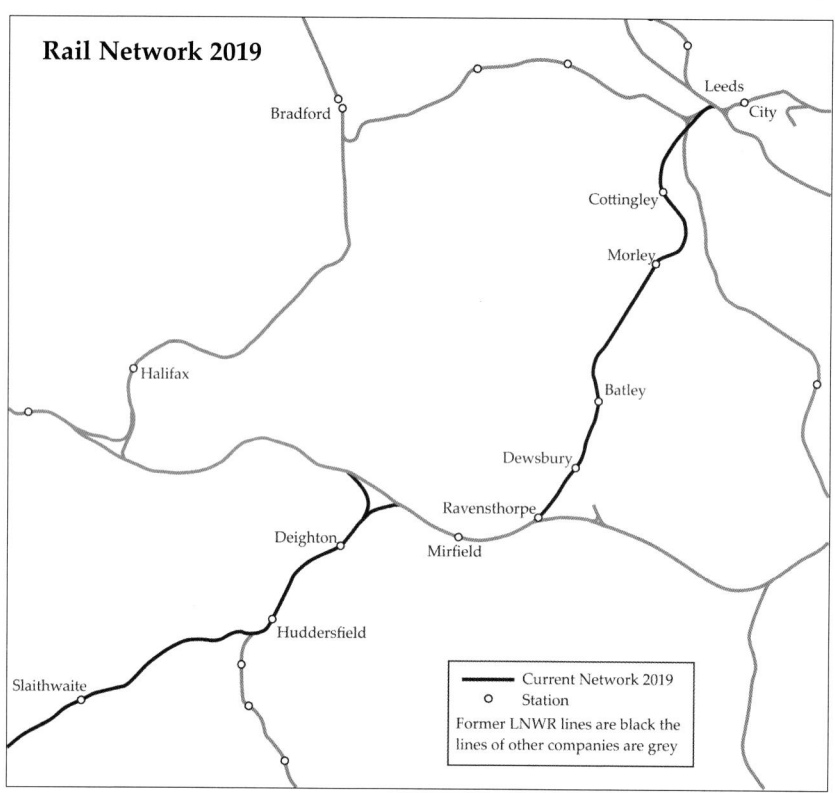

East Lancashire and North East Cheshire (SELNEC) towards ending the Stockport – Stalybridge service heard the second proposals in 1972 rejected. Had it been approved the line between Dukinfield Junction and Stalybridge would be closed entirely. A 30 page Heads of Information compared existing facilities and alternative suggestions. The objectors included 282 individuals, two MP's, 17 local authorities and four petitions bearing 1,806 signatures. A 25 page amended Heads of Information contemplated Trans-Pennine passenger trains stopping at Ashton (Charlestown) instead of Stalybridge to make better connection with SELNEC-operated Trans Lancs Express buses, acclaimed as an ideal substitute at peak hours. Alternate rail routes between Manchester Victoria and Piccadilly stations were suggested in response to some objectors. One example allowed no more than 10 minutes during the morning peak to allow passage between those places!

In West Yorkshire a Bullseye ticket was introduced offering competitive fares over a 30 mile radius and with it the first glimmer of hope for the future! Government plans to reduce still further the national rail network were upset when the *Sunday Times* disclosed that in the West Riding the annual decline in ridership of 5 per cent changed to a 2.2 per cent increase or 8.8 per cent in receipts as a result of a 'take a new look at your railway service' and a further increase of 5 per cent was expected in 1973. By October 1973 the increase in patronage between Leeds and Huddersfield was 13.2 per cent with a total of 62,243 or 7,283 passengers more than in the corresponding months of 1972. A further initiative was undertaken on 5th March, 1974 when a new Tuesdays-only shoppers' train commenced between Huddersfield and Manchester, instituted at the behest of SELNEC Passenger Transport Executive (PTE).

The Renaissance Unfolds

Local government reorganization of 1974 gave both West Yorkshire and Greater Manchester PTE's responsibility for all passenger services by municipalities and control of private operators. Services from Leeds to Huddersfield had some trains extended to Marsden while the Day Rover ticket which started in July 1976 provided unlimited travel by train and bus. Electric traction between Guide Bridge and Ashton Moss North ceased on 1st August, 1970. Park Bridge viaduct was demolished in 1971, less than 10 years after it had been rebuilt.

The up loop Gledholt to Standedge was closed on 31st January, 1971. In 1973 the remaining buildings at Greenfield were demolished and the Huddersfield National Carriers Ltd warehouse closed on 26th January, 1974 as the £4,000 annual rate bill had made it uneconomic. Huddersfield viaduct had three arches cleaned at the expense of the local authority, the first of many so treated. Maintenance work on Huddersfield's two tunnel shafts resulted in the newer one having its height reduced by 30 feet in January 1974.

On 1st March, 1975 the 14.40 dmu ex-Leeds hit the buffers at Huddersfield station platform 6. In the same month the issue of Edmundson tickets at Huddersfield came to an end. 1976 saw the closure of Hillhouse coal depot on 29th June and its siding was cleared for the final time on 2nd July.

The York – Shrewsbury TPO was discontinued on Saturdays and Sundays from 9th October. New footbridges were installed during the year at Wards Sidings, Morley and Diggle. Marsden station was given a facelift. The remaining stub of the Mickluhurst line between Stalybridge and Hartshead Power station was closed 5th May, 1976 when 08602

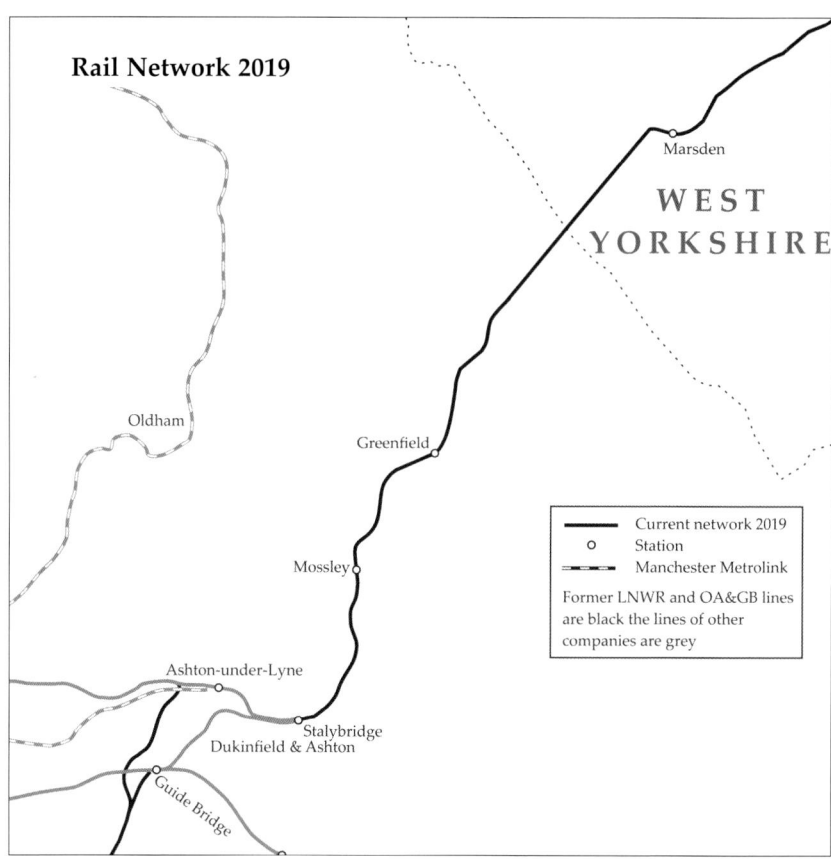

worked an inspection train. Gledholt Junction box was closed 1st March, 1976 and later class '56' No. 56006 appeared on 1,102 ton test trains over Standedge.

On 5th September, 1977 there was an accident at Farnley Junction, 47402 was diverted from the up main line to the Farnley Mineral branch and collided with the 20.40 Liverpool – Hull train which caused the death of both drivers. The accident was due to signal maintenance error. In August and September 1977 the Huddersfield north tunnel was under repair, the roof in particular was given attention.

In February 1978 the Greenfield station subway was replaced by a bridge that formerly served at Watford Junction. Longwood Goods box closed in July 1978. The bridge over John William Street, Huddersfield was, after local representations, repainted in the ornate style required by its enabling Act of Parliament.

On 18th June, 1979 'Deltic' No. 55015 *Tulyar* began to operate regularly between York and Liverpool. It also put in some appearances on the 21.50 ex-York TPO as far as Stockport, returning with the eastbound TPO to York. 1979 saw Trans-Pennine services radically altered (14th May, 1979) and Huddersfield booking hall was remodelled. On 4th August, 1979 parcel traffic was transferred to Bradford Forster Square which led to the closure of the old LMS Road Motor Engineers' Department on Park Drive, Huddersfield. The year also saw a derailment at Heaton Lodge Junction on 11th July.

Restoration of Farnley viaduct started on 2nd May, 1980 to enable it to be used by Leeds, Wakefield and Doncaster trains as from 2nd May, 1981. The prototype class '140' dmu was used between Leeds and Marsden, but the use of 'Deltics' finished on 4th January, 1982. On 11th November, 1980 No. 46229 *Duchess of Montrose* worked a Liverpool – York special over 'The Yorkshire Lines'. From that time onwards locomotive-hauled trains became rarer.

Work on Huddersfield tunnel was completed on 17th September. A new platform was added at Marsden and used by up trains in 1981. The general carriage of parcels came to an end, apart from the Red Star premium service in 1981. The viaduct line at Huddersfield was remodelled in July 1981. New girders were fitted to the eastern end of Huddersfield tunnel in September with a new pediment which cost £350,000 and the whole project £500,000.

The girders of the footbridge close to Bank House Lane at Paddock (known to generations of Huddersfield enthusiasts as Cuckoo Bridge) were taken down and renewed during August and September 1981. The bridge re-opened on 16th October.

1981 saw the first visit to 'The Yorkshire Lines' of a High Speed Train. In December a new Slaithwaite bridge was installed. A further steam appearance was of former Southern Railway 4-6-0 *Lord Nelson* in June 1981 which returned in July in company with LMS No. 5305 and 46229 *Duchess of Hamilton*.

At Oldham Clegg Street the new parcel depot ended its life in June 1981. A month earlier a class '40'-hauled rail tour ran between Heckmondwike curve and the Charrington-Hargreaves depot at Liversedge, the only such tour to operate on the line. In September 1981 the BR Bill for the next Parliamentary session included reactivating part of the Kirkburton branch to British Dyes Sidings and part of the OA&GB between Guide Bridge and Ashton Moss North Junction.

In 1982 the last of the Swindon Trans-Pennine dmus was withdrawn as were 'Deltic' locomotives. General feelings of the use of the 'Deltics'

The viaduct carrying the approach road to Cleckheaton station on the Leeds New line, 25th March, 1982, the viaduct was listed in 1984 and now carries a footpath. *Author*

The deep cutting, spanned by many bridges, that took the Leeds New line through the centre of Heckmondwike. The single track line extended to Liversedge oil terminal.

Author

through Huddersfield on a regular basis could be described as inspirational. Opening occurred of a new station at Deighton on 26th April, located on the main line and not on the Kirkburton branch as the earlier station had been. Slaithwaite station followed in December. On 3rd September, 1982 class '25' No. 25151 ran out of control to crash at Hillhouse sidings. On 14th January the Liverpool – York service was extended to Scarborough. As from 17th May, 1982 an improved stopping train service began to Manchester. The bridge in Gledholt Bank was renewed in October 1982.

1983 saw the renewal of Ravensthorpe station bridge and the LD&M line was closed for repairs to the bridge over the Calder and Hebble Navigation. Ravensthorpe station displayed the paint date 1984. Class '141' dmu was inaugurated in September 1984 and in June 1984 the bridge carrying the Dobcross ironworks' branch over the Huddersfield Narrow Canal was demolished. Due to the liquidation of the Charrington-Hargreaves company, the line to Liversedge Spen was closed and later lifted. The oil terminal had been mothballed since 1984.

By September 1987 'Sprinter' and 'Pacer' diesel units were in regular use. 1987 also saw the Marsden canal bridge replaced between 28th and 30th November, a major undertaking. The Bradley Wood branch was used for the final time by diverted trains from Manchester to Huddersfield on 20th September, 1987. The Farnley viaduct's tight curves made it unsuitable for electrification and the last scheduled train passed over it on 11th October, 1987. Most of the track was lifted soon after except for a spur

The newly opened (basic) station on the main line at Deighton, 26th April, 1982. *Author*

Ceremonial opening of Cottingley station on 25th March, 1988. *Author*

at the station end, that too was deemed surplus to requirements in 2000. on On 2nd December, 1987 the Royal Train arrived at Huddersfield from Crigglestone conveying HRH Prince Charles. The train, which was hauled by class '47' *Ely Cathedral*, returned empty to Wolverton.

In 1988 the remodelling of Heaton Lodge Junction was completed. Cottingley station, between Morley and Leeds, was opened on 24th April. The York – Shrewsbury TPO carried passengers for the last time on 13th May and henceforth ran via Manchester Piccadilly. On 10th July the final newspaper trains from Manchester Victoria ran over 'The Yorkshire Lines' as did the corresponding 'Red Bank empties'. These two trains had used the former (island) platforms 4 and 5 at Manchester Exchange station.

From 15th May, 1989 new timetabling saw services running via Manchester Piccadilly. Starting on 7th October, 1989 remodelling track at Huddersfield station took place. The end came (except for one train Fridays only) for the Stockport – Stalybridge service.

In November 1989 a collision occurred on Huddersfield viaduct between two dmus which caused injury to 35 passengers and railwaymen.

In 1989 Speedlink freight service ceased. The Farnley Mineral branch closed. At Mirfield the bridge by the station was struck by a lorry which was driven away carrying one of the girders! A new platform 111 yards long on the up slow line at Mirfield was brought into use in May 1990.

Dewsbury had its third line reinstalled (down) and Leeds, Whitehall Road depot closed in March 1991. It was the last active former LNWR 'Yorkshire Lines' goods depot, in its time the most modern installation in Leeds. In May 1990 work finished on Huddersfield track remodelling. Freight via Standedge remained at just four trains daily, while a new freight from Scunthorpe to Stalybridge was the only new traffic hauled over 'The Yorkshire Lines'. In 1991 the Whitehaven – Huddersfield TPO ended its operation.

A derailment to a ballast train occurred at Marsden on 29th March, 1993. The Bangor Mail ended its long life without any ceremony in May 1994. The year also included the long awaited removal of scaffolding from the front of Huddersfield station. In May 1995 the former Whitehall Road goods station became the construction depot for the Aire Valley electrification.

In May 1996 the Liverpool – Newcastle service was simplified. During 1998 Golcar station bridge was half renewed, the portion over the up and down main lines. In February Northern Spirit, operator of the Trans-Pennine services introduced a Premier class of travel, available on payment of supplementary fare. In a section of coach divided from the rest of the train, improved comfort, lighting and facilities were provided. Also in July the £150M modernization of Leeds City station was inaugurated, due for completion in 2001 to enable the

Whitehall Road goods depot, Leeds (LNWR/L&YR joint), in 1959. The depot closed in March 1991 and was afterwards used as the contractor's yard for the Aire valley electrification scheme. *Author*

Thomas Grainger's skew arch, built to carry the Leeds, Dewsbury & Manchester Railway over Gelderd Road in Leeds. The photograph was taken on 11th May, 2000, when the arch was temporarily uncovered during the replacement of the girder bridge which spans the abutments in the foreground. *Author*

station to deal with almost a third more trains than before. English, Welsh and Scottish Railways foresaw a vast increase in freight traffic using the route and envisaged reopening one of the two disused Standedge tunnels. In March 1999 Greenfield box was removed and signalling between Stalybridge and Diggle Junction modernized, whilst at the OA&GB Junction a modern small timber BR box dating from 1957 was also removed.

During 1999 the Canker Lane Bridge at Huddersfield was renewed in respect of up and down north lines. Bradley Wood branch was re-laid in September 1999. A temporary single platform station, Leeds Whitehall, was built in 1999 to serve trains diverted during the Modernization Scheme. The temporary station was at the edge of the former Whitehall Road goods depot, adjacent to Whitehall Junction. Work on the Leeds Modernization Scheme included reconstruction of Globe Road bridge at Christmas 1999.

As the millennium passed the future looked much healthier than for many years. A future where safety, congestion and the environment would be accorded their real significance.

Reinforcing abutments of Gelderd Road bridge, Leeds.

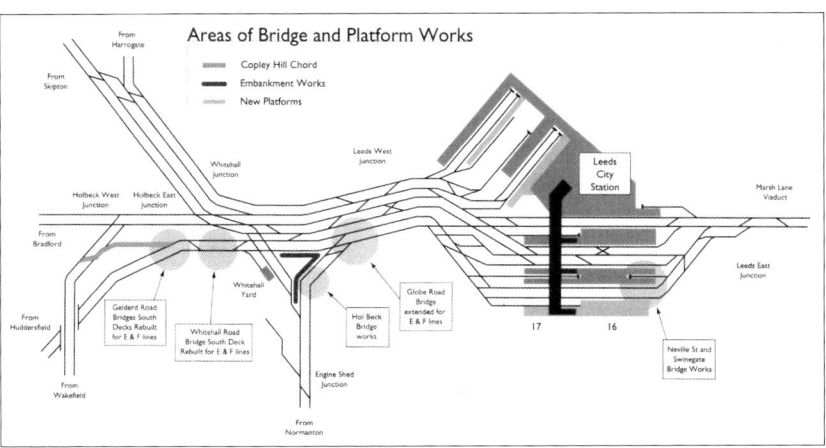

Leeds modernization.

Platforms 16 and 17 under construction

Leeds Canal Junction, May 1960, with City station in the background.   *Author*

Reconstruction of the bridge at Canal Junction Leeds, 6th May, 1961.   *Author*

APPENDIX ONE

Lists of Copley Hill Engines as given by two stalwart drivers. A number of apparent anomalies will be noted.

COPLEY HILL ENGINES 1858. From a list by driver John Wells.

Single Wheel Sharps Nos. 444 *Aldham*, 445 *Brook*, 446 *Huddersfield* 426, 453 *Meteor*, 454, 455, 456, 457, 458.
Single Trevithick No. 115. Four-coupled 203 *St George* 482.
Single Wheel *Nasmyth* No. 451.
Six-coupled Sharps Nos. 465, 466, 467, 271 *Minotaur*, 275 *Vulcan*, 295, 302 *Hector*, 308 *Booth*, 309 *Huish*. Stephenson six-coupled 463. E.B. Wilson six-coupled 438 and 416 possibly with Sharps Gab motion. Stephenson mid feather firebox 463.
Mr Wells also recalled in his cleaning days 459, 460.
462 Sharps six-coupled goods non mid feather firebox.
Ramsbottom 452, 345 *Turk*, 519, 558, 220 *Waterloo*.
65 Woodstock (Wheatstone).
And single wheel types 64 *Odin*, 128 *Swallow*, 79 *Belted Will*, 14 *Witch*, 194 *Ruby* and 366 *Nestor*.
The list concludes with the remark 'got an engine in eight years''.

COPLEY HILL ENGINES 1858-9 by George Hinchcliffe

14 *Witch*	6 feet single
51 *Turk*	6 feet single
64 *Odin*	6 feet single
79 *Belted Will*	6 feet single
81 *Greystoke*	5 feet 2-4-0
115 *Meteor*	6 feet single
271 *Minotaur*	0-6-0 Sharp Stewart
275 *Vulcan*	0-6-0 Sharp Stewart
276 *Pluto*	0-6-0 Sharp Stewart
295 *Penmaenmawr*	0-6-0 Sharp Stewart
304 *Hector*	0-6-0 Sharp Stewart
303 *Booth*	0-6-0 Sharp Stewart
309 *Huish*	0-6-0 Sharp Stewart
459	0-6-0 Sharp Stewart
425	7 feet single Sharp Stewart (worked by pumps)
453	7 feet single Sharp Stewart (worked by pumps)
454	7 feet single Sharp Stewart (worked by pumps)
455	7 feet single Sharp Stewart (worked by pumps)
456	7 feet single Sharp Stewart (worked by pumps)
457	7 feet single Sharp Stewart (worked by pumps)
458	7 feet single Sharp Stewart (worked by pumps)
469	7 feet single Sharp Stewart (worked by pumps)
436	E.B. Wilson 0-6-0 (all wheels in front of firebox)

437	E.B. Wilson 0-6-0 (all wheels in front of firebox)
438	E.B. Wilson 0-6-0 (all wheels in front of firebox)
462 *Stephenson*	E.B. Wilson 0-6-0 (all wheels in front of firebox)
463	E.B. Wilson 0-6-0 (all wheels in front of firebox)
464	E.B. Wilson 0-6-0 (all wheels in front of firebox)
465	E.B. Wilson 0-6-0 (all wheels in front of firebox)

The final entry is 410, 415 same as 425.

APPENDIX TWO

ASSISTANT ENGINES

This expression was used in the LNWR working timetable and appendices. An assistant engine could take many forms. An express train would be supplied with an assistant engine over part of a route, but it was never 'piloted'.

For the LNWR a bank engine was a locomotive that assisted a train to climb an incline, either from the front, or more commonly, from the rear. The bank engine was added to the train at the foot of the incline and was detached, at the top. When not assisting, its duties might include shunting at a smaller yard or trip working between two places.

The term 'pilot' described a particular duty eg passenger pilot at a large station where there may be an up side pilot or a down side pilot. In goods yard or sidings there might be the top yard pilot, low yard pilot or coal chutes pilot. It was rare for the LNWR to 'bank' their trains but exceptions did arise eg *Chequerbent, Shap* etc.

APPENDIX THREE

STABLING VEHICLES

It was common practice for wagons placed in sidings, especially those with a handbrake on one side only to be secured by a number of safeguards.

A hinged chock with a screw down section was located near to the siding exit. Any vehicle running against this would be derailed. Sometimes a chain would be placed between the wheel spokes and then fastened round the rail and locked. It was not uncommon for a loose wagon to run out onto the main line, often in a strong wind.

APPENDIX FOUR

TUNNEL NAMES

Until BR times Standedge was the name given to the canal tunnel. The railway tunnels were known to drivers and guards from Manchester or Liverpool as Marsden tunnel. Likewise Yorkshire personnel called it Diggle tunnel. Butterhouse tunnel on the Micklehurst line had the alternative name of Ryefields. Lydgate tunnel on the Oldham branch was known as either Springhead, Grasscroft or Grotton and at one time in early LMS days bore a painted board 'Grotton Tunnel 1334 yards' at the Oldham end.

APPENDIX FIVE

CLOSURES

Howley Park	1930
West End	1930
Morley Gas Works	1940
Bottom Hall Sidings	1949
Dewsbury	2nd June, 1952
Farnley and Wortley (up sdgs 6/67)	3rd November, 1952
Battyeford	5th October, 1953
Northorpe Higher	5th October, 1953
Fieldhouse Siding	1953
Grotton and Springhead	2nd May, 1955
Gildersome	13th June, 1955
Linthwaite	1st November, 1958
Liversedge Spen	2nd May, 1960
(Charrington Hargreaves Depot 1963-1986)*	
Cleckheaton	2nd May, 1960
Micklehurst	14th February, 1962
Droylsden LNWR/L&Y	24th November, 1962
Birstall	18th June, 1962
Carlinghow	18th June, 1962
Tunnel End	3rd January, 1963
Stalybridge TE Sidings	11th January, 1963
Mirfield Yard	14th October, 1963
Black Rock Sidings	11th January, 1963
Droylsden Lumb Lane	15th July, 1963
Delph branch	4th November, 1963
Diggle	4th November, 1963
Lees	16th December, 1963
Park Bridge	1st February, 1964
Oldham Glodwick Road	13th April, 1964
Greenfield – Oldham	13th April, 1964
Staley and Millbrook	20th April, 1964
Uppermill	15th June, 1964
Ravensthorpe	10th August, 1964
CEGB Sidings	18th January, 1982
Heaton Lodge Sidings	1st October, 1984
Slaithwaite	5th October, 1964
Marsden	5th October, 1964
Dobcross Iron Works Sidings	1st November, 1964
Mossley	30th November, 1964
Friezland Goods	21st February, 1965
BD Siding – Kirkburton	5th April, 1965
Deighton	5th April, 1965

* To reach the Charrington Hargreaves depot all trains to and from Stanlow ran to Healey Mills and reversed before proceeding to the Heckmondwike curve.

Gomersal	2nd August, 1965
Birstall Town	2nd August, 1965
Mirfield Goods	6th September, 1965
Hillhouse Yard	3rd July, 1965 partial
	1st November, 1965 total
Stalybridge LY Yard	27th February, 1965
Spen Valley Junction - Heckmondwike	29th November, 1965
Copley Hill Yard	December 1965 final
	(5 siding up side June, 1964)
Longwood Goods	4th April, 1968
Scarwood (Shaws) Siding	4th April, 1966
Liversedge - Farnley	11th January, 1966
Copley Hill – Three Sig Br Junction	1st March, 1966
Ashton LNWR Goods	20th June, 1966
Standedge single line tunnels	29th October, 1966
Diggle Junction – Staley and Millbrook	30th October, 1966
Farnley Junction C'l Junction	18th November, 1966
Leeds Central	29th April, 1967
Oldham Clegg Street – OA&GB	21st May, 1967
Sutcliffe Sidings	1967
Royal George Siding	1967
Stalybridge Bayley Street LNW/GC	27th April, 1967
Stalybridge South	22nd July, 1967
Leeds Goods High Level	16th December, 1967
	2nd March, 1970
Oldham Clegg Street	1st January, 1968
Stalybridge Junction line	1st July, 1968
Gledholt Sidings	5th August, 1968
	reopened 23rd April, 1970
	final close October 1970
Greenfield	29th April, 1968
Dukinfield and Ashton	1st July, 1968
Huddersfield Goods	4th August, 1969
Hollidays Sidings	1971
Hartshead Power Station	June 1972 last train,
	line closed by earth slip 1976

INDEX

Accidents, 27-28, 30, 32, 38-39, 44, 49, 53, 58-60, 62-63, 67-69, 71-72, 74-75, 77, 78, 80, 88, 93, 106, 107, 110, 112, 115, 121, 124, 129, 135, 137, 139, 147, 149, 159, 161, 186, 193; Diggle, **158**; Friezland, **140**; Mirfield, 124; Springwood Junction, **32**
Aldam, William, 9
Ambulance train, 147
Bangor Mail, 28, 35, 46, 60, 67, 71, 120, 131, 141, 199
Batley, 13, 30, 41, 42, **43**, 58, **62**, **64**, 73, 76, 126, 146, 177, 178, 183, 185; accidents, 103; Birstal branch, 13, 41, 43; Lady Anne Crossing, **58**, **61**, 183
Batley Carr, 45, **45**, 83, 149
Beeching, Dr Richard, 169
Birstal branch, 13, 23, **25**, **42**, 73, 83, 108, 110, 139, 168, 171, 183, 189
Board of Trade, 66, 81, 123; accident inquiry, 68, 72; line inspection, 40, 49, 65, 69, 129
Booth, Henry, 11, 13, 14, 18
Bradford, 33, 44, 99; proposed LNWR lines to, 10, 13, 30, 31, 35, 40
Bradford Canal, 78, 81, **82**
Bradley Wood branch, 10, 16, **20**, 21, **21**, 54, 79, 92, 163, 188, 189, 191, 197, 200
British Dyes, 145, 146, 160, 176, 183, 191
Brook, Joseph, 9, 13, 15, 23
Brook, William Leigh, 15
Brooke, Colonel Thomas, 102, 107, 113, 120, 137
Bus services, 153, 154, 155, 161, 165, 175, 181
Calder and Hebble Navigation, 18, 56, 162, 197
Captain Laws, 7, 8
Copley Hill shed, 19, 28, 33, 63, 84, 86, 91
Delph branch, 8, **22**, 23, 33, 39, 85, 87, 110, 141, 156, 165, 174, 183
Dewsbury Junction Railway, 73, 82
Dewsbury station, **12**, 18, **50**, 83, 85, 101, 112, 171, 183, 185, 188, 189, 199; accidents, 68, 69, 70; demolition of LD&M building, 171; warehouse, 52, 146
Dewsbury viaduct, 41, **41**
Diesel dmu trials, 168
Diesel first services, 167
Electrification, 197, 199
Excursions, 27, 31, 37, 44, 53, 70, 76, 79, 108, 122, 159
Farnley; ironworks, 43, 57; Junction, 83, 129, 147, 169, 174, 178, 183, 184, 186; mineral branch, 57, **174**; North Junction, 88; shed, 91, 99, 161, 175, 188
Farnley viaduct, 90, 172, 177
Franco-Prussian war, 66
Frederick Swanwick, 7
Gladstone Agreement, 29
Gooch, T.L., 7
Gott, John, 13, 14, 15
Grainger, Thomas, 8, 13, 200
Great Northern Railway, 8; Batley, 30, **61**, 184; Leeds Central station, 49, 50; London services, 29, 31, 44, 53; Wakefield line172, 180

Guide Bridge, 39, 40, 72, 78, 82, 84, **89**, 91, 107, 149, 177, 193
Halifax; L&Y services to Huddersfield, 21, 61, 80, 92; LNWR services, 29, 33, 37, 46, 99; proposed Huddersfield lines, 45, 55, 57, 60, 66, 75, 92, 106
Healey Mills Yard, 174, 176
Hillhouse, 81, 85, 87, 91, **152**, 174, 176, 191, 193; accidents, 68, 95, 98, 103, 112, 137, 143, 186, 187, 197; wrong site for shed, 19; shed, 59, 158, 184, 188
Hirst, William Edwards, 53, 56, 70, 79, 89
Huddersfield and Leeds Railway, 7
Huddersfield and Manchester Railway and Canal Company, 8, 9, 19; armorial device, **19**; engineering features, 16; inaugural service, 13; Motto, 19
Huddersfield Broad Canal, see Sir Ramsden Canal
Huddersfield Canal, 8, 76, 113, 116, 120, **179**; closed by drought, 98, 131; deviations, 16, 83, 84; lock reconstruction, 63; tolls, 123; water supplied for locomotives, 70
Huddersfield
Huddersfield; accidents, 33, 45, 53, 54, 59, 68, 69, 80, 84, 86, 88, 93, 96, 97, 100, 106, 112, 115, 135, 139, 159, 191, 193, 198; goods warehouse, 33; goods yard, 178; improvements to station, 35, 64, 77, 94, 99, 109, 111, 115, 128, 159, 181, 185, 195, 198, 200; John William Street bridge, 85, **94**, **95**, 194; not worth stopping for, 8; platform renumbering, 167; poor facilities at station, 43, 56, 61, 65, 72, 79, 81, 97; proposed low level line, 7; speaking tube to Standedge tunnel, 83; station, 10, 16, 19, 21, 76, 81, 151, **153**, 158, 160, **162**, **165**, **166**, **172**, 185, **190**; Royal Train, 95, 101, 110, 191, 198; temporary wooden platforms, 61, 65; turntable removed, 183; tunnel, 10, 53, 68, 78, 80, 81, 88, 90, 94, 97, 105, 107, 184, 194, 195; tunnel, ventilation shafts, **6**, 193; viaduct, 10, 11, 12, 78, 85, 89, 94, 191; widening of line, 78, 81, 85, 89
Hull, 107, 117, 120, 131, 139, 143, 145
Irish Mail, 101, 135
Jee, Alfred S., 8, 9
Kirkburton; accidents, 62, 72, 73, 84, 95, 98, 115, 117; branch, 45, 50, 56, 57, 60, 63, 70, 95, 107, 137; horse bus, 64; mail for Clayton West, 95; proposed lines to, 54, 107; emporary platforms at Huddersfield, 61, 65
Lancashire & Yorkshire Railway; amalgamation with East Lancashire Railway, 33; amalgamation with LNWR, 72, 149; Bangor Mail, 28; Holbeck viaduct, 29; Huddersfield to Halifax route, 21; L&Y, LNWR conversion of Bradford Canal to Railway, 78, 81; L&Y, LNWR Huddersfield to Halifax line, 75; main line, 8, 46, 94, 97, 113, 117, 121, 130, 160, 185; Manchester

and Leeds Railway, 7, 13; operating LNWR trains, 14; opposition to LNWR Halifax line, 55, 61; running powers on Bradley Wood curve, 16, 79, 92; trains using Dewsbury route to Leeds, 14, 24, 28; Wakefield Road Yard Bradford, 99; Whitehall Road Goods Depot, 76, 87, **199**

Leeds and Thirsk Railway, 8, 9

Leeds Central Station, 14, 15, 17, 24, 118, 171, 180, 184, 189; GNR, 29, 49, 65; Joint Committee, 8

Leeds City station, 156, 168, 169, 171, 178, 181, 187, 199, **201**

Leeds New line, 113, 117, 123, 125, 127, 129, **130**, 174, 189, 191, **196**; accidents, 129

Leeds New station, 54, 65, 75, 81, 83, 85, 87, 107, 117, 120, 125, 128, 157, 159, 171; accidents, 124; becomes Leeds City, 156; fire, 117

Leeds (Holbeck) viaduct, 13, 15, 18, 50, **87**, 178

Leeds Wellington station (Midland), 14, 37, 54, 81, 91, 95; as Leeds City (North), 171, 178, 181; LNWR services, 14, 118; Royal Train, 146

Leeds Wellington Street station, 14, 24; proposals, 8

Leeds, Dewsbury and Manchester Railway, 8, 9, 11, 13, 15, 18, 19, 24, 28, 141, **200**; main line, 43, 93, 113, 130, 146, 178, 183, 197; workers' housing, **86**

Leeds, North Yorkshire and Durham Railway, proposal, 49

Loch, George, 9, 11

Locke, Joseph, 8, 26

London Midland & Scottish Railway, 150, 151, 153, 154, 155, 156, 158, 159, 162, 176

M62 Motorway, 189, 191

Mail train, 28

Manchester and Leeds Railway, 7, 13

Manchester Exchange station, 96, **112**, 122, 178, 181, 185, 198

Manchester Victoria, 16, 29, 72, 99, 185, 192, 198

Marcus, Henry, 23, 27

Marindin, Major Francis, 90, 91

Micklehurst line, 84, 90, 93, 94, 97, 98, 99, 100, 103, 126, 136, 137, 140, 146, 155, 158, 161, 173, 176, 183, 184, 186, 193

Midland Railway, 23, 29, 30, 33, 50, 54, 63, 65, 117, 165, 169; at Huddersfield, 65, 66, 78, 79, 81; proposed lines, 54, 75

Midland Railway, Wellington station, 14, 54

Moon, (Sir) Richard, 29, 64, 70, 78, 101, 102, 107, 116

Morley tunnel, 13, 18, **48**, 85, 113, 141, 149, 157, 165; accidents, 125, 128, 159

Nelson, Thomas, 69

Nicholson, Thomas, 10

Normanton; accident, 49; facilities, 53, 58, 93, 108, 188; Joint Station Committee, 35, 46, 84; Joint Uniforms, 61; proposed LNWR line to, 33

Official opening, 15

Oil depot, Liversedge, 174, 176, 196, 197

Oldham; accidents, 121, 133; branch, 10, 26, **27**, 110, **142**, 143, 153; Clegg Street station, 40, 43, 130, 195; Mumps station, 40; horse-drawn train, 29; Mossley-Oldham proposed railway, 10; opening, 29

Oldham, Ashton and Guide Bridge Junction Railway, 30, 33, 39, 40, 43, 46, 53, 65, 69, 72, 74, 77, 130, **142**, 159, 167, 195, 200; traffic, 43, 78, 92, 105, 107, 108, 143, 144, 167

Pritchett, J.P., 11, 16

Ramsbottom, John, 19, 27, 28

Rich, Colonel F.H., 95, 103

River Aire, 7, 18, 54

River Calder, 7, 18, 51, 56, 57, 60, 72, 97, 117, 123, 127, 130, 157, 168, 184

Roberts, R.F., 65, 78

Rochdale Canal, 110, 117

Royal Train, 31, 95, 101, 110, **137**, 146, 156, 162, 163, 191, 198

Runaways, 30, 33, 41, 62, 73, 77, 88, 98

Sheffield, Ashton-under-Lyne and Manchester Railway, 8; proposed merger with H&MR&CC, 9

Sir Ramsden Canal (Huddersfield Broad Canal), 8, 57, 60, 69, 76, 78, 123

Sleeper car, 135

Snow, 27, 67, 87, 93, 160, 161

Stalybridge, 8, 15, 16, 72, 82, 83, 84, 90, 93, 94, 99, 108, 116, 119, 125, 139, 162, 173, 175, 177, 183, 184, **188**, 192; 49, 59, 75, 77, 88, 93, 144, 159

Standedge; accidents, 59, 67, 68, 72, 74, 110, 114, 115, 158, 159, 191; canal tunnel, 8, 102; water troughs, 83, 186

Standedge tunnel, 16, 30, 64; blocked by snow, 160; Cathedral, 69; channel tunnel trials, 186; corrosion to telegraph wires, 41, 106; diversion of MS&L trains, 87; first (Nicholson) tunnel, 8, 16, *173*, 186, 200; pilot, 9, 69; second, (Nelson) tunnel, 57, 67, 69, **173**, 186, 200; third tunnel, 108, 113, 117, 119, 121, **173**

Strikes, 143, 144, 149, 153, 167

Trams, 129, 137, 145

Transport Users Consultative Committee, 173, 175, 176

Travelling post office, 101, 120, 132, 141, 147, 173, 186, 193, 195, 198, 199

Tyler, Captain Henry, 43, 68

Wakefield, proposed lines, 13, 30

Whitehall Road goods yard, 76, 87, **182**, 199, **199**

Wool trade, 79, 99, 131, 133

Yolland, Colonel William, 40, 65, 66, 69, 86

Front cover: A down express crossing the Calder at Ravensthorpe 1958.   *Author*
Back cover: Class '5MT' 2-6-0 No. 42856 passes Delph Junction with an up goods train on 25th June, 1960. In the foreground are the disused platforms of Moorgate halt.   *Author*